WITHDRAWN

HARVARD LIBRARY

WITHDRAWN

A PHILOSOPHICAL
PRIMER ON THE
Summa Theologica

A PHILOSOPHICAL

PRIMER ON THE

Summa Theologica

RICHARD J. REGAN

Franciscan University Press

Copyright © 2018 by Franciscan University Press
All rights reserved.
No part of this publication may be reproduced or transmitted in any form or means, electronic or mechanical, including photography, recording, or any other information storage or retrieval system, without permission in writing from the publisher. Requests for permission to make copies of any part of the work should be directed to:

Franciscan University Press
1235 University Boulevard
Steubenville, OH 43952
740-283-3771

Distributed by:
The Catholic University of America Press
c/o HFS
P.O. Box 50370
Baltimore, MD 21211
800-537-5487

Design and composition: Kachergis Book Design
Cover Image: St. Thomas Aquinas, from tapestry, circa 1480–1500; courtesy The Cloisters Collection, 2014, Metropolitan Museum of Art, New York.
Printed in the United States of America.

Cataloging-in-Publication Data available from the Library of Congress
Casebound: ISBN: 978-0-9995134-3-9
Paperback: 978-0-9995134-4-6

CONTENTS

Preface	vii
Abbreviations	xi
1. Introduction	1

ST 1

2. God	49
3. Creation and Governance of the Universe	73
4. The Soul	78

ST 1-2

5. The Human End	97
6. Human Acts	100
7. Moral Goodness and Malice	110
8. Love	114
9. Habits	117
10. Virtue	121
11. Law	127

ST 2-2

12. Faith	147
13. Hope	163
14. Charity	167
15. Prudence	187
16. Justice	206
17. Fortitude	253
18. Temperance	259
Glossary	275
General Commentaries	287
Index of Persons	288
Topical Index	289

PREFACE

Historians consider Thomas Aquinas a great philosopher-theologian, and the ST one of the great books of Western civilization. Although the ST is expressly theological, Aquinas therein provides strictly philosophical analyses of many topics (e.g., God, creation, the human soul) as well as scriptural and theological arguments. Such topics are important, and the enquiring general reader and philosophical neophyte should be readily able to understand the analyses on their own terms, at least with the aid of a glossary and, in some cases, a dictionary. I hope that this primer will assist the educated general public and philosophical neophytes to become better acquainted with Aquinas' thought on the topics. (The reader should keep in mind that this work is only a primer, and that it omits relevant philosophical material in the ST.) The primer expresses Aquinas' positions and arguments in his own terms, albeit summarily, with only a minimum of clearly distinguishable commentary, and so the reader is advised to consult a comprehensive commentary for further treatment. The reader will find a list of excellent commentaries at the end of the book. The introductory chapter describes the academic context in which Aquinas lived and wrote and provides an overview of his philosophical thought.

 I include the theological virtues largely because of their moral and political ramifications (e.g., the treatment of heretics and apostates under faith, and of killing and war under charity). I have omitted treatment of the angels, except for a brief mention of them in the introductory chapter in order to contrast the views of Aquinas against the Franciscan school. The reader should especially note that Aquinas radically distinguishes the angelic way of knowing from the human, and the primer develops his understanding of the latter, however summarily. The primer also omits most of the objections that Aquinas raises and his replies to them. It does, however, include the objections and replies that involve the most important distinctions relevant to the questions at issue. The format is innovative in that it positions the objections and responses to them after Aquinas' statement of his position, and I structure the objections in syllogistic form to assist the reader to understand more clearly the point of the objections. To supplement this anthology of the ST, the reader may consult the original translation of the ST by the English Dominican Fathers (New York: Benziger Bros., 1947–48) and the works listed in the General Commentaries.

My translation and redaction of the ST here are based on two previous works of mine: *A Summary of Philosophy* (Indianapolis: Hackett, 2003) and *The Cardinal Virtues* (Indianapolis: Hackett, 2005), to which I have added new material on the theological virtues (faith, hope, and charity). The introductory chapter includes material from the introductions to the aforementioned works and from the introduction to *Law, Morality, and Politics* (Indianapolis: Hackett, 2002). I have revised and expanded the introductions here, especially regarding the contributions of Plato, Aristotle, Plotinus, and Avicenna to Aquinas' theory of participation. Hackett has graciously granted permission to incorporate and adapt the cited works. In the present work, I aim to make available in one volume the texts and introductions now available in the several works and so provide a more integrated view of Aquinas' philosophy in the ST.

I have retained the scholastic philosophical terminology used by Aquinas. To do otherwise might be insufficiently precise and mislead the reader. Instead, I have retained the technical words and added an extensive glossary of the terms with illustrative examples. Such an extensive glossary, which is often absent from works on Aquinas, should greatly help the reader to understand the technical terms.

While this book should be of interest and utility to the educated public without specialization in philosophy, it may also be of interest and utility to philosophy students and professors themselves. Students and professors may find it useful for review purposes and for locating precisely where and how Aquinas treats a particular subject (e.g., the immortality of the soul) in the ST. In addition, instructors may find it a good outline for course lectures, which they will be able to supplement with other materials and their own analyses.

Richard J. Regan
Fordham University

ABBREVIATIONS

A., AA.	article, articles
Cor.	Corinthians
CT	*Compendium of Theology*
dist.	distinction
Ex.	Exodus
Gen.	Genesis
Hos.	Hosea
Jer.	Jeremiah
Mt.	Matthew
NE	*Nicomachean Ethics*
PG	*Patrologia Graeca*
PL	*Patrologia Latina*
Q., QQ.	Question, Questions
Rom.	Romans
SCG	*Summa contra Gentiles*
ST	*Summa Theologica*
Tim.	Timothy

I

✥

INTRODUCTION

Thomas Aquinas flourished in the second and third quarters of the thirteenth century of our era (AD 1224/1225–1274). A Dominican friar, he lectured at the University of Paris and taught Dominican friars at Naples. Toward the end of his life, he wrote a summary of theology, the ST, to introduce beginners to the study of the discipline, probably future Dominican preachers in training.

The entire ST is, in effect, Aquinas' answer to the question: What is the meaning of human life? The central purpose of the ST is to show why human beings exist, their destiny, and how they can achieve it. He argues that human beings exist to know God, that their destiny is to enjoy the vision of him in the next life, that they need to act properly in this life in order to be worthy of their destiny, and that the Church's sacraments are the means to do so. The ST represents a major attempt to introduce the method and principles of Aristotle (384–327 BC) into the study of Christian theology.

The first part of the ST (ST 1) treats of God, creatures, and human nature. The first half of the second part (ST 1-2) deals with the human end and the role of human acts and virtues in achieving the end. The second half of the second part (ST 2-2) deals with specific virtues and the moral character of particular acts. The third (and never completed) part of the ST (ST 3) considers the life, death, and resurrection of Christ and the role of the sacraments in the lives of the Christian faithful. In the course of summarizing Christian theology in the first two parts of the ST, Aquinas explicitly deals with many topics of philosophical interest and advances explicitly philosophical arguments—that is, arguments based on reason rather than Scripture or Church authority—as well as the explicitly theological themes in connection with the virtues of faith, hope, and charity. This introduction attempts to recapitulate the background to the major themes developed in those parts of the ST, as well as the themes themselves.

The first section of the introduction describes the problem posed by the introduction of major texts of Aristotle into Western Europe in the twelfth and thirteenth centuries, especially at the University of Paris. The second section considers the epistemological problem of universals, not because that problem was a major focus of concern for scholastic theologians at that time, but in order to indicate the moderate realist foundation on which they based their philosophical speculation. The third section considers the metaphysical problem of the oneness and the multiplicity of being, the problem of the oneness and the multiplicity of material things belonging to the same species, and Aquinas' solutions to the problems. The fourth section considers Aquinas' philosophy of God and his philosophical cosmology. The fifth section considers Aquinas' philosophical psychology. Succeeding sections consider ethical topics: the end of human beings, human actions, and the virtues.

The Intellectual Context

To understand why Aquinas chooses to treat the philosophical topics he does, the reader needs to be conscious of the intellectual climate in which he worked.

INTRODUCTION 3

The chief educational institution in which Aquinas studied and taught was the University of Paris. Beginning at Bologna in the eleventh century of our era, universities arose in Western Europe to provide scholarly and professional education beyond that provided by cathedral and monastic schools.[1] The University of Paris, which developed from the cathedral school of Notre Dame in the last quarter of the twelfth century, was, like other contemporary universities, a corporation of students and masters free to govern itself.

The University of Paris was composed of four faculties: arts, medicine, law, and theology. In addition to the arts of writing and speech (grammar, rhetoric, and logic) and the mathematical arts (arithmetic, geometry, astronomy, and music), the arts faculty taught Aristotelian scientific and philosophical subjects (biology, physics, psychology, ethics, and metaphysics). Although Aquinas taught in the theological faculty, he strongly contested certain positions of the arts faculty that he regarded as heretical and/or contrary to reason.

The theology faculty of the University of Paris was the most distinguished in medieval Christendom and boasted of such masters as Alexander of Hales (AD 1170/1185–1245), Albert the Great (AD ca. 1200–1280), Bonaventure (AD ca. 1217–1274), and Aquinas himself. The lecture format in theology typically consisted of a master's commentary on the *Sentences* of Peter Lombard (AD ca. 1100–1160), but the public disputation provided the discipline's cutting edge. In these disputations, students or masters would defend theses before all comers. Those defending theses would recapitulate objections, state and explain the defenders' contrary position, and reply specifically to the objections. The ST adopted this basic question-and-answer format.

The chief intellectual event of the twelfth and thirteenth cen-

---

1. On medieval universities generally, see Hilda De Ridder-Symoens, ed., *A History of the University in Europe, Volume I: Universities in the Middle Ages* (Cambridge: Cambridge University Press, 1991).

turies of our era was the reintroduction of the texts of the major works of Aristotle into Western Europe.[2] Aside from Aristotle's works on logic and rhetoric, his scholarship had been lost to the West since the collapse of the Roman Empire, although medieval scholars knew citations of the works by Latin authors like Augustine. In the twelfth century, James of Venice translated *Physics*, *De anima*, and *Metaphysics* into Latin. In the thirteenth century, Robert Grosseteste produced the first complete translation of *Nicomachean Ethics*, and William of Moerbeke revised the translations of James and translated other works of Aristotle. In short, by the last quarter of the thirteenth century, the basic corpus of Aristotle's philosophical work was readily available to Latin-literate scholars of the universities of Western Europe. The Arabic works of Averroes (AD 1126–1198) had also been translated into Latin by AD 1240.

Reconciling Aristotle with the tenets of the Christian faith posed serious problems.[3] Aristotle held that the world was uncreated and could be read to hold the common Greek view that the world always and necessarily existed, but the Christian Church taught that the world had a beginning, that it could have not existed, and that God freely created it. Aristotle's Prime Movers were self-absorbed intelligences that had no providential design for the world or its human inhabitants, but the Christian God was an intelligence that providentially created the world and each human being. Aristotle never explicitly affirmed the personal immorality of the human soul, and he considered proper human behavior exclusively as a prerequisite for human happiness in this life, but the

---

2. For an older but useful survey of the reception of Aristotle in the West until 1277 AD, see Fernand van Steenberghen, *Aristotle in the West: The Origins of Latin Averroism*, trans. L Johnson (Louvain: E. Nauwalaerts, 1955). For a more recent survey, see Mark D. Jordan, "Aristotelianism, Medieval," *Routledge Encyclopedia of Philosophy*, ed. Edward Craig (London, Routledge, 1998).

3. On Aristotle generally, see J. L. Ackrill, *Aristotle the Philosopher* (Oxford, UK: Oxford University Press, 1981), and J. Barnes, *Aristotle* (Oxford, UK: Oxford University Press, 1982).

Christian Church unequivocally affirmed the immortality of each individual human soul and unequivocally conditioned blessedness in the next life on proper behavior in this one.

The nearly simultaneous introduction of Averroes as the most authoritative interpreter of Aristotle compounded the problems.[4] Where Aristotle could be interpreted to suppose rather than to affirm that the world was necessary and eternal, as Aquinas interpreted him (ST 1, Q. 46, A. 1), Averroes explicitly affirmed that the world was such. Where Aristotle could be interpreted to hold that the individual human soul was intellectual and so immortal,[5] as Aquinas interpreted him,[6] Averroes categorically denied that the individual human soul was intellectual by its own power and held that the individual human soul perished with the dissolution of the human composite (body-soul). And Averroes asserted not only that philosophical reason and religious faith are different ways of knowing, but also that the way of reason, that is, the way of philosophy, is superior to the way of faith, that is, the way of theology. (Needless to add, the latter position particularly aroused

---

4. On Averroes generally, see M. R. Heyoun and A. de Libera, *Averroes et l'averroisme* (Paris: Presses Universitaires, 1991), and O. Leaman, *Averroes and His Philosophy*, 2nd ed. (Richmond, UK: Curzon, 1997). On Averroes and the intellect, see H. A. Davidson, *Alfarabi, Avicenna, and Averroes on Intellect* (New York: Oxford University Press, 1992).

5. Aristotle seems to have held that the human soul as such perishes with the dissolution of the composite. He held that the potential intellect, the intellect that actually understands, passes away with the composite, but that the active intellect, the intellect that causes the potential intellect to understand, is immortal (*De anima* III, 5.430a 17–25). He is ambiguous about whether the active intellect is a faculty of each human being or of a separate spiritual substance operative in mature human beings during their lifetime. If he means the former, which is unlikely, the individual human soul as such would presumably not be immortal, although an unconscious part of it would be. If he means the latter, which is likely, there would evidently be no immortality of any part of the individual human soul.

6. Aquinas, partially on the basis of a faulty Latin translation, so interpreted Aristotle (*Commentary on the De anima*, Lecture 10, nos. 742–45).

strenuous opposition from contemporary Muslim theologians and imams.)

Some masters of the arts faculty of the University of Paris enthusiastically embraced a radical form of Aristotelian thought regarding the world and the human soul similar to the views of Averroes, although probably not derived from him. Prominent among such masters were Siger of Brabant (AD ca. 1240–1281/1284) and John of Jandun (AD ca. 1286–1328). Since radical Aristotelian views about the world and the human soul were evidently in conflict with central tenets of Christian belief, masters who openly taught such views risked condemnation by Church officials. Whether for this practical reason or for theoretical reasons, radical Aristotelians like Siger and John seem to have held what orthodox adversaries called a "theory of double truth." Such a theory would hold that a proposition could be true from the perspective of reason and philosophy and simultaneously false from the perspective of faith and theology.

Augustine of Hippo (AD 354–430) was the foremost Western patristic theologian, and the theology faculty of the University of Paris regarded his explanation and exposition of Christian doctrine as authoritative and quasi-normative. His theology reflected the dominant Neo-Platonist philosophical tradition of his time.[7] Christian thinkers like Augustine rejected the aspects of Neo-Platonist tradition that were contrary to Christian teaching. The Neo-Platonist theory of emanation, for example—the theory that the material world necessarily originated by a series of hierarchically descending radiations from their infinite source—is clearly contrary to the Judeo-Christian theory of creation. But there are other elements of Neo-Platonism that were attractive to Christian thinkers like Augustine. The infinite perfection of the One of

---

7. On Augustine generally, see Henry Chadwick, *Augustine* (New York: Oxford University Press, 1986). On Neo-Platonism in the Latin tradition, see S. Gersh, *Middle-Platonism and Neo-Platonism: The Latin Tradition* (Notre Dame, IN: University of Notre Dame Press, 1986).

Neo-Platonism is compatible with the infinite perfection of the Christian God. The ideal Forms of Neo-Platonism, if interpreted as ideas in the mind of God regarding the natures of the things he creates, would ground the intelligibility of the world and God's providence. And the Neo-Platonist emphasis on the superiority of spirit over matter resonated with Christian doctrine.

On the other hand, the Aristotelian approach to philosophy was attractive from many perspectives. Aristotle's explanation of human intellectual activity, rooted in sense perception and not merely occasioned by it, seemed to correspond more closely to human experience. Where Neo-Platonists regarded material things as ephemeral and unintelligible apart from the ideal forms of which they were obscure reflections, Aristotle regarded material things as unqualifiedly real and intelligible by reason of their proper forms. Where Neo-Platonists argued to the existence of the One from internal data (ideas), Aristotle argued to the existence of the Prime Movers from external data (motion and change). Some of the arts faculty of the University of Paris embraced the Aristotelian perspective without qualification, but theologians like Albert, Bonaventure, and Aquinas adopted it only cautiously.

The Problem of Universals

Some traits and specific or generic identities seem to be common to many things, and so human beings predicate common words to signify the traits and identities. For example, we say that John is a human being, and so is Joan. What is the ontological status of such predicates and the concepts underlying them? On the one hand, every existing thing is singular. On the other hand, existing material things and human composites of mind and matter seem to possess common characteristics and specific identities that validate general concepts representing the characteristics or identities. From the singularity of existing things, radical empiricists argued that universal concepts represent nothing existing in external reality. In other words, they held that universals are nothing more than either arbitrarily assigned words or purely conceptual constructs subsuming different existing things under a common heading, as, for example, we use the words *member of the armed forces* as a predicate of both soldiers and sailors. These philosophers have come to be known as nominalists. Conversely, radical idealists like Plato (ca. 428–348/347 BC) argued that material things do indeed have common specific identities, and that universal concepts of such identities reflect ideal Forms that transcend their material manifestations. The highest Forms were the One and the Good (perhaps the same Form), and the lesser ideal Forms shared in the perfection of the highest Forms.

Aristotle took a middle position. Universals as such do not exist, since every existing thing is singular, but the content of universals, that is, what they represent, exists in things in a concrete, individual way. Aquinas and most medieval theologians accepted this explanation. (Nominalists on the arts faculty of the University of Paris, of course, did not.) But Aquinas and his contemporaries grounded the content of universal ideas about natural things in God himself. If universals truly represent the natures and essences of things, and if created things partake of God's essence, then the natures or essences of things need to exist in God in an unshared, infinite way. The natures or essences of things are then the different ways in which various kinds of things can partake of God's essence in finite ways. Plato's ideal Forms do exist, not as such but as the ways in which creatures can partake of God's existing.

The debate over the ontological status of universals is no mere quibble. In the fourteenth and fifteenth centuries, nominalists concentrated attention on linguistics and logic, with much gain for those disciplines and much loss for metaphysics. The implication of nominalism for ethics is particularly important. If there is nothing in external reality corresponding to the idea of human nature beyond perceived similarities and causal relations, we cannot ground moral obligation on an order of nature, that is, a natural law. (Kant and others, however, have striven to derive such obligation from a purely internal moral law, and utilitarians to derive it from a calculus weighing subjectively desirable consequences against subjectively undesirable consequences.) And nominalism, of course, precludes any conceptually meaningful theology.

Participation of Finite Things in Existing and of Material Things in Specific Forms

In Western thought, classical Greek philosophers were the first to raise questions about the oneness of being and the multiplicity of beings, on the one hand, and the oneness of a specific form and the multiplicity of individual things with the form, on the other.

Plato, for example, considered the relation between the objects of our intellectual knowledge and the objects of our sense perceptions. According to him, the objects perceived by the intellect in its necessary judgments are changeless and universal realities, and the objects perceived by the senses singular, unstable, and ever-changing realities of the material world. Are both worlds real, or is only one truly real?

Plato thought that the Forms (Ideas) provided the key to the solution. The Forms were the true and eternal essences of things. They were unique existent, singular, substantial realities but not constituent sources in union with corporeal matter. Nonetheless, deficient images of the Forms were in some way linked to the matter in the sensibly perceptible world, and so singular material things could imitate the Forms and participate in their perfection. Moreover, there were above the Forms of generic and specific essences more perfect Ideas: the Form (or Forms) of the Good, the One, and Absolute Beauty. Plato described the Idea of the Good as "the universal cause of all things right and beautiful, the source of truth and reason" (*Republic* VII, 517B). The Good causes true being, since true being is identical with the intelligible.

Aristotle rejected Plato's theory of the Forms. For Aristotle, a form could be only a singular complete spiritual substance or else the intrinsic specific form of a material substance. The process of change, he argued, requires that a material subject undergoing change be composed of two incomplete and contrary intrinsic sources (material causes). In any change, there must be a perfection that is lost and a perfection that is acquired, and there must be a subject, a substratum, that endures before, during, and after the process of change. In an accidental change (e.g., getting sunburned), the subject that remains throughout the process of acquiring the accident (e.g., the sunburn) is a substance (e.g., the one getting sunburned). In a substantial change (e.g., digested food becoming part of the animal digesting it), the subject is the underlying purely potential source undergoing the substantial change. Aristotle called this source prime, that is, first, matter, which, as such, lacks any determination and receives its specific determination and perfection from its substantial form. (Second matter is the complete material substance with its quantity and qualities.)

For Aristotle, unlike Plato, form is an intrinsic constituent source of the singular material essence, and prime matter is the other constituent source. The union of the two produces the specific nature, or essence, of material substances. By positing an analogous pair of intrinsic sources in material substances, namely, substance and accidents, Aristotle also resolved the problem of accidental change. The composite substance of matter and form is the determinable source, and accidental forms, namely, quantity and qualities, determine a material substance to have such-and-such characteristics.

Aristotle proposed his theory of the composition of prime matter and substantial form in material things as a solution to the problem of substantial change, not to the problem of participation, namely, how many things can share in an actuality. He never proposed that multiplication of an actuality requires its reception in a potentiality. Such a theory would require one to hold that pure actuality as such is unlimited, that is, infinitely perfect. This no classical Greek philosopher did. For them, the infinite meant the completely imperfect, the complete lack of determination, the boundlessness of matter. The classical Greek philosophers and their culture regarded the definite limits of a form (e.g., the form of a champion athlete in action) as perfection. The determinations of form give being and intelligibility to the boundless indetermination of matter.

Neo-Platonists completely inverted the classical Greek idea of the infinite and the finite. For them, the infinite meant the completely actual and perfect, not the completely indeterminate and imperfect. For example, the Neo-Platonist Plotinus (AD 205–270) held that the First Hypostasis, the One, was pure actuality as such, completely supreme, and the first source of all other things, which were necessary, eternal, and uncreated emanations from it and finite.

Christianity was simultaneously spreading in the Roman Empire and would soon dominate it. The Hebrew Bible and the New Testament, both of which Christians held to contain divine revelation, taught that God was infinitely perfect, and Christian theologians were well aware of that. They could accordingly accept the Neo-Platonist idea of the infinite and identify the Neo-Platonist One with the Christian God in that respect but not in other respects. In particular, Christian theologians could not accept the Neo-Platonist idea of finite, necessary, and uncreated emanations from the One. Medieval Christian philosopher-theologians then faced the problem of explaining how finite created things participated in the actuality of existing that was infinite in God, and they developed two principal lines of analysis: that of Thomas Aquinas and that of the Franciscan school.

The central postulate of Aquinas' theory was that existing is an actuality and indeed the first and chief actuality. God, being infinite, is the pure actuality of existing: subsistent existing itself. In the case of finite things, Aquinas invoked the Aristotelian principles of actuality and potentiality to explain the limited existing of finite things: the actuality of existing in finite things is limited to and by the potentiality of their particular essences (angelic, human, animal, and vegetative). Thus Aquinas expanded the principles of actuality and potentiality beyond an explanation of change to an explanation of the limitation of finite things.

The medieval Islamic philosopher Avicenna (AD 980–1030), who authored a synthesis of Neo-Platonic and Aristotelian elements, provided an idea that resembled the position of Aquinas on the actuality of existing. According to Avicenna, the One is an essence with which existing is identical. In all other beings, which are emanations from the One, existing is not identical with their essences. Besides the necessarily existing One, there are possible essences. When a possible essence is brought into existence, it receives existing as an accident, not an intrinsic constituent of the essence itself.

Aquinas agreed with Avicenna that existing is an actuality, and that it is not a constituent part of the essence but held that existing is the actuality of the essence rather than merely an accident added to the essence. Classical Greek philosophers understood being not only as what exists but also as what could exist, namely essences or forms. In effect, Aquinas recasts being to comprehend existing things, not abstract essences of forms.

To explain the multiplicity of individual material things having the same specific form, Aquinas postulated that they have the actuality of the same specific form, but that the potentiality of prime matter limits the form to the individual material thing. The source individuating the thing is the quantity designating the prime matter for the form. Quantification enables prime matter to be capable of many particular parts, each of which can be united to a numerically different but substantially same form. Purely spiritual forms, namely, those of angels, are unlimited in one respect. Being purely immaterial, they have no matter to distinguish one angelic form from another. Therefore, each angel exhausts the perfection of its species, and angels differ from one another as one species from another.

Medieval philosopher-theologians of the Franciscan school had a different theory of participation: universal hylomorphism. They held that all finite things, both corporeal and spiritual, are composed of the potentiality of matter and the actuality of form. Thus purely spiritual things, namely, angels, belong to the same angelic species, which spiritual matter individuates. Some Franciscans thought that spiritual matter differs specifically from corporeal matter, but others, like Bonaventure, held that spiritual and corporeal matter were specifically the same.

Medieval philosopher-theologians of the Franciscan school also opposed the Thomist theory that each individual material thing has only one substantial form. For example, they held that each human being has a form of corporeity (the form making a material thing three-dimensional), a vegetative soul, a sensory soul, and a rational soul, each of which corresponds to the ascending grades of perfection in material composites.

The Franciscan Duns Scotus (AD ca. 1266–1308) extended the theory of plural substantial forms in material composites to a form that individuates a thing, that is, makes a material composite this particular thing. "Thisness" is added to the composite after it has received its last specific form.

God and the World: ST 1

Contrary to some popular and scholarly misconceptions of yesteryear, twelfth- and thirteenth-century theologians raised and discussed central philosophical problems of human concern, not least the problem of God. There was ongoing intellectual debate among orthodox Christian thinkers (e.g., between Bonaventure and Aquinas) and between Christian thinkers and their Muslim and Jewish counterparts. In addition to Avicenna and Averroes, Christian thinkers knew and studied the writings of Alfarabi (AD ca. 870–950) and Moses Maimonides (AD 1138–1204), among others.

From the earliest days of Christianity, Paul of Tarsus (first century AD), in the course of preaching to the pagans, claimed that human beings, without the aid of special divine revelation, could perceive the invisible God in the visible things he created (Rom 1:20). Later, Augustine advanced explicitly philosophical arguments for God's existence that he deemed demonstrative. Paul and Augustine, from different perspectives, advanced these arguments to convince pagans in a predominately pagan world of the reasonableness of Christianity. Medieval Christian theologians, on the other hand, lived in a predominantly Christian world. Why, then, did the medieval theologians bother to articulate arguments for God's existence? For the believer, surely, no proof should be necessary.

There is a short and a long answer to this question. The short answer is that there were agnostics and possibly atheists in medieval Christendom, however atypical they were. Few were so bold as to assert categorically that there is no God. But a number of those in the arts faculty of the University of Paris were denying the Judeo-Christian idea of a transcendent, provident God. The philosophical God of the so-called Latin Averroists was finite, purely immanent, and disinterested in human affairs. Nor did the logical inconsistency of a putative theory of double truth preclude the possibility that radical Aristotelian views about God were true. One implicit atheist regarding the Christian idea of God, David of Dinant (AD 1150–1206), claimed that God was prime matter—that is, the eternal substratum of material things—and so purely immanent and potential. In addition to refuting the arguments of such agnostics, the faith of the weak needed to be confirmed.

Thus there were apologetic reasons for advancing proofs for the existence of God and the chief predicates of him. But there was another, ultimately more important, reason for doing so. An intellectually vibrant faith seeks understanding. Faith transcends reason, but reason enlightens faith. Theologians were naturally concerned about what reason could say about God, and his existence and predicates about him were prerequisites for such an inquiry.

Aquinas, in contrast with early modern and many contemporary philosophers, devotes only a few pages of the ST to questions related to knowledge of God's existence (Q. 2, AA. 2, 3). His five ways of proving the existence of God rest on two principles: (1) the principle of intelligibility, or sufficient reason; and (2) the inability of contingent causes, severally or collectively, to explain adequately the very existence of contingent things or their activities. The more serious question for him concerned how to know God and the cognitive status of our predications about him.

If God transcends finite things, which Aquinas thought he had demonstrated by proving that God is the uniquely necessary and perfect being, then we, by denying intrinsically finite perfections of him, know what he is not. For example, we can know that God, as perfect being, is not material, changeable, and so forth, and so we can make true negative statements denying such predicates of him.

But if God transcends finite beings, then no finite intellect unblessed by the vision of God himself can know what God is in himself, that is, in his infinite perfection.[8] And if finite intellects in this life do not know what God is in himself, then it would seem that human beings could not make true affirmative statements about him except that he exists and causes everything else to exist. For example, Maimonides claimed that human beings could predicate positive perfections of God only metaphorically,[9]

---

8. Even those blessed with the vision of God do not and cannot know him comprehensively. Cf. ST 1-2, Q. 3, A. 8, *ad* 2.

9. Moses Maimonides, *Guide to the Perplexed*, part 1, chap. 58.

and many Christian theologians followed the negative theology of Pseudo-Dionysius. Aquinas in the ST dealt directly with the position of Maimonides and implicitly qualified Pseudo-Dionysius' theology

Aquinas agreed with Maimonides that human beings by the use of reason in this life do not and cannot know anything about what God in his infinite self is. Our concepts are derived from sense perceptions, and the senses perceive material things. And so material things are the proper object of our intellect, and we can in this life understand the nature of spiritual things only in relation to material things, that is, as not material. Moreover, although we can experience spiritual perfections like intellection and willing, and understand that they, as such, imply no imperfection, we cannot know what such perfections without imperfection are in God. We necessarily understand the perfections of understanding and willing, as they exist in us, in a finite way.

But we do know God as he is reflected in created things, and we can truly predicate of God pure perfections, that is, perfections that as such signify no imperfection (e.g., intellection), despite the fact that we have no proper knowledge of what intelligence is in him. Predicates applied to God and human beings are not univocal, that is, predicated of both in exactly the same sense, as we predicate *human* of each and every human being. Nor are such predicates purely equivocal, that is, identical written or spoken words predicated of different things in completely different senses, as in the case of puns. Rather, pure perfections attributed to God and human beings are predicated analogously, that is, understood and predicated of each in partially the same sense and in partially different senses. We predicate *intelligent* of God and human beings in partially the same sense because God creates the human intelligence we understand, and every effect is like its cause either univocally or analogously. And we predicate *intelligent* of God and human beings in partially different senses, since the way in which God understands (i.e., by simply and completely understanding himself) is totally different from the way in which we understand (i.e., by successively and incompletely understanding material things, by affirmative and negative judgments, and by rational argument).

There is a paradox here. We do not have proper knowledge of God, that is, knowledge of God as he is in himself; and yet we can properly predicate pure perfections of him in a transcendentally eminent way because we know him through the perfections of the things he creates. Moreover, such perfections are not synonymous, since the multiple perfections of creatures reflect his unique perfection in different ways.

The demonstrations of God's existence indicate that he is the first cause of the existence and activity of every contingent thing. And if he is the fullness of being, then contingent things share his infinite perfection in different, finite ways. And if he is intelligent, then he creates intelligently, that is, purposefully and providentially.

In Aquinas' view, the existence of the material world depends on God, its primary cause. Contrary to the view of Aristotle and Greek philosophers generally, the finite world cannot sufficiently explain its existence, nor can finite causes sufficiently explain their activities. The world needs to be created by God, and its activities need his concurrence. In this sense of radical dependency, the world does not exist necessarily. But Aquinas does not think that one can demonstrate that the material world had a beginning, that is, that there was a first moment of time (Q. 46, A. 2). Nonetheless, he affirms as a tenet of Christian faith based on Genesis 1:1 that the world had a beginning, and he argues in the preceding article that reason can demonstrate that the world does not have to be coeternal with God.

The presence of evil in the world, of course, poses a severe challenge to the biblical belief in a providential creator. How can a supremely wise and good God foreordain human suffering and death? From the faith perspective, Christians can regard such physical evils as punishment of sin, whether Adam's collectively imputed sin (cf. Gen 3, Rom 5:12–13) or the actual sins of his descendants (cf. Job). Christians can then regard such physical evils as the vindication of God's justice (cf. Q. 49, A.2). From the rational perspective, the suffering of human beings may help them to develop and exercise certain moral virtues (e.g., courage, patience, compassion). Regarded either way, human suffering is not intrinsically evil, and God will accordingly will it for the sake of a greater good (cf. Q. 2, A.3, *ad* 1). These explanations are not likely to convince the nonbeliever or fully satisfy the believer, but they may be the most that reason can understand about human suffering without recourse to the role of Christ's suffering and of human beings' sharing in it in accord with God's plan of salvation.

But reconciling the presence of moral evil in the world with God's goodness is more difficult, since God evidently cannot cause moral evil without himself being responsible for moral evil itself. The presence of moral evil in the world challenges the very existence of a providential God in various ways. If God does not cause moral evil, how can he foreknow it? If he has the power to prevent it, why doesn't he? If he doesn't prevent things like the Holocaust, how can he be good? I shall consider these questions in connection with human freedom.

Reconciling the physical evil of human suffering with divine providence posed no problem for Aristotle, since the Prime Movers neither created the world not preordained cosmic activities for the particular benefit of human beings. For Aristotle and Greek philosophers generally, the world of nature is indeed orderly, but the order results from the necessary effects of physical causes, with some effects good and some effects bad for particular human beings. This view of a cosmos unrelated to the destiny of human beings contrasts sharply with the biblical view of a provident God creating and directing the universe for the benefit of human beings. In this regard, Greek religion to some extent compensated for what Greek philosophy lacked, since the Greeks invoked the favor of generally capricious gods to avert or remedy physical harm.

The Human Soul and the Human Being: ST 1

Contemporary philosophers today are accustomed to speaking of the mind-body problem. Does the mind have activities irreducible to physical and sensory activities? If the mind's ability to universalize and to reflect on itself transcends physical and sensory powers, how is the mind united to the body? If we substitute the ultimate source of intellectual activity, the soul, for the proximate source of such activity, the mind, we shall be considering the problem from the perspective of medieval scholastic theologians.

Christianity promises the believer everlasting life. This would seem to presuppose that each human being has an immortal soul that is united to the body in this life but is capable of surviving dissolution of the human composite. For Augustine, the leading Western patristic theologian, as for Nemesius, a leading nearly contemporaneous Greek patristic theologian (late fourth century AD), the soul as such was a spiritual substance, albeit united in this world to a body.[10] Insofar as the unity of the human composite was concerned, this position echoed the Neo-Platonist view that the human being *is* the soul, and everything else in a human being is merely accidental,[11] although the union of the soul with the

---

10. On Augustine and the soul as a complete substance, see *City of God* XIII, 2. His position on the creation of the human soul with that of the angels before generation of the human composite also presupposes that the soul is a complete substance. See *On the Literal Meaning of Genesis* VII, 24–28 (PL 34:368–72). On Nemesius and the soul as a complete substance, see *On the Nature of Human Beings* 2 (PG 40:589, 592).

11. E.g., see Plotinus, *Enneads* IV, tr. 7, chap. 8. On Plotinus generally, see L. P. Gerson, *Plotinus* (London: Routledge, 1996).

body is for Augustine and Nemesius natural and necessary. But insofar as the origin of the soul is concerned, Augustine rejected the Neo-Platonist doctrine of emanation and held the orthodox Christian doctrine of creation. The individual human soul, as purely spiritual, cannot be fashioned out of anything preexisting and so needs to be created *de novo* by God.

Aristotle held a different view of the human soul. For him, a soul is the substantial form of all living material things, whether animal or vegetable, whether rational or irrational animal, that is, the soul is the intrinsic component that determines living material things to be what they specifically are. The human soul is the substantial form determining human beings to be specifically human and the ultimate source of all their vital activities, including those of the body. The human soul and the body comprise an integral human substance, but such a view of the human soul as the form of the body seems to entail the conclusion that the human soul, like all other souls and forms, ceases to exist when the composite dissolves. Such a conclusion would be clearly contrary to Christian doctrine.

Aristotle's view of the human soul as the form of the body was reintroduced into Christendom under the mantles of two influential interpreters. One was Avicenna. For him, an Aristotelian deeply influenced by Neo-Platonism, the individual human soul emanates from a subsistent pure intelligence, itself the tenth successive emanation from the supreme intelligence. The human soul comes into existence with the body but is united with it only temporarily. Because the soul is spiritual, its existence does not depend on the body, and so the human soul is immortal. This spiritual being is called a soul or form because of its relation to the body, not because of its essence.[12] This understanding of the human soul, however unacceptable to Christian thinkers because of its origin by emanation, was acceptable to them regarding its spiritual nature,

---

12. Avicenna, *De anima* I, 1.

and early thirteenth-century scholastics followed Avicenna in the latter regard. For Albert the Great, Aquinas' teacher, the spiritual soul was the perfection and actualization of the body without being a form in the strict sense, that is, limited by its reception into matter.[13] For Bonaventure, both the soul and the body were complete substances, although the two were naturally united to each other.[14]

The other major interpreter of Aristotle was Averroes, whom Aquinas regarded as *the* commentator on the former. For Averroes, the human soul comes into existence by human generation and perishes with the dissolution of the human composite at death. Like other souls and forms, the human soul exists solely by reason of its composition with matter. The active and potential intellects (the intellect causing understanding and the intellect brought to understanding, respectively) are indeed spiritual, but they are the common, collective powers of a separate substance, a pure intelligence, not intellects belonging to individual human beings. In short, the human soul is not essentially intellectual and so not essentially spiritual and immortal.

Aquinas distinguished himself from the positions of both interpreters. As one would expect of any orthodox Christian thinker, Aquinas agrees with Avicenna that the individual human soul is spiritual and immortal. But he disagrees with Avicenna's (and Augustine's) view that that the human soul is a complete substance. Aquinas agrees with Averroes that the human soul is the form of the body in the proper sense, that is, the ultimate source of all the activities of human beings, including those of the body. But he disagrees vigorously and passionately with Averroes' view about the relation of the human soul to the powers of intellection.

13. Albert wrote a treatise on the soul (*De anima*). On Albert generally, see A. de Libera, *Albert le Grand et la philosophie* (Paris, Vrin, 1990).

14. On Bonaventure generally, see Etienne Gilson, *The Philosophy of Bonaventure* (Paterson, N.J.: St. Anthony's Guild, 1965), and G. Bougerol, *Introduction to the Works of Bonaventure*, trans. J. de Vinck (Paterson, N.J.: St. Anthony's Guild, 1964).

Contrary to Averroes, Aquinas holds that each human soul possesses its own active and potential powers of intellection, and so each human soul is spiritual and immortal. In short, the individual human soul, like other substantial forms, is only part, albeit the determinative part, of one human substance, but the individual human soul is unlike other substantial forms by reason of its spiritual nature and so cannot perish.

Many of Aquinas' theological contemporaries, especially those of the dominant Augustinian school, thought it theologically and philosophically impossible for the spiritual soul to be the form of the material body. (In fact, a few years after Aquinas' death, the Archbishop of Paris, at the instigation of the Augustinians, expressly condemned the proposition that the human soul is the form of the body.) Were the human soul to be the form of the body, they argued, the soul would be incomplete without a body and so incapable of existing apart from the body. But Aquinas thought that experience justified his conclusions that the substance of a human being is a composite of body and soul, *and* that the soul engages in intellectual activities intrinsically independent of matter. However paradoxical it may be that something intrinsically subsistent could be part of something else, and that a part of something could be intrinsically subsistent, he did not hesitate to follow where the evidence of experience and the analysis of reason led him. Moreover, his position supplied a rationale for Christian belief in the resurrection of the body, since the soul reunited to the glorified body will again be a human composite.

Earlier Christian theologians had disagreed about when human souls were or are created. Some said that each soul is created at the time of human generation.[15] Others said that all human souls were created with the angels and came to exist in particular human bod-

---

15. E.g., Basil, *On the Six Days of Creation*, homily 2 (PG 29:29); Ambrose, *On the Six Days of Creation* I, 7–8 (PL 14:135ff.); John Chrysostom, *On Genesis*, homily 2 (PG 53:31).

ies at the time of human generation.¹⁶ Aquinas, in common with other thirteenth-century theologians, holds that human souls are created individually at the time of each human generation, not collectively with the angels before any human generation (Q. 90, A. 4). But Aquinas does not claim that the human soul is created at the first moment of conception.¹⁷ Rather, he holds that the human soul is created and infused into the body as its form about three months later. Like Aristotle, he reasons that an embryo would not have developed sufficiently to be suitable to receive a rational soul. (This, incidentally, in no way lessened his opposition to abortion during any part of pregnancy, since the embryo is already part of the process of human generation, and human beings should not, in his opinion, directly thwart the process.)¹⁸

The Human End: ST 1-2

Every kind of thing has a nature that aims to achieve its specific perfection, which is its end. Seedlings grow into mature plants and trees capable of exercising vegetative functions, colts grow into mature horses capable of fully exercising animal as well as vegetative functions, and babies grow into mature adults capable of fully exercising rational as well as vegetative and animal functions. Accordingly, human beings differ from other kinds of living material things (and, of course, from all purely material things) in that human beings possess the power to understand and reason.

16. E.g., Origen, *On First Principles* I, 6 (PG 11:165), and II, 9 (PG 11:225); Augustine, *On the Literal Meaning of Genesis* VII, 24–28 (PL 34:368–72).

17. Cf. Aquinas, SCG II, 89.

18. Aquinas does not explicitly treat of the morality of abortion in the ST or the SCG. But it is evident that he would regard abortions after the infusion of the human soul, that is, during the second and third trimesters of pregnancy, as subject to the precept against the direct killing of innocent human beings (cf. ST 2-2, Q. 64, A. 6), although the principle of double effect might be applicable when abortions would be necessary to save the life of the mother. And he would regard abortions in the first trimester of pregnancy as subject to the precept against contraception (cf. ST 2-2, Q. 154, A. 11).

Aquinas, following Aristotle, understands happiness to be the objective state of perfection of human beings, not a subjective state of euphoria (Q. 1, A. 7). He rejects the position that human happiness consists only of material goods, although material goods (e.g., a healthy body and adequate means of economic support) are necessary in this life. Rather, similarly following Aristotle, Aquinas holds that human happiness is a condition of the soul produced by activities of reason itself and other, namely, animal, activities according to reason.

But when Aquinas specifies the object of human happiness, he decisively parts company with Aristotle. The object of perfect happiness, says Aquinas, is the intellectual vision of God's essence, albeit not a comprehensive vision (Q. 3, A.8). He argues that human beings will not be perfectly happy as long as there remains something more for them to know, that nature constitutes them to know God, and that they cannot in this life know what God is in himself. (As presently constituted, the human intellect depends on sense images and knows God only through his perceptible effects, that is, only as the cause of perceptible things and the possessor of those things' perfection in an infinitely superior way.)

Aristotle was satisfied with the limited, albeit daunting, goal of theoretical wisdom as one of the two essential ingredients of human happiness. Human beings readily understand the principle of causality, namely, that things coming to be are caused by something else, and discover the ultimate causes (efficient, final, formal, and material) of changeable things. In doing so, human beings become theoretically wise and attain the perfection of their specifically rational nature. For Aristotle, the other essential ingredient of human happiness was practical wisdom, that is, prudence, which concerns human action. Aquinas agrees that theoretical and practical wisdom are important ingredients of human happiness in this life, but he insists that the happiness attainable in this life is incomplete and imperfect, a pale reflection of the perfect happiness of beholding God's essence, and that nothing material or created, including human friendship, is essential to such happiness.

Both Aristotle and Aquinas recognized that human happiness in this life requires practical wisdom, or prudence—that is, right reason to govern human action—and moral virtue—that is, a rightly ordered will regarding one's actions and emotions. But Aquinas goes beyond Aristotle to maintain that rectitude of the will is necessary for human happiness, not only because happiness results from the proper direction of the will, but also because willing to do so entails loving as good whatever God loves and wills (Q. 19, A. 4). For Aquinas, there is no complete rectitude of the will without conformity to God's will and commands, which reason and revelation communicate.

Happiness in the life hereafter consists of beholding God himself, a vision human beings are incapable of achieving by their natural power. The vision of God, however, is not superimposed on the natural end of human beings like a tower on a building. Rather, human beings have only a single end in the concrete order of salvation: incomplete happiness in this life as they advance in both supernatural and natural virtues, and complete happiness in the next life as they rest content in the vision of God. Indeed, since human beings naturally desire to know complete truth, they *naturally* desire to know God as he is in himself. Therefore, they cannot be completely happy without the vision of God, although no finite intellect can behold him without him enabling them to do so.

Thus, despite the large measure of agreement that Aristotle and Aquinas share regarding the human end, they differ sharply about the sufficiency of theoretical and practical wisdom in this life for the complete happiness of human beings. On the one hand, the pagan Aristotle did not conceive of his Prime Movers in providential terms and so did not look to human happiness in a future life. On the other hand, the Christian Aquinas conceives of God as providential and so cannot look to the theoretical and practical wisdom accessible to human beings in this life, or even a more complete theoretical wisdom in the next life without the beatific vision, as the ultimate human end.

Other medieval Christian theologians, preeminently Bonaventure, while agreeing that perfect human happiness is only possible in the heavenly union with God, argued that it is the love of God, not the knowledge of his essence, that makes human beings who enjoy the beatific vision perfectly happy. The significance of this dispute may be greatly exaggerated. On the one hand, Aquinas holds that perfect love of God accompanies the cognitive vision of God, since the will necessarily seeks goodness, and God's essence is goodness itself. On the other hand, Bonaventure holds that the cognitive vision of God necessarily accompanies perfect love of God, since the will is the faculty of intellectual desire and so can find perfect satisfaction only insofar as the intellect knows God. Nevertheless, there is a difference of emphasis reflecting the larger question of the relative rank of cognition and affection in the rational life of human beings.

Aquinas focused his attention solely on the concrete end that God envisions for human beings in his plan of salvation. Later theologians posed a hypothetical, a "what if," question about the possibility of a purely natural human end: If God had chosen not to bestow the vision of himself on those worthy, what would have been the human end? Complete happiness in the vision of God, something evidently not possessed in this life, would also have been inaccessible in the next life. But relatively complete happiness, that is, as much happiness as could be achieved by acquiring theoretical and practical wisdom in this life and by enjoying theoretical wisdom in the next life, would be possible.

How the vision of God complements and fulfills human nature is a theoretical question. But how Christians should integrate their dual membership in earthly and ecclesial societies is preeminently a practical problem. Much of medieval history resolves around conflicts between Church and State, and much of medieval political theory revolved around attempts to distinguish and integrate the respective roles of these institutions.

Aquinas explains the two roles. He calls the earthly society secular, its end the secular common good, and its structure of authority the secular power. And he calls the ecclesial society spiritual, its end the spiritual common good, and its structure of authority the spiritual power. In his view, the pope is the supreme ruler in medieval Christendom and in the Church, but he ordinarily exercises secular power only in the Papal States. Secular rulers exercise secular power elsewhere, even to the point of putting persistent public heretics to death (ST 2-2, Q. 11, A. 3). They should also defer to the spiritual power of the Church in cases of conflict between religion and public morals.

Aquinas' subordination of secular society to the Church, of course, is inconsistent with the democratic principle of personal religious freedom. The secular-spiritual terminology may have contributed to the inadequate distinction of the two societies, since secular matters may involve spiritual matters (e.g., public policies may have moral dimensions), and spiritual matters may involve secular matters (e.g., safety regulations applied to churches and religious assemblies). Enlightenment thinkers made a conceptually sharper and more functionally useful distinction. They distinguished the secular order from the *sacral*, or strictly religious, order, not the *spiritual* order, and they explicitly denied to the State any competence in religious matters as such and to the Church any competence in secular matters as such. This distinction is now normative in the Western world.

As already noted, the presence of moral evil in the world singularly challenges the idea of a provident God. Its presence supposes that human beings freely choose to desire and act contrary to God's will, howsoever communicated, whether by reason or revelation. Reflection on human experience, in Aquinas' opinion, fully justifies that supposition. And reflection on God's role as the first cause of every finite action leads him to the conclusion that God both knows and permits the presence of moral evil in the world he creates. If so, how can God know what human beings will freely do, and how can he allow moral evil without being its cause? Aquinas' answers to these questions largely follow the analysis of Augustine.

Moral evil as such, like physical evil as such, is not a thing, an entity. Rather, moral evil is the absence of the requisite conformity of human desires and actions to God's will. Thus God can cause human desires and actions as entities without causing their moral deficiencies.

But if human beings alone are responsible for the moral defects of their desires and actions, how can God know them from all eternity? Material things and human beings exist in time, and their internal and external acts succeed one another in time. From our perspective, therefore, there are past, present, and future events. From God's perspective, however, all of world history, both material and human, is equally present to him and known by him from all eternity, since his knowledge is identical with himself, and he is eternal. Physical causes, given the requisite conditions and the absence of outside intervention, necessarily produce certain physical effects. But human beings freely produce acts of the will and external acts when they deliberately desire and do things. God knows both kinds of effects *in the way in which they exist*, namely, as necessarily or freely caused. And so God knows everything that human beings have desired or done, are desiring or doing, and will desire or do in the course of human history, just as he knows everything that physical causes have caused, are causing, or will cause in the course of cosmic history.

This means that God knows the morally good desires and deeds of human beings as well as their morally evil desires and deeds. But morally good desires and deeds by themselves cannot bring human beings to merit the blessed vision of God. Only the grace of God can elevate them to that, and consistent natural moral virtue is itself impossible without grace. There is thus an asymmetry between the human potential for, and the reward merited by, natural moral virtue as such, on the one hand, and the purely human potential for, and punishment merited by, natural moral vice as such, on the other. Natural moral virtue as such cannot merit salvation, but natural moral vice as such is due solely to the human will and so can merit damnation. This poses the problem of predestination, namely, that some human beings with the help of God's efficacious grace are predestined to heavenly blessedness, albeit with their free cooperation, while other human beings without that help can be predestined to eternal damnation, albeit by their own free choice.

Catholic theologians of the sixteenth and seventeenth centuries, principally members of the Dominican and Jesuit religious orders, did not think the Augustinian-Thomist explanation completely sufficient, especially in the context of Protestant theories of predestination.[19] How can God know with certainty what free human beings will do? Without further explanation, does not the Augustinian-Thomist analysis divorce the course of human history from God's foreknowledge and providence?

To remedy this perceived inadequacy, Dominican theologians postulated that God causes the predestined to choose moral good and reject moral evil, although human beings freely cooperate with his grace, and that the damned receive no like predetermination to do so. The Dominican explanation seemed to Jesuit theologians to vindicate divine omnipotence at the price of human freedom. For their part, Jesuit theologians postulated that God foreknew what human beings would freely do in the world he chose to create. The

---

19. For a general description of the controversy, especially as the Roman authorities became involved, see James Broderick, *Robert Bellarmine* (Westminster, MD: Newman, 1961), 189–216.

Jesuit explanation seemed to Dominican theologians to vindicate human freedom at the price of divine omnipotence. How, they asked, could God know that human beings *will* be morally good in the actual world, or that they *would* be morally good in a hypothetical world, without predetermining their actions to be such?

In my opinion, these "further explanations" are unnecessary. Aquinas' analysis, derived from Augustine, links God's knowledge of free human acts to their reality as such. That, of course, leaves in place a question about the responsibility of the omnipotent creator for moral as well as physical evil.

It is interesting to contrast the Reformation and Counter-Reformation concern about how to reconcile human freedom with God's power, and contemporary concern about how to reconcile moral evil and its consequences with God's justice. How can a just and good God tolerate moral evil and resulting injustice? Is it just or good for God to create human beings who he knows will be damned (assuming there should be any such)? Is it just or good for God to allow human beings to be subject to injustices, often monstrous, by other human beings? In Aquinas' view, human freedom itself involves the possibility of moral evil and its consequences, and God could not create human beings without them possessing the power of free choice. Moreover, regarding actual moral evil and its unjust consequences, God ultimately vindicates justice by punishing the sinner, perhaps in this world but certainly in the next.

Human Acts and Virtue in General: ST 1-2

The human soul's intellectual activity is not only cognitive but also affective, since human beings desire things they understand, and they can and do will such things for themselves and others. The propriety of desiring and willing particular things depends on whether the desired or willed things befit human nature and the human end. Concretely, every conscious activity is either in accord with reason or contrary to it, and certain activities may be always contrary to reason because of their object (e.g., hatred of others and the direct killing of an innocent human being).[20] By good acts of the will, human beings develop moral virtues, good habits of action, the chief of which are justice, fortitude, and temperance; and the intellectual virtue of prudence, that is, practical wisdom, determines the appropriate means to achieve the moral virtues and so govern desires and actions.

Human beings enjoy the power of free choice. They can knowingly and willingly act in accord or discord with right reason regarding particular goods. Aquinas devotes the second part of the ST to consideration of moral good and evil in general (ST 1-2) and particular virtues and vices (ST 2-2). In considering these topics, he reflects much of Aristotle's ethical theory but goes much further, especially regarding the nature of moral obligation. As provident creator, God foreknows and foreordains human nature, its end, and the proper means to achieve the end. In doing so, God commands that human beings act in ways befitting their nature as *rational* animals, and human beings, using their reason, perceive his commands regarding their human nature and carry out the commands in their actions.

The intellect directs, that is, structures what the will wills, but the will is free to choose imperfectly good things and not even determined to will the perfect good, God, since the intellect in this life imperfectly understands that good (Q. 10, A. 2). Practical reason deliberates about (Q. 14) and decides (Q. 13, A. 1, *ad* 2) what to do or not to do, and the will, by consenting, chooses to do or not to do it (Q. 15).

Human acts derive their moral goodness from the suitability of the acts' objects for the ultimate human end (Q. 18, A. 2), from the observance of requisite circumstances (Q. 18, A. 3), and from the goodness of the ends for the sake of which one acts (Q. 18, A. 4).

---

20. On intrinsically evil acts generally, see ST 1-2, Q. 18, A. 2. On the intrinsic evil of directly killing innocent human beings, see ST 2-2, Q. 64, A. 6.

Conversely, human acts derive their malice from the lack of any of these things. The goodness of the will itself depends exclusively on the will's object and so on reason, which presents the object to the will as in accord or discord with right reason (Q. 19, AA. 1–3). Since natural law is the light of human reason participating in the eternal law, the goodness or malice of the will depends on the conformity or deformity with the natural law or divinely revealed law (Q. 19, A. 4). Every will that acts contrary to reason, even erroneous reason, is evil (Q. 19, A. 5), but acts of the will in accord with erroneous reason are not necessarily good, since they will be evil if human beings will not to know, or neglect to know, what they can and should know (Q. 19, A. 6).

The most striking contrast between Aquinas' treatment of human acts and Aristotle's lies in the attention that Aquinas pays to the moral goodness or malice of *individual* human acts. Aristotle was largely concerned about the character of human acts in connection with the development of moral virtue, that is, with the relation of morally good or bad acts to the acquisition of morally good or bad habits. Aquinas, although similarly concerned about the relation of morally good or bad acts to the acquisition of virtues or vices, is also and chiefly concerned about the consequence of such acts for meriting happiness in heaven or punishment in hell.

For Aristotle, a virtuous life constitutes its own reward, and a vicious life its own punishment. For Aquinas, a virtuous life in this world does not bring complete happiness to a human being, and a vicious life in this world does not sufficiently punish the guilty with unhappiness. Moreover, morally bad acts, in his view, are not only contrary to the dictates of right reason and so morally bad for their perpetrators, but also contrary to the dictates of God and so deserve fitting retribution from him. Accordingly, the morality of every human act involving serious matter is of supreme importance for human beings. For example, murder is not only contrary to the humanity of the murderer and unjust to the victim, but also a serious offense against God and so deserves the punishment of hell. Conversely, just acts are not only virtuous for the actor and just to others, but also acts that, by God's grace, merit the reward of heaven.

Aristotle held that certain emotions (e.g., spite and envy), insofar as they are subject to reason, are always morally wrong (NE II, 6. 1107a9–27), since such emotions as such are disordered, that is, contrary to right reason and virtue. He also cited there acts of adultery, murder, and theft as always morally wrong, presumably because they involve injustice against the husband of the woman in the case of adultery, and injustice against the victims in the case of murder and theft. And so the unjust acts disorder the perpetrator's soul. But Aquinas, going beyond Aristotle's concern and mode of analysis, holds that some external acts are always evil because they frustrate the intrinsic ends of the acts, even if the acts involve no victims, and that no larger purpose, however good, can render the acts morally good. For example, Aquinas argues that lying is always morally wrong because it frustrates the purpose of communicative speech, although much speech (e.g., actors' speech) is not communicative (ST 2-2, Q. 110, A. 1). Similarly, he argues that some sexual acts (e.g., masturbation, bestiality, homosexuality, and contraception) are always morally wrong, since they are contrary to the intrinsic reproductive purpose of sex (ST 2-2, Q. 154, A. 11). In short, Aquinas was more of a moral absolutist about human acts than Aristotle.

Natural Law: ST 1-2

For Aquinas, moral obligation is a matter of legal obligation. He defines law as the rational ordering of means to an end, for the good of the community, by one or more persons with authority over the community, and promulgated to the community (Q. 90), and he applies the definition to God's act of creation (Q. 91, A. 1).

In that act, God rationally orders things, including human beings, to their ends and the good of the universe, obviously has the authority to do so, and manifests this order in the natures of the things that he creates. And because the act of creation, although the things created have a beginning in time, is identical with God's eternal substance, Aquinas calls this order the eternal law.

Irrational creatures have no freedom regarding their actions, and human beings are not free to decide their end or the objective rectitude of acts (ST 1, Q. 82, A. 1). But human beings are free to choose to act or not to act in ways conducive to their end, and so human beings participate rationally and freely in the eternal law. If human beings decide and freely choose to act in accord with their nature, they rationally and freely share in God's plan for themselves regarding their individual good and the common good of human beings and the universe. And so Aquinas properly calls this participation in the eternal law the natural law (Q. 91, A. 2).

Aquinas considers creation and the natural law from the Christian perspective, namely, as one aspect of God's plan of salvation for humankind. Whereas Aristotle rested content with human goodness in a self-sufficient and rightly governed human community, Aquinas is concerned as well with Christian holiness and obedience to God's commands, explicit or implicit, in God's plan of salvation. In this regard, the natural law has a supernatural dimension, namely, that observance of the natural law can be a grace-filled act, and failure to observe it is a sinful act. In Aquinas' view, divine revelation plays a supportive role in recognizing the demands of the natural law, and divine grace an indispensable role in consistently and substantially observing it. Moreover, love of God, that is, the theological virtue of charity, is the guiding source of the morally virtuous activity of the Christian faithful.

But the natural law is accessible to reason. Reason can discern an order of nature that imposes demands on human behavior. Since these demands derive from the order of nature, their observance rewards human beings with fulfillment, and nonobservance of them punishes human beings with lack of fulfillment. From this perspective, we can say that Aquinas introduces God's creative act to provide the ontological ground for a eudaemonist ethic. He brings God into the act, so to speak, to support, not supplant, such an ethic. We should strive to act in accord with right reason both because we are so constituted, and because God so constitutes us.

The first principle of practical reason, that is, the first principle of human action, is that human beings should seek things that are good for them as human beings and avoid things that are bad for them as human beings (Q. 94, A. 2). This principle is self-evident. Human beings, simply by understanding the terms *human good* and *things to be sought by human beings*, and the terms *human evil* and *things that human beings should avoid*, can without any reasoning process understand the necessary connection between the respective terms.

Because good is the end of action, human beings can understand that those things toward which human nature inclines them are human goods, and that contrary things are human evils. Aquinas, reflecting on the data provided by the senses about human activity, identifies three classes of things toward which human nature inclines human beings (Q. 94, A. 2). First, nature inclines human beings, in common with all substances, to strive to preserve themselves in existence. Second, nature inclines human brings, in common with all animals, to seek sexual union, to beget offspring, and to educate them. Third, nature inclines human beings, precisely as human beings, to know truths about God and his plan of creation and to live in community with other human beings. Practical reason, on understanding these things to be the objects of inclinations from nature, articulates the primary precepts of the natural law. Human beings should preserve their lives in reasonable ways, mate and beget children in reasonable ways, learn truths about God and his plan of creation, and live peacefully and cooperatively with other human beings in organized society. As in the case of the first principle of practical reason, human beings, on understanding the precepts' terms, can assent to them without any process of reasoning.

Reason, with the knowledge gained from experience, can draw conclusions about particular kinds of human acts by applying the primary precepts as principles, and these conclusions constitute secondary precepts of the natural law (Q. 94, A. 4). Aquinas admits that some secondary precepts may be so formulated as to be valid only for the most part. For example, one formulation of a secondary precept of the natural law prescribes that one should return property held in custody to its owner on the owner's request for its return, but it is obviously contrary to reason to return a gun to an owner with a homicidal intention. Moreover, Aquinas admits that some persons and peoples may not recognize the truth of valid secondary principles of the natural law. For example, a secondary precept of the natural law prescribes that one should not steal the property of another, but emotions, habits, and customs may blind the reason of some persons or peoples from recognizing the precept in particular circumstances.

Aquinas, by contrasting the conclusions of practical reason with those of theoretical reason, explains why secondary precepts of the natural law may be so formulated as not to be universally valid (Q. 94, A. 4). Theoretical reason deals with necessary things, and so its conclusions are as universally valid as its premises. But practical reason deals with contingent things, and such things vary widely. There is also an essential difference between the methods of theoretical and practical reason. Theoretical reason draws conclusions in a categorically deductive way in mathematics and Aristotelian science, which includes theology, but practical reason, namely, ethics, draws conclusions by relating contingent things to general principles.

The distinction within the class of secondary precepts between those that are proximate and those that are remote is perhaps as important as the distinction between primary and secondary precepts (Q. 100, A. 1). The relation of some human acts to the primary precepts is so easily understood that reason can promptly, that is, with little reflection, conclude that a person should or should not, at least generally, act in a particular way. The relation of other human acts to the primary precepts is complex, and so considerable reflection is required before reason can conclude that an individual or a community should or should not act in a particular way. The latter remote conclusions are the province of those Aquinas calls the wise, that is, professional experts prudent and knowledgeable about their subject matter. For example, by applying the primary precept to live cooperatively in organized society, one can with little reflection conclude that one should not commit murder, but it requires considerable reflection to decide if or when a particular cause justifies killing another (e.g., when, if ever, is war justified? If and when it is, what are the rules of just war conduct?)

Both Aristotle and Aquinas hold that human beings need to form a body politic in order to promote their proper human development—to develop themselves intellectually and morally as well as materially. But Aquinas goes further and links human law to the natural law. In his view (Q. 95, A. 2), human law is either itself a conclusion based on natural law (e.g., laws prohibiting and punishing murder, robbery, and theft) or a further determination, or specification, of natural law (e.g., laws regulating traffic). This linkage is absolutely necessary if human law is to qualify as law at all and be morally obligatory (Q. 96, A. 4).

Human laws are just if they are directed to the common good, fall within the power of the lawmakers, and lay proportionately equal burdens on citizens. Conversely, human laws are unjust if they depart in any way from these prerequisites, and then, absolutely speaking, citizens are not morally obliged to obey them. Citizens, however, may be morally obliged to obey unjust laws for the sake of the common good, namely, to avoid civil unrest and the breakdown of legal observance. Human laws may be unjust in another way: if they command things contrary to the natural or divinely revealed law. In such cases, human beings are not only not obliged to obey the laws but also morally obliged to *dis*obey them (Q. 96, A. 4).

Specific Virtues and Particular Acts: ST 2-2

ST 2-2 explains the specific virtues to be cultivated in Christian life and the contrary sins to be avoided. There are two kinds of virtues connected with human action: the supernatural theological virtues of faith, hope, and charity, and the naturally acquired virtues of prudence, justice, fortitude, and temperance. Three of the natural virtues (justice, fortitude, and temperance) are moral virtues, and the fourth (prudence) is the practical intellectual virtue governing moral decisions. The theological virtues, because they concern human action, involve moral acts that can be in accord with the virtues or contrary to them. For example, a Christian is in certain circumstances morally obliged to profess the faith publicly, and a Christian is in certain circumstances morally obliged to assist a neighbor in need. Indeed, Aquinas treats some matters (e.g., war) under the virtue of charity, although the matters manifestly also involve justice.

The act of faith is supernatural, that is, impossible for human beings relying on their natural human powers and possible only with the help of God's grace (Q. 6, A. 1). But the act is nonetheless a *human* act and specifically the act of a human intellect (Q. 4, A. 2). In the act of faith, the believer's intellect assents to the truth that God has revealed in Scripture and Tradition through the authority of the Church and the pope, who is the Vicar of Christ (Q. 1, AA. 9, 10). The believer does not assent because the evidence conclusively demonstrates the revealed truth (Q. 1, AA. 4, 5). Rather, the will *commands* the intellect to assent, that is, the will inclines the intellect to adhere to God, who is truth itself and is revealing himself and his plan of salvation (Q. 2, AA. 1, 2). The act of faith is a meritorious free act insofar as the will is free, with the aid of God's grace, to command the intellect to assent (Q. 3, A. 9). In this respect, the act of faith differs from demonstrative knowledge.

This may seem to be a version of Kierkegaard's celebrated leap of faith. Not quite. Aquinas, unlike Kierkegaard, does not consider the intellect's assent altogether blind, that is to say, without evidentiary support. In Aquinas' view, the miracles and fulfilled prophecies recorded in Scripture support the assent but not sufficiently to compel it (Q. 2, A. 10). Modern thinkers have challenged the possibility of miracles and the veracity of claims of fulfilled prophecies. For example, Enlightenment philosophers claimed that natural causes could explain all events in the physical world, and that claims of fulfilled prophecies were *vaticinia ex eventu* (prophecies made after the fact). Moreover, modern scriptural scholarship has demythologized purely literal interpretation of the miracles and prophecies recorded in Scripture.

It is impossible in this short introduction to consider adequately the epistemological status of biblical miracles and prophecies. It will be enough here to note that modern Christian apologists do not follow Aquinas and pre-modern theologians in claiming that biblical miracles necessarily occurred outside the order of natural causes—although the incarnation of Christ and his resurrection from the dead certainly would—or that biblical prophecies need to be literally interpreted. Indeed, modern apologists rely much more on post-biblical moral miracles as evidence for faith (e.g., the holiness of those who live exemplary Christian lives). In any case, Aquinas did not fully articulate a rational apologetic in favor of Christian faith, although he thought that one was possible. One seeking an epistemological and psychological examination of faith will need to look elsewhere (e.g., in John Henry Newman's classic *Grammar of Assent*).

Aquinas struggled to reconcile the so-called preambles of faith (the existence of God and the rationally demonstrable predicates about him) with articles of faith regarding them. If human reason can demonstrate the existence of God, for example, as Aquinas held, then the human intellect assents to it because it is demonstrable, not because of faith in God revealing it. Why then do Christians profess: "I believe in one God"? Aquinas' principal answer is that the creedal article is necessary because many persons are unable to demonstrate that God exists, and it is for their sake that the Nicene Creed incorporates the article (Q. 2, AA. 4, 10). He also points out that the Christian professes faith in the true God, who is more than the god of the philosophers and different from the god or gods of the pagans (Q. 2, A. 4). In any case, Aquinas is clear that the human intellect can demonstrate God's existence, and that when it does, the intellect's assent is based on philosophical demonstration, not faith.

In considering the sins contrary to faith, Aquinas distinguishes four kinds of unbelievers: (1) pagans (including Muslims); (2) Jews; (3) heretics, who dissent from particular articles of the Creed; and (4) apostates, who completely abandon the Christian faith (Q. 10, A. 5; Q. 12, A. 1). (He considers schismatics, who deny the primacy of the pope, in connection with sins against charity [Q. 39].)

With regard to pagans and Jews, Aquinas distinguishes two situations: one in which they know of the Christian faith and the evidence in support of it; the other in which they do not (Q. 10, AA. 1, 8). In the first situation, which prevailed in medieval Christendom and much of the Mediterranean basin, Aquinas presumed that pagans and Jews are guilty of sinning against the faith, but the rites of the pagans may be tolerated to avoid greater evils, and the rites of Jews may be tolerated because the rites prefigure the Christian religion (Q. 10, AA. 8, 11). In the second situation, pagans and Jews do not sin against the faith, since they know nothing of the Christian religion.

With regard to public heretics, they are to be given two successive pointed admonitions to recant. If they do not, or if they do but relapse twice, they are to be executed (Q. 11, A. 3). The death sentence for adamant heretics is draconian and indefensible,[21] but the cultural context may explain, although not excuse, the grim prescription. First, Aquinas and other medieval theologians could not conceive how a person raised Catholic could become a heretic without serious sin. Second, he and most contemporary theologians conceived society as sacral, not purely secular, that is, that organized society should be committed to the Catholic religion, and that secular authority should accordingly safeguard and promote the spiritual welfare of the Catholic Church. Third, some medieval heretics (such as the Cathars) may have deserved some punishment if they harassed orthodox Christians, disturbed public peace, or engaged in activities contrary to public morals.

With regard to apostate rulers, their subjects are absolved from any obligation to obey them (Q. 12, A. 2). (The same would presumably apply in the case of a heretical ruler, but Aquinas, quite reasonably, does not deem this likely in the cultural climate of medieval Christendom.) He quite evidently considers public heresy and apostasy species of treason, and necessarily, not merely presumptively, sinful.

As to hope, Aquinas' treatment is relatively short. He defines the conditions for hope (QQ. 17, 18) and analyzes different levels of fear of God (Q. 19). He identifies two kinds of sin contrary to hope: despair (Q. 20) and presumption (Q. 21). With respect to despair, one should note the absence of psychological analysis that might lessen or eliminate moral culpability (e.g., clinical depression).

As to charity, Aquinas compares the Christian virtue to the Aristotelian ideal of friendship and the love of benevolence (Q. 23,

---

21. One should also note that Aquinas held untenable views about women. For example, he considered them purely passive partners in the process of procreation, as well as mentally inferior to men.

AA. 1, 3; Q. 27). The Christian virtue transcends the Aristotelian ideal in that, while Aristotle is concerned only with particular human friendships and their relation to human fulfillment and good life in the *polis*, Christian charity is concerned with human-divine friendship and universal human fellowship. Indeed, Aquinas argues that the virtue of charity is the form of every moral virtue: it directs the moral virtues to the ultimate end of human beings, namely, God (Q. 23, A. 8). In other words, charity infuses supernatural virtues to supplement and elevate the naturally acquired moral virtues.

Aquinas lists ten sins contrary to charity: hate, spiritual apathy, envy, discord, contention, schism, war, strife, sedition, and scandal (QQ. 34–43). In the course of describing these sins, he shows his typical care to distinguish different actions, different motives, and different situations. Some of these sins, which he considers as contrary to charity, are also contrary to justice. The fact that he considers war only from the perspective of charity (Q. 40) leads him to omit consideration of the principle of double effect in just war conduct, which he does discuss in connection with the justice of killing a human being in self-defense (ST 1-2, Q. 64, AA. 6, 8).

After treating of the theological virtues, Aquinas considers the cardinal virtues: prudence, justice, fortitude, and temperance. These are naturally acquired virtues, to which charity adds supernatural prudence and supernatural moral virtues (ST 1-2, Q. 65, A. 2). Prudence is the first cardinal virtue (QQ. 47–56). Human action should be according to reason, and theoretical reason understands the ends of the moral virtues (to be just in relation to others, brave in confronting mortal dangers and other evils, and moderate in sense desires and pleasures) (Q. 47, A. 6). It is the function of prudence, or practical reason, to determine means to achieve the ends of the moral virtues (Q. 47, A. 7). Prudence is an intellectual virtue but concerns practical, not theoretical, things (Q. 47, A. 2). It has integral, that is, constitutive, parts, such as memory and understanding (QQ. 48, 49). It has subjective parts, that is, subdivisions (QQ. 48, 50). The principal division is between the common prudence that ordinary citizens exercise and the particular, higher prudence that those who govern exercise (Q. 47, AA. 12, 13; Q. 50, AA. 1, 2). It has potential, or related, parts: good deliberation, good judgment according to general law, and good judgments about exceptions to general law (Q. 51). One can sin against prudence by diverging from the rules of right reason, which is imprudence (Q. 53), and by lack of due care, which is negligence (Q. 54).

Justice is the second cardinal virtue QQ. 57–122). Justice as a special virtue concerns one's social relations with others and so is evidently the most important moral virtue (Q. 58, A. 12). Right is the object of justice (Q. 57, A. 1), and Aquinas, like Aristotle, understands right as the objectively right order of social relations, not the subjective right of individuals. For example, it is right that human beings do not deliberately kill innocent human beings. Of course, the necessary consequence of this objective right order is that individual innocent human beings have a subjective right not to be deliberately killed. But the rights of individuals are the focus of Enlightenment philosophers, not that of Aquinas. Natural, divine, and human laws prescribe the right moral order of social relations (Q. 57, A. 2).

Justice in general is moral virtue in general, as directed to the common good (Q. 58, A. 6), and particular justice concerns relations to other individuals (Q. 58, A. 7). Particular justice has two subjective parts (subdivisions): commutative justice, which concerns the quid pro quo relations between individuals; and distributive justice, which concerns the allocation of common goods to individuals in proportion to their contribution to the common good (Q. 61). In connection with commutative justice, Aquinas considers the problem of restitution (Q. 62).

Human beings sin against distributive justice if they give favorable treatment to particular persons irrespective of the persons' deserts (Q. 63). Human beings sin against commutative justice by deeds against another's person (e.g., murder [QQ. 64, 65]) or property (e.g., theft [Q. 66]). Human beings sin against commutative justice by word in the criminal judicial process. In particular, Aquinas examines what justice requires of judges (Q. 67), accusers (Q. 68), defendants (Q. 69), witnesses (Q. 70), and lawyers (Q. 71). He also considers ways in which human beings sin against commutative justice outside the criminal judicial process (QQ. 72–76). Then he considers commutative justice in connection with merchants buying and selling goods and with lenders exacting interest or any monetary equivalent on money lent to borrowers (QQ. 77, 78).

There are two integral (constitutive) parts of justice: avoiding injustice, that is, acts contrary to justice, and doing justice, that is, acts required by justice (Q. 79, A. 1). Conversely, one sins against justice by transgression, that is, by acting unjustly, and by omission, that is, by failing to perform actions required by justice (Q. 79, AA. 2, 3). Aquinas contends that sins of transgression are, for the most part, more serious than sins of omission (Q. 79, A. 4).

There are potential (related) parts of justice (e.g., acts of religion, filial devotion, and truth telling) (QQ. 80–119).

Lastly, Aquinas relates the Aristotelian principle of equity, that is, fundamental fairness, to justice and argues that application of legal principles to particular cases sometimes fails to effect justice (Q. 120). In such cases, reason requires that fundamental fairness trump the letter of the law.

Fortitude, or courage, is the third cardinal virtue (QQ. 123–40). As a special virtue, fortitude guards the will against withdrawing from the good prescribed by reason out of fear of the most grievous bodily harm, namely, mortal danger (Q. 123, A. 4). The virtue disposes the will to stand firm against the fear and to counterattack it with moderate boldness (Q. 123, A.3). Standing firm against fear is the chief act of the virtue of fortitude, since it is more difficult to withstand fear than to moderate boldness (Q. 123, A. 6) Fortitude consists of the mean between too much fear (timidity) and too little fear (temerity) (QQ. 125, 126), and the moderation of boldness by reason (Q. 127). The corresponding sins against fortitude are timidity, temerity, and excessive boldness.

Fortitude has integral (constitutive) and potential (related) parts but no subjective parts (subdivisions) (Q. 128). The integral parts in standing fast are patience and perseverance (QQ. 136–38). The integral parts in counterattacking fear are mental confidence, which Aquinas equates to magnanimity, and bold action, which he equates to magnificence (QQ. 129–35). Fortitude has potential parts insofar as human beings courageously withstand and overcome fear of things other than mortal bodily harm (e.g., fear of losing one's job unless one commits sin) (QQ. 129–38).

Temperance, or moderation, is the fourth cardinal virtue (QQ. 141–70). As a special virtue, temperance guards the will against choosing sense desires and pleasures contrary to the good prescribed by reason (Q. 141, AA. 2, 3), and one sins against temperance when one chooses such desires and pleasures (Q. 142). The subjective parts (subdivisions) of temperance concern moderation in food (QQ. 143, 146–48), sobriety in alcohol (QQ. 143, 149, 150), and chastity in sexual behavior (QQ. 143, 151–54). The integral (constitutive) parts involve a sense of shame regarding intemperate acts, and a sense of honor (QQ. 143–45). The potential (related) parts are continence, humility, meekness, mercy, good order, proper attire, parsimony (self-sufficiency), and moderation (simplicity) (QQ. 143, 156–70).

ST I

2

✣

GOD

The ST begins with questions about God. The order is precise. First, after defending theology as necessary and scientific in the Aristotelian sense (Q. 1), Aquinas quite logically begins with questions about God's existence. Second, he deals with God's so-called attributes—characteristics that we predicate of the Godhead itself apart from God's activity. Third, Aquinas explains our knowledge of God and assesses our predications about him. Fourth, he examines characteristics that we predicate about God regarding his immanent activity (knowing and willing). Lastly, he analyzes aspects of his transitive activity regarding creatures, especially human beings (providence, predestination, power).

Existence

Aquinas asks three questions about God's existence: Is knowledge of his existence self-evident, that is, does one know that he exists when one understands what the term *God* means? If one does not, can one demonstrate his existence? If one can, how does one?

The answer to the first question is that God's existence, although self-evident in itself, since the predicate *exists* necessarily belongs to the subject *God*, is not self-evident to us, since we do not in this life know what God is—we do not know God's essence in itself (Q. 2, A. 1).

Aquinas poses the following objection, which explicitly articulates Anselm's so-called ontological argument. A proposition is self-evident if one knows its truth as soon as one understands its terms, and we know that God exists as soon as we understand the term *God*, since God exists in our intellect as soon as we understand the term *God*, and that term means that than which nothing greater can be conceived. But what exists in fact is greater than what exists in the intellect alone. Therefore, the existence of God is self-evident. Aquinas makes three points in reply. First, there are some who believe that God is a material substance and so do not understand that the term *God* means that than which nothing greater can be conceived. Second, even supposing that one understands that God means that than which nothing greater can be thought, it only follows that such a one would understand that the meaning of the term would exist conceptually, not that it would actually exist. Third, one cannot prove that God really exists unless one admits that something than which nothing greater can be conceived really exists, a proposition that atheists and agnostics do not concede.

Can we nonetheless demonstrate that God exists? Aquinas claims that we can do so by tracing known existing things to God as their cause, although we thereby have no knowledge of what God in himself is (Q. 2, A. 2).

He then proposes five ways to demonstrate God's existence (Q. 2, A. 3). The ways presuppose the principle of intelligibility, or sufficient reason—that things need to have a sufficient reason that explains why they exist or happen. We, when we understand the terms, immediately recognize the truth of this principle, and that of the related principle of causality—that things happen because other things cause them to happen. Philosophers commonly call the principles analytic, or self-evident.

The first way focuses on observed locomotion and alterations to material things. These changes are only intelligible if something else causes the changes, and there cannot be an infinite regress of caused causes, which themselves need to be moved or changed from inactivity to activity. Therefore, there exists an uncaused cause that is pure actuality.

The second way focuses on the same fact of accidental changes in the world from the perspective of the causes of the changes and reaches the same conclusion.

The third way argues from the difference between the possible and the necessary. Some things come to be and pass away, and so they can exist or not exist. But it is impossible that all such things always exist, since what can not-exist, at some point of time does not exist. Therefore, if everything can not-exist, there was a time when nothing really existed. But if this is so, nothing would now exist, since something nonexistent begins to exist only through the agency of something existent. Therefore, if nothing existed, nothing would begin to exist, and so nothing would now exist. But this conclusion is obviously false. Therefore, not every being is capable of nonexistence, and there is a necessary being. But everything necessary either has or does not have the ground of its necessity from another source, and there cannot be an infinite regress of necessary things having the ground of their necessity in another source. Therefore, we need to posit something intrinsically necessary, something that does not have the ground of its necessity from another source. This intrinsically necessary being is God.

The third way is difficult to interpret, and many, if not most, scholars, including some generally sympathetic to Aquinas, find the argument flawed. The central problem concerns interpretation of the temporal references. Is Aquinas assuming hypothetically that the world always existed, that is, that the world had no first moment? (Or, conversely, is he assuming the biblical view that the world had a beginning?) Is he claiming that if the world has existed eternally, and if only substantially changeable things were to have existed, then everything would have ceased to exist by now? Is he assuming the possibility of time before things come to be or pass away?

But the temporal references need not be interpreted in a strictly temporal sense. When Aquinas says that intrinsically contingent things, that is, substantially changeable things, did not exist at one time, he may simply mean that such things are things that come to be and pass away, and that something necessary needs to cause the intrinsically contingent things to come to be. And when he says that if every existing thing were to be intrinsically contingent, there was a time when nothing existed, he may simply mean that nothing at all would exist, since there would be nothing to cause the intrinsically contingent things to come to be.

If the argument is so interpreted, it can be summarized as follows: We observe that material things do not exist necessarily but come to be and pass away, and so material things are intrinsically contingent. But such things cannot exist by their own power. Rather, they can do so only by the power of something that does not come to be and pass away, that is to say, such things exist by the power of something intrinsically necessary. Therefore, if everything were to be intrinsically contingent, nothing would exist. But this is contrary to fact. Therefore, there needs to exist a necessary being that causes the existence of intrinsically contingent things, and ultimately an absolutely necessary being, one that is not only intrinsically necessary like the angels but also does not depend extrinsically on any other necessary being. In short, intrinsically contingent beings can neither severally nor collectively account for their coming to exist, and only an absolutely necessary being, God, can. This interpretation of the third way is logically consistent and compatible with similar arguments that Aquinas advances in the *Summa contra Gentiles* (I, 15) and *Compendium of Theology* (I, 6).

The fourth way begins with the observed grades of existing and perfection in the world. We call things more or less excellent insofar as they approximate something more excellent and existing in the highest degree, and this most excellent thing, as the most in the transcendental genus of being, causes the being and excellence of everything else. This way argues from the perfection of observed things to the *existence* of an absolutely perfect exemplar, but the exemplar is a concrete reality, not an abstract idea, and the efficient cause, not merely the exemplar, of everything else.

The fifth way begins with the observed regularity of natural material things in the world. The regularity indicates that the things act purposively, and yet they lack the intelligence prerequisite for purposeful activity. Therefore, there needs to be an intelligent being that orders the things of nature to their ends. Alone of the five ways, the fifth explicitly argues to the existence of an *intelligent* source that ordains the activities of material things. The fifth way is also unique in not explicitly concluding to the existence of God as the efficient cause of the world's existence and processes of change. Aquinas' argument is not the design argument of William Paley (AD 1743–1805). Aquinas here argues from the fact that *particular* things act in regular ways, not from the fact that the cumulative activities of particular things produce an ordered universe, a cosmos, although he indeed holds that to be true.

Aquinas cites a perennial objection to the existence of God: the problem of evil, a problem that he will later deal with extensively in connection with creation. The objection runs as follows: If God were to exist, nothing evil would exist. But evil things do exist. Therefore, God does not exist. Aquinas answers summarily that God is the highest good, and so it belongs to his infinite goodness to permit evil things and bring forth good things from them.

Essential Predications

Aquinas next considers things we predicate of God essentially, that is, of God considered in himself apart from his activity. People frequently refer to these predicates as his attributes, but God, strictly speaking, has no attributes. He is the fullness of being, pure actuality, and so does not "have" anything over and above his substance.

First, God is identical with his essence or nature, since, like the angels and unlike human beings, he has no composition with matter, and so his individuality does not differ from his essence or nature (Q. 3, A. 3).

Second, God's essence and existing are identical, since an essence distinct from existing would be a potentiality and would need to receive existing, but he is pure actuality (Q. 3, A. 4).

Third, God is most perfect, since he, as the first efficient cause of all other things, is most actual (Q. 4, A. 1). He possesses the perfections of all things, since he is their first cause, and effects preexist in their cause (Q. 4, A. 2). Conversely, creatures have an analogical likeness to God (Q. 4, A. 3). Aquinas poses the following objection: if creatures are like God, God is like creatures. He answers that, although creatures are like God, God is not like creatures, since there is no mutual likeness in causes and effects of different orders (e.g., a portrait is like a human bring, but not vice versa).

Fourth, we attribute goodness to God inasmuch as all desired created perfections flow from him as their first cause, and he is accordingly the highest good (Q. 6, A. 2). Aquinas poses an objection: Highest signifies comparison. But things not belonging to the same genus are not comparable (e.g., sweetness is not greater or lesser than a line). Therefore, since God does not belong to the same genus as other things, we cannot call God the highest good in relation to other things. He replies as follows: Things not belonging to the same genus are in no way comparable if they belong to different genera. But God is outside genera and is the source of every genus. Therefore, we compare him to other things by superfluity, and the highest good signifies such a comparison.

Fifth, God is infinite, since his existence is not received in anything (Q. 7, A. 1).

Sixth, God is altogether immutable, since he is pure actuality without admixture of any potentiality (Q. 9, A. 1).

Seventh, God is eternal, since he is immutable, and time is based on change (Q. 10, A. 2.).

Lastly, there is only one God, since he includes within himself the *whole* perfection of existing (Q. 11, A. 3).

Our Knowledge of God

Aquinas affirms that the human intellect has a potentiality to know God, since he, as pure actuality, is most knowable in himself, and human happiness consists of intellectual activity that would not be satisfied without knowledge of him in himself (Q. 12, A. 1). But natural reason knows him in this life only through his effects, namely, sensibly perceptible things (Q. 12, A. 12).

Our Predications about God

Aquinas defends the truth of human predications about God. We know him from creatures by his causal relationship to them and by way of eminence and elimination (Q. 13, A. 1).

Aquinas poses several important objections. One runs as follows: Every predicate is either abstract or concrete. But concrete predicates are not proper to God because he is simple, and abstract predicates are not proper to him because they do not signify a complete and subsistent being. (Abstract predicates [e.g., *wisdom*] signify forms apart from subjects, and concrete predicates [e.g., *wise*] signify forms in subjects. Therefore, the objection argues, the proposition *God is wisdom* fails to signify God's subsistence, and the proposition *God is wise* fails to signify his simplicity.) Therefore, we can apply no predicate to God.

Aquinas gives an unusually long response. We know God from creatures, and we apply predicates to him from them. Therefore, the predicates signify in the way proper to material creatures. But what is complete and subsistent in such creatures is composite, and the forms of such creatures are not complete subsistent things. Therefore, the predicates we apply to signify complete subsisting things signify things in their materiality, since materiality belongs to composite things. And the predicates we apply to signify simple forms signify the sources whereby things are such-and-such (e.g., whiteness signifies the source whereby something is white). Therefore, since God is both simple and subsistent, we attribute to him both abstract predicates to signify his simplicity and concrete predicates to signify his subsistence and completeness. But both such predicates fall short of his way, since our intellect in this life cannot know him as he is.

The second objection runs as follows: Nouns signify substances qualitatively, verbs and participles signify substances temporally, and pronouns signify substances demonstratively or relatively. But none of these parts of speech are proper to God, since he lacks qualities, accidents, and time, and we cannot sensibly perceive him so as to point him out. Nor can we signify him relatively, since relative pronouns record the aforementioned nouns or particles or demonstrative pronouns. Therefore, we cannot apply a predicate to God in any way.

Aquinas gives another long reply. To signify a substance qualitatively is to signify an individually existing subject with the determined nature or form in which it subsists. Therefore, as we give predicates to God in their materiality in order to signify his subsistence and completeness, so do we give him predicates that signify him qualitatively. And we predicate of him verbs and participles connoting time because eternity includes all time. But we can absolutely understand subsistent things and signify them absolutely only by way of composite things. Therefore we can understand absolute eternity and give expression to it only by way of temporal things and because our intellect is innately ordered to composite and temporal things. Additionally, we predicate demonstrative pronouns of God insofar as they point to what we understand, not to what we sensibly perceive. Thus also we can signify God by relative pronouns in the way in which we predicate nouns, participles, and demonstrative pronouns of him.

Some affirmative predicates signify the divine substance (e.g., God is good), although they deficiently represent him (Q. 13, A. 2). Such predicates belong to God in the proper sense as to what they signify, but not as to their way of signifying, namely, as they belong to creatures (Q. 13, A. 3).

Aquinas poses an objection: Every predicate we apply to God comes from creatures. But we predicate creatures' perfections of God metaphorically, as when we say he is as strong as a lion. Therefore, we apply every predicate to God metaphorically. Aquinas answers the objection with an important distinction. Some predicates signify perfections that come from God to creatures in such a way that the imperfect way itself whereby a creature shares in a divine perfection is included in the very meaning of the predicate (e.g., a lion's strength signifies in a material way), and we can apply such predicates to God only metaphorically. But other predicates signify the perfections themselves absolutely, without any mode of sharing being included in their meaning (e.g., being, good, living, and the like), and we apply such predicates to God in the proper sense.

Predicates signifying the divine substance are not synonyms, since they represent different aspects of God's perfection reflected in the multiplicity of created perfections (Q. 13, A. 4). We neither univocally nor purely equivocally but analogously, that is, in a sense partly the same and partly different, apply predicates to both God and creatures (Q. 13, A. 5). We are able to do so because effects are in some way like their cause, and God causes the perfections of creatures. We apply temporal predicates to God because of changes in creatures, not because of changes in him (Q. 13, A. 7).

The predicate and subject in a true affirmative proposition about God signify something really the same in one respect, namely, God himself, and something conceptually different, namely, the subject and the predicate (Q. 13, A. 12).

Aquinas poses an objection: Every act of the intellect that understands an object otherwise than the object exists is false. But God exists without any composition, and every affirmative judgment understands an object as composite. Therefore, we cannot formulate true affirmative propositions about God.

Aquinas answers the objection by pointing out that it is ambiguous to say that a judgment that understands an object otherwise than the object exists is false, since the adverb *otherwise* can modify the verb *understands* as regards what is understood or as regards the one who understands. If the adverb modifies the verb as regards what is understood, the proposition is true, and it means that any judgment that understands something to be otherwise than it is, is false. But this is irrelevant, since our intellect in formulating a proposition about God asserts that he is simple, not composite. If, however, the adverb modifies the verb as regards the one who understands, then the proposition is false, since the intellect's way of understanding differs from the object's way of existing (e.g., our intellect understands in an immaterial way material objects inferior to itself without understanding the objects to be immaterial). Similarly, when our intellect understands simple beings superior to itself, it understands them in its own way, namely, a composite way. And so the judgments of our intellect are not false when they form composite propositions about God.

Aquinas easily defends the truth of negative predications about God, predications that deny imperfections in him (e.g., God is not material, finite, etc.). But affirmative predications about God pose a serious problem, since our intellect in this life is dependent on sense images and so cannot know God as he is in himself. Aquinas claims that we can affirm pure perfections, that is, perfections that as such do not imply imperfections (e.g., goodness, knowing, willing), of God. We can predicate those perfections of God in a sense partly the same but completely different insofar as he infinitely transcends creatures. Aquinas thus proposes a via media between complete rationalism and complete agnosticism: We can know that God causes the perfections in the universe and that effects are like their cause. Therefore, created perfections without any admixture of imperfection can be predicated of him analogously.

Knowledge

Understanding is immaterial (e.g., the knower knowing a stone possesses the form of stone but not the concrete, individual matter of a stone). Because this is so, and because God is most immaterial, he is most knowing (Q. 14, A. 1). God's power to know is as great as his actuality, and so he knows himself as much as he is knowable, that is, comprehensively (Q. 14, A. 3). God's understanding is an immanent activity identical with his substance, since otherwise the divine substance would be a potentiality in relation to the activity (Q. 14, A. 4).

In knowing himself, he knows other things as his essence contains the likeness of those things (e.g., he knows what human beings are by knowing how they share in his perfection and imitate him in a limited way) (Q. 14, A. 5).

His knowledge, in conjunction with his will, causes the things he creates, just as a craftsman's knowledge causes the things he crafts (Q. 14, A. 8), to which Aquinas poses an objection. In positing a cause, we posit its effect. But God's knowledge is eternal. Therefore, creatures exist from eternity if God's knowledge causes things. Aquinas gives the following answer: God's knowledge causes things as they belong to his knowledge. But it was not part of his knowledge that things would exist from eternity. Therefore, although God's knowledge is eternal, it does not follow that creatures would exist from eternity.

God knows possible as well as actual things, since possible things exist in his power, and his knowledge of actual things extends across the whole spectrum of time and to everything that has existed, does exist, or will exist (Q. 14, A. 9). By pure understanding, that is, understanding without any recourse to deductive reasoning, he knows both the universal and the individual particular (Q. 14, A. 11).

He knows future contingent things, that is, things that may be or not be, both in their proximate causes and in their actuality. Although contingent things come to exist successively and are future in relation to proximate causes, he knows all of them at once. Everything in time is present to God from eternity, both because the natures of things are present to him, and because his sight is borne from eternity over all things as they exist in their presence to him (Q. 14, A. 13).

Aquinas poses a key objection: Everything we know necessarily exists, and God's knowledge is more certain than ours. Therefore, everything God knows necessarily exists. But no future contingent thing necessarily exists. Therefore, God does not know any future contingent thing.

Aquinas answers the objection at length. We successively know things brought into actuality in time, but God knows such things in eternity, which transcends time. And so we cannot be certain of future contingent events, since we know them as contingent, but God and only God, whose understanding transcends time, can be certain of them. For example, travelers on a road do not see travelers on the road behind them, but someone with a view of the whole road from a height sees at once all the travelers on the road. We cannot know future contingent things as such, and so the things we know need to be necessary, namely, as they are in themselves. But the things God knows need to be necessary in the way in which they are subject to his knowing but not absolutely necessary in relation to their particular causes.

And so also we distinguish the proposition *everything God knows necessarily exists*. The proposition can be about the things

God knows or the statement. If we understand the proposition to be to be about those things, it is a simple one and false, and its meaning is that everything that God knows is necessary. If we understand the proposition to be about the statement, it is a compound one and true, and the meaning is that the statement, namely, that the things God knows exist, is necessary.

The Divine Ideas

God's ideas consist of his knowledge of the forms of things. The theory has its roots in Plato's Ideas, or Forms, which Augustine located in the mind of God. Since God, in creating things, acts with understanding, he knows the forms of the things he creates (Q. 15, A. 1). He intends the order of the universe and so has an idea of that order, and he cannot contemplate the whole without contemplating the particular natures of the things out of which the whole is constituted (Q. 15, A. 2). The ideas as exemplars belong to practical knowledge, but the ideas as sources of knowledge are related to everything God knows, whether actual or possible, in its own nature in a theoretical way (Q. 15, A. 3). In answer to an objection arguing that God has no idea of evil and so no idea of everything, Aquinas points out that God does not know evil by its own nature but by the nature of good. And so God has no idea of evil, either as an exemplar or as a nature.

Life

Aquinas distinguishes the immanent activity of different living material things: plants, animals, and human beings. Plants activate themselves only in executing their powers of nutrition, growth, and reproduction. Irrational animals activate themselves not only regarding vegetative functions but also by forms acquired through the senses, forms that cause animals to act (e.g., cats to chase mice). Human beings, rational animals, activate themselves regarding chosen ends (e.g., to cook dinner). But the human intellect needs to be activated by the first principles of theoretical understanding (e.g., the principle of contradiction) and the final end of practical activity (happiness). Since God's nature is his understanding, nothing is needed to activate his intellect, and so he has the highest degree of immanent activity (Q. 18, A. 3).

Aquinas poses an objection: Living things move themselves. But being moved does not belong to God. Therefore, neither does life. Aquinas answers the objection with further explanation of immanent activity. There are two kinds of action. One kind (transitive action) passes into external matter (e.g., heating things). The other kind (immanent action) remains in the cause (e.g., understanding, sense perception, willing). The first kind perfects the object. The second kind perfects the cause. Because motion is the actuality of a movable object, we call the second kind of action the motion of the cause by this analogy: as motion is the actuality of something imperfect, so the second kind of action is the actuality of the cause. Although motion is the actuality of something incomplete (i.e., something with potentiality), the second kind of action is the actuality of something complete (i.e., something that has actuality). Therefore, something that understands itself moves itself in the way understanding is motion. And God moves himself in this way, not in the way of something incomplete.

God's Will

An intellectual nature has a disposition to rest in possession of an understood good or to strive for it if it is not possessed, and this disposition belongs to the intellectual appetite, the will. And so there is a will in everything that has an intellect. Since there is an intellect in God, a will needs to be in God, and his will is identical with his existing (Q. 19, A. 1). He wills himself as the end and other things as means to that end, as it befits his goodness that other things share in it (Q. 19, A. 2).

To this Aquinas poses an objection: Objects move appetites,

and willed objects move the will. Therefore, if God causes things other than himself, something else will move his will. But this conclusion is impossible. Aquinas answers the objection. Human beings can will things both for the sake of something else and for their own sake. But God wills things other than himself only for the sake of his goodness. Therefore, it does not follow that anything other than his goodness moves his will. And so, just as he understands other things than himself by understanding his own essence, he wills other things than himself by willing his own goodness.

His will is necessarily related to his goodness, and so he necessarily wills his goodness, but he wills other things only insofar as they are related to his goodness as their end. It is only hypothetically necessary that he will other things than himself, that is, it is necessary for him to will them only if he should happen to do so. Any thing that he wills conditionally (e.g., that human beings obey his laws, which is conditioned on them freely doing so) need not happen (Q. 19, A. 3).

To this Aquinas poses an objection: God necessarily knows everything he knows, but God's will, like his knowledge, is his essence. Therefore, God necessarily wills everything he wills. Aquinas answers the objection. As God's existing is intrinsically necessary, so also are his willing and knowing. But God's knowing has a necessary relationship to what he knows, and God's willing does not have a necessary relationship to what it wills. This is so because knowledge concerns things as they exist in the knower, and the will concerns things as they exist in themselves. But all things other than God himself have a necessary existence as they exist in God, and no absolutely necessary existence as they exist in themselves. Therefore, God necessarily knows everything that he knows, and he does not necessarily will everything that he wills.

God causes things by his will but not by a necessity of nature, since an intellect needs to predetermine the end and the necessary means to the end for causes that act by nature (e.g., an archer predetermines the target and path of an arrow), and God is the first efficient cause of nature (Q. 19, A. 4).

He is the universal cause of everything, and so his will necessarily achieves its effect (Q. 19, A. 6). To this Aquinas poses an objection: St. Paul says that God wills that every human being be saved (1 Tim 2:4). But his does not turn out to be so. Therefore, God's will is not always fulfilled. Aquinas gives a lengthy reply, the first two points of which try to qualify the words of Paul: they may only mean that God wills that all the saved be saved, or that human beings of every condition be saved.

The third point is Aquinas' principal response. We can understand the words about universal salvation to be about God's antecedent, not his consequent, will, and we understand this distinction to be on the part of the things willed, not the divine will itself. To understand this, we need to consider that God wills everything insofar as it is good. Moreover, things can be good or evil in their primary aspect, as we consider them absolutely, and yet they have the contrary character as we consider them with something added, which is a secondary aspect. For example, it is good, absolutely considered, that human beings live, and it is evil that they be killed; but, if we add about this human being that he is a murderer or a threat to the community as long as he lives, it is good that he be killed, and it is evil that he live. And so a just judge wills antecedently that every human being live, but consequently that a murderer be hanged. Similarly, God wills antecedently that every human being be saved, but consequently that some individuals be damned, as justice requires.

And yet we will in one respect, not absolutely, what we will antecedently, since the will relates to things as they in themselves exist, and they as such exist in particular ways. And so we will things absolutely as we will them with all their particular circumstances taken into consideration, and this is to will consequently.

And so a just judge wills absolutely that a murderer be hanged but would in one respect will that the murderer live, namely insofar as the murderer is a human being. Such a qualified willing is a wish rather than an absolute willing.

In summary, Aquinas concludes that everything that God wills absolutely happens, even if what he wills antecedently does not always.

His will cannot vary, but he can will that things change (Q. 19, A. 7). To this Aquinas poses an objection: According to Jeremiah 17:8, God would repent of the evil he had planned to inflict on Israel if the people were to repent. Therefore, God can, so to speak, change his mind.

To this Aquinas gives a lengthy reply. God's will, as the first and universal cause, does not exclude intermediate causes with the power to produce some effects. But intermediate causes have less power than the first cause. Therefore, there are many things in God's power, knowledge, and will that are not included in the order of inferior causes. And so, in the case of Lazarus after his death, an observer who regarded only inferior causes could say that Lazarus will not rise from the dead, and an observer who regarded the divine cause could say that Lazarus will rise from the dead. God wills that things sometimes happen by inferior causes, and that things at other times will happen by the superior cause (or the converse). Thus God sometimes declares that something will happen insofar as the thing is included in the order of inferior causes (e.g., as nature or merit so disposes), and yet the thing does not come to be, since it is otherwise regarding the superior cause. Therefore, we should understand the statement of Jeremiah in a metaphorical sense, since human beings seem to repent when they do not carry out what they threatened to do.

Things that he wills both come to be and come to be in the way he wills them to come to be, sometimes necessarily (e.g., effects of the law of gravity) and sometimes contingently (e.g., automobile accidents, human observance of his laws) (Q. 19, A. 8).

He in no way wills sin, which takes away the proper order to the divine good, but he does coincidentally will natural evils in connection with willing order in the universe (e.g., that this thing passes away when something else comes to be) (Q. 19, A. 9).

Aquinas poses an objection: The propositions *evils exist* and *evils do not exist* are contradictory. But evils exist, and so God, whose will is always fulfilled, does not will that evils not exist. Therefore, God wills that evils exist. Aquinas replies that the two given propositions are contradictory. But the proposition *God wills evils to exist* and the proposition *God wills evils not to exist* are not contradictory, since both propositions are affirmative. God neither wills that evils exist, nor that they not exist. Rather, he wills to permit evils to exist, and this is good.

Since God does not necessarily will other things, he enjoys free choice regarding them (Q. 19, A. 10).

Love

Since acts of the will tend toward good, and love concerns good in general, love is by nature the first act of the will, and since God wills, he loves (Q. 20, A. 1). Aquinas poses an objection: Love is a unifying and binding force. But there cannot be such in God, since he is simple. Therefore, God does not love.

Aquinas replies with an explanation of love. An act of love tends toward two things: the good that one wills for someone, and the one for whom one wills the good. To will good for someone is in the proper sense to love that one. And so persons, insofar as they love themselves, will good for themselves. And so they seek to unite that good to themselves as much as they can. And so love is a unifying force even in the case of God. But the good he wills for himself is only himself, who is by his essence goodness. Therefore, his love implies no composition in him. In loving another, one wills the good for the other. But one rejoices in the other as if in oneself, judging the good for the other as the good for oneself. And so love is a binding force, since love, being disposed toward the other as toward oneself, unites the other to oneself. But God wills goodness for others, and so God's love for others is a binding force without any composition in him

And since his will causes every other existing thing, and existing as such is good, he wills some good for everything. Moreover, his love pours out the very goodness of things (Q. 20, A. 2).

Aquinas poses an objection: There are two kinds of love, namely, the love of desire and the love of friendship. But God does not have a love of desire for irrational creatures, since he needs nothing beside himself. Nor does he have a love of friendship for irrational creatures, since one cannot have such a love. Therefore, God does not love everything. Aquinas replies that there can be friendship only between rational creatures, among whom there can be mutual love and shared activities, and for whom things may turn out well or ill, just as there is benevolence in the proper sense toward such creatures. But irrational creatures cannot attain to loving good or sharing the intellectual and blessed life God enjoys. Therefore, God, properly speaking, does not love them with a love of friendship. But he does love them with a love of desire inasmuch as he ordains them for rational creatures and even for himself. He loves them because of his goodness and their benefit to us, not because he needs them. We likewise desire some things both for ourselves and for others.

And so he loves everything but not equally, willing greater good for some than for others (Q. 20, A. 3).

Justice and Mercy

God's justice consists of creating things with due order and proportion. But creatures are ultimately due something only because of the mercy of his goodness, and he dispenses to creatures more than anything proportional (Q. 21, A. 4).

God's Providence

God causes the good in creatures by his intellect in conjunction with his will, and so his plan ordering things to their ends needs to preexist in his mind. This plan is providence in the strict sense (Q. 22, A. 1). His causality reaches to all things as to their specific and individual causes and as to both destructible things (material things) and indestructible things (human souls and angels). And so he necessarily orders everything to its end, and every existing thing is subject to his providence. Even acts of free choice by human beings are traceable to God as their first efficient cause (Q. 22, A. 2).

To this Aquinas poses several objections. The first runs as follows: Nothing foreseen is fortuitous. Therefore, if God had foreseen everything, nothing would be fortuitous, and so there will be no chance or luck. But this is contrary to the common opinion. Aquinas replies that the universal cause and particular causes differ. Things can depart from the order of particular causes, since things are taken away from the order of some particular causes by other particular causes preventing the order (e.g., the action of water prevents wood from burning). But all particular causes are included under the universal cause. Therefore, no effect can escape the order of the universal cause. Therefore, there are effects by chance or luck with respect particular causes but not with respect to the universal cause. For example, the meeting of two slaves, although by chance on their part, is nonetheless foreseen by their master, who knowingly sends them to the same place without either knowing about the other.

A second objection runs as follows: Things left to themselves are not subject to the providence of anyone directing them. But God leaves human beings, especially the wicked, to themselves. Therefore, some things are not subject to divine providence. Aquinas replies. Rational creatures by free choice move themselves to action. But we need to trace the very acts of free choice back to God as their cause. Therefore, deeds done by free choice need to be subject to his providence. But God does not allow anything to happen that would definitively prevent the salvation of the just. Therefore, he provides for the just in a more excellent way than for the wicked. But God does not entirely exclude the wicked from his providence. Otherwise, they would fall into nothingness if his providence were not to preserve them.

He directly provides for everything, but he communicates his causal powers to creatures to execute his order (Q. 22, A. 3). His goodness is the chief end of his providence, but the secondary end is the perfection of the universe. His providence has prepared necessary causes to produce effects that necessarily come to be (e.g., thunder and lightening), and contingent causes to produce effects that contingently come to be (e.g., human acts of free choice) (Q. 22, A. 4).

Predestination

Part of God's providence is to convey human beings to him, their final end, which they cannot attain by their own power. This part of providence is predestination (Q. 23, A. 1). As predestination is part of providence regarding those he orders to eternal life, so damnation is part of providence regarding those who fall away from their end. Damnation includes his will both to allow some to fall into sin in this life and to cause the sinners to be eternally punished in the next life (Q. 23, A. 3).

Aquinas poses an objection: Damnation would need to be related to the damned in the same way that predestination is related to the predestined. But predestination causes the salvation of the predestined. Therefore, condemnation will cause the destruction of the damned. But this is false. Therefore, God does not damn anyone. Aquinas replies that damnation causes in a different way than predestination does. Predestination causes both what the predestined hope for in the future life, namely, glory, and what exists in the present life, namely, grace. But damnation does not cause what exists in the present life, namely, sin, although damnation causes abandonment by God. Sin results from the free choice of those damned and bereft of grace, but damnation causes what is rendered the damned in the future life, namely, eternal punishment.

Human beings cannot cause the effect of predestination in general, but God can order a particular effect of predestination (merit) to be the cause and reason of another particular effect of predestination (glory) (Q. 23, A. 5).

Aquinas poses an objection: It seems unfair to give unequal benefits to those who are equal. But all human beings are equal as regards both their nature and original sin, and human beings are unequal as regards the merits or demerits of their own acts. Therefore, God prepares unequal rewards for human beings by predestining some and damning others only because he foreknows their merits or demerits.

Aquinas gives a lengthy reply. We can understand from God's goodness why he predestines some and damns others. God made everything to manifest his goodness. But his goodness needs to be manifested in many ways, since created things cannot attain his simplicity. And so different grades of things are required to fill up the universe, and some things in the universe have high rank, and other things low rank. And so, to preserve the multiplicity of grades in things, God allows some evils to occur. Consider the whole human race as the entire universe. God willed to manifest his goodness in some human beings—those he predestines—by his mercy, by sparing them, and in others—those he damns—by his justice, by punishing them. And this is the reason why God chooses some and damns others.

But why he chose these human beings and damned those has no reason except God willing it so. Similarly, we can ascribe the reason why God established parts of prime matter under different forms, namely, that there be a diversity of species in things of nature. But why this particular part of matter is under this particular form depends on God's absolute will, as it depends on the absolute will of a craftsman that this particular stone is in this particular part of a wall.

Still, there is no unfairness in God if he prepares unequal benefits for equal things. Regarding things bestowed as a favor, one can at one's pleasure, without detriment to justice, give more or less to whomever one wishes, provided that one does not take away from another what is due to the other.

Power

God is pure actuality and so most properly an active source, that is, an efficient cause, without being acted upon in any way. Therefore, he has active power in the highest degree (Q. 25, A. 1). Since his existing is unlimited, possessing in itself beforehand the perfection of all existing, he can make anything that can exist. Only nonbeing, something simultaneously signifying existing and not existing, is absolutely impossible and beyond his power (Q. 25, A. 3). Since his will causes whatever he creates, and his will is not determined by nature and necessity to create the things created, he can make other things than those he has (e.g., different kinds of plants or animals) (Q. 25, A. 5). With respect to the goodness that belongs to a thing's essence, he cannot make anything better than he has (e.g., an essentially better human being). But with respect to the goodness over and above a thing's essence, he can better the things he has made (e.g., a better human digestive system). And he can make something else better than anything he has made (e.g., a better plant or animal) (Q. 25, A. 6).

Aquinas poses an objection: What is best cannot be made better. But all things made by God are collectively best, since the beauty of the universe consists of them all. Therefore, God cannot make a better universe. Aquinas replies that God assigned the most becoming order to the things he made, and the good of the universe consists of that order. Therefore, presupposing the things God made, the universe cannot be better. But God could make other things or add other things to those he made, and so such a universe would be better.

3

CREATION AND GOVERNANCE OF THE UNIVERSE

The Cause of Creation

God is the first efficient cause of every existing thing, since the first being, intrinsically subsistent existing, needs to cause everything that shares in different ways of existing (Q. 44, A. 1). The cause of things as beings needs to cause whatever belongs in any way to their existing, and so the universal cause of beings also causes the substratum of material things, prime matter (Q. 44, A. 2). And exemplars (models) are necessary to produce things with definite forms, as his essence is imitable in different ways (Q. 44, A. 3). Efficient causes, since they act to produce particular effects, act to achieve ends. The first efficient cause, God, acts to communicate his goodness, and the goodness of creatures is a likeness of his goodness. And so his goodness is the final cause of all things (Q. 44, A. 4).

The Manner of Creation

The emanation of the whole of being from the universal cause does not presuppose comings-to-be by particular emanations, and so the emanation of the whole of being in general from the first cause cannot presuppose any beings, that is, the emanation comes "out of" nothing (Q. 45, A. 1). God's proper effect in creating is existence without qualification, and so nothing else can act dependently and instrumentally to produce that effect (Q. 45, A. 5).

The Beginning of Creation

Since God did not need to will that anything other than himself exist, the world need exist only as long as he wills it to exist (Q. 46, A. 1). Although God has revealed that the world had a beginning, we cannot demonstrate the impossibility of the world having always existed (Q. 46, A. 2).

The Diversity in Creation

The multiplicity and diversity of things comes from the intention of their first cause, God. The goodness that exists simply and uniformly in God exists diversely and disparately in creatures (Q. 47, A. 1). There is only one world, since there is an integrated order of all creatures (Q. 47, A. 3).

Evil

Following Augustine, Aquinas holds that evil as such cannot signify a form or a nature, since the existence and perfection of every nature possesses goodness. And so, since evil signifies the absence of good, it is neither anything existing nor anything good (Q. 48, A. 1).

Aquinas poses an objection: Every constitutive difference is a nature. But evil is a constitutive difference in moral matters, since evil habits differ specifically from good habits. Therefore, evil signifies a nature. He replies that moral matters take their species from their ends, that is, the object of the will. But good has the nature of end. And so good and evil are uniquely specific differences in moral matters, good as such and evil as taking away a due end. But taking away a due end constitutes a species in moral matters only insofar as the taking away is connected to an undue end. And so the evil that constitutes a specific difference in moral matters is a good linked to the privation of another good (e.g., an intemperate person aims to gain a sensibly perceptible good apart from the order of reason, not to be deprived of the good of reason). And so evil—by reason of a connected good, not evil as such—constitutes a specific difference in moral matters.

Some things can and do pass away and so thereby lack goodness, and evil consists of lacking goodness. And so there is evil in things (Q. 48, A. 2).

Aquinas poses an objection: *Being* and *thing* are convertible terms. Therefore, if evil is a being in things, evil is a thing. But this is contrary to what the preceding article said. He replies that we speak of being in two ways. Being in one way signifies the reality of something, and being in this sense is convertible with thing. But no privation is a being in this sense, and so neither is any evil. Being in the second way signifies the truth of a proposition, and the word *is* indicates composition of the subject and the predicate, in which the truth of a proposition consists. Being in this sense answers the question: Is it? In this sense, we say that there is evil.

Evil is the privation of good in things, and the things subject to the privations are good (e.g., blindness is the privation of sight in a human being, who, as such, is good) (Q. 47, A. 3). Good things cause evil, since causes are beings, and beings are good. But good things cause evil incidentally (i.e., incidentally to seeking some good), not intrinsically (i.e., as the object striven for). Evil results from the deficiency of a cause (e.g., Down's syndrome in offspring from the recessive genes of parents) or from the indisposition of matter (poor produce from poor soil) (Q. 48, A. 4). Since there is no defect in God, the evil resulting from particular deficient causes cannot be traced to him. But the evil in things passing away is traceable to him insofar as he intends the good order of the universe, in which some things can and do pass away (e.g., plants pass away when animals eat them, and this is evil for the plants but good for the animals). He does not cause the evil of sin, but his order of justice requires that sinners be punished (Q. 49, A. 1).

There is no first cause of evil comparable to the first cause of good, since nothing is evil by its essence—nothing is wholly and completely evil—and something good intrinsically causes every evil. And so there is no supreme evil that causes every evil (Q. 49, A. 3).

Governance

Two considerations show that the universe is governed: the fixed order of things toward ends, and the nature of God's goodness, which requires that he bring things to their ends (Q. 103, A. 1). Since the universal end of all things is a universal good (God's goodness), which is intrinsically and essentially good, and the particular ends of particular things are only good by sharing in the universal good, the end of the universe needs to be extrinsic to it (Q. 103, A. 2). And since the world's governance is intrinsically good, it needs to be the best, and the best governance is by one ruler, namely, God (Q. 103, A. 3). Regarding the end, governance of the universe has only one effect, which is to imitate the supreme good. Regarding the means, governance of the universe has two general effects: preservation of the goodness of created things and the goodness of things that created things cause. And governance of the universe has countless particular effects (Q. 103, A. 4). As nothing can exist that God does not create, so nothing can exist that is not subject to his governance (Q. 103, A. 5). God's providence governs everything directly, but he executes his providence by means of some created things causing other things (Q. 103, A. 6). Since God is the first, universal cause, nothing can happen outside of his governance (Q. 143, A. 7).

Aquinas poses an objection: Nothing preordained exists by chance. Therefore, if nothing happened in the world outside the order of God's governance, then nothing in the world would exist by chance. Aquinas replies. Things exist in the world by chance in relation to particular causes, and such things happen outside the disposition of those causes. But nothing in the world happens by chance in relation to God's providence. Also, because God is the first universal cause, nothing, whether natural or voluntary, can resist his order (Q. 103, A. 8).

God preserves all things intrinsically and directly, since every creature's existence depends on him (Q. 104, A. 1). Created things preserve other created things indirectly and incidentally by removing destructive causes (e.g., salt prevents meat from putrefying) or directly and intrinsically as intermediate causes (e.g., the sun sustains life) (Q. 104, A. 2).

God acts in three ways in everything that acts. First, as final cause, God causes created action as its end: real or apparent goods sharing a likeness to the highest good, namely, God. Second, in subordinated efficient causes, the second created cause acts in the power of the first, universal cause, namely, God. Third, as to forms, God moves things to act by applying their forms and powers to actions, gives created efficient causes their forms, and preserves them in existence (Q. 105, A. 5). Moreover, he can do things outside the regular order of secondary causes (Q. 105, A. 6). Such things are miracles, that is, wonderful events whose cause is absolutely hidden from everyone (Q. 105, A. 7).

4

✥

THE SOUL

Essence

Aristotle and Aquinas called the primary source of life in a material thing the soul. This primary source of life is the actuality, that is, the *form*, of a living material substance, not the material substance itself (Q. 75, A. 1). The human soul is the primary source of intellectual cognition, and the intellect, unlike the senses, can know every kind of material thing. Therefore, the human soul is intrinsically subsistent (Q. 75, A. 2), and the souls of irrational animals are not (Q. 75, A. 3). The human being is a composite of soul and body, not simply the soul alone (Q. 75, A. 4). The human soul does not have matter, since it, as a form, that is, an actuality, excludes the pure potentiality of matter, and since it, as intellectual, namely, as capable of knowing the forms of material things, is pure form (Q. 75, A. 5). The human soul cannot pass away when the human composite does, since it is intrinsically subsistent (Q. 75, A. 6).

Union of the Soul with the Body

Aquinas here addresses a series of questions about the human soul. Is the soul the form of the human body and thereby the source of all the vital activities of human beings? Is there one intellectual soul, or intellect, in all human beings collectively? Do human beings have other souls than the intellectual soul? Do human beings have other substantial forms than the intellectual soul? Is the human soul in every part of the body?

His answer to the first question is crucial and puts him at variance with Augustine and even his formative teacher, Albert the Great. Aquinas forcefully defends the proposition that the intellectual soul is the primary source of all the vital activities of human beings, appealing to the unity of intellectual activity and other vital activities in the experience of human persons (Q. 76, A. 1). He thereby rejects every kind of substantial dualism regarding the source of human vital activities (e.g., the body-mind dualism of Descartes). The position aroused considerable contemporary opposition, since traditional theologians of the Augustinian school thought it entailed denial of the soul's immortality.

Aquinas poses several objections. The first runs as follows: A form is the source whereby something exists, and so the very existing of a form does not belong to the form as such. Therefore, what intrinsically possesses existing is not united to a body as the body's form. But the source of intellection, as such, possesses existing and is subsistent. Therefore, the source of intellection is not united to the body as the body's form. He then replies that the soul communicates to corporeal matter the existing in which the soul itself subsists, and the corporeal and the intellectual soul form one thing in such a way that the existing belonging to the whole composite also belongs to the soul itself. This does not happen in the case of other living material forms, which are not subsistent. For this reason, the human soul abides in its own existing when the body dissolves, and the other forms do not.

The second objection runs as follows: What belongs to something as such always belongs to it. But being united to matter belongs to material forms as such. For a material form is essentially, not accidentally, the actuality of matter; otherwise, matter and material form would be one thing accidentally, not substantially. Therefore, material forms cannot exist without their matter. But the source of intellection, since it cannot pass away, abides apart from the body after the body dissolves. Therefore, the source of intellection is not united to the body as the body's form. Aquinas replies with an allusion to an article of Christian faith, the resurrection of the body at the last judgment: being united to the body belongs to the soul as such, and the human soul, when separated from the body, abides in existence with a *natural* disposition and inclination for union with the body.

The answers to the succeeding questions derive from the answer to the first. If the intellectual soul is the substantial form of human beings, then one and the same form cannot belong to several numerically different human beings, and so there cannot be one intellect in all human beings collectively (Q. 76, A. 2). If the intellectual soul is the substantial form of the body, then there cannot be several essentially different souls informing one and the same body (Q. 76, A. 3). Nor can there be any other substantial form, since then the intellectual soul would not without qualification confer existing on the body (Q. 76, A. 4). And the intellectual soul, if it is the form of the body, actualizes the whole body and every part of the body, although the soul is not in every part of the body regarding every one of the soul's powers (e.g., the power of sight is in the eyes, not the hands) (Q. 76, A. 8).

Vegetative Powers

A living body needs three vegetative powers: nutrition, growth, and reproduction. The human soul, as the form of the body, has these powers. The powers of nutrition and growth produce effects in the living things exercising the powers, but the power of generation produces its effect in another body (Q. 78, A. 2).

Cognitive Sense Powers

Aquinas distinguishes the five external senses by what properly and intrinsically belongs to each, namely, the external things each sense perceives (e.g., sight perceives color). The senses require an immaterial change, which produces the representation of a sensibly perceptible form in a sense organ. In senses other than sight, there is also a natural change either on the part of the object (place in the case of sound, and heat in the case of odor) or on the part of the sense organ (heated hands in the case of touch and moistened tongue in the case of taste). Several senses, in the course of perceiving their own proper objects, also perceive quantitative forms like size and shape (Q. 78, A. 3).

Aquinas poses several objections. One runs as follows: Size and shape and other things we call commonly perceptible are not by chance perceptible. But the intrinsic differences of powers' objects distinguish powers, and size and shape differ more from color than sound does. Therefore it seems that there ought much more to be a different sense power cognitive of size and shape than there ought to be different sense powers cognitive of color and sound.

Aquinas replies that things peculiarly perceptible by one sense primarily and intrinsically affect that sense, but we trace all the things perceptible by several senses to quantity. Size and number are forms of quantity, and shape is a property that concerns quantity, since the essence of shape consists of the limitation of size. And we perceive motion and rest as their subject is in one or several ways disposed regarding the subject's size (as to growth) or regarding the magnitude of the subject's spatial distance (as to locomotion) or regarding perceptible qualities (as in change). And so perceiving motion and rest is in a way to perceive one thing and many things. But quantity is the proximate subject of the qualities that cause change (e.g., surfaces are the proximate subjects of color). And so things perceptible by several senses do not primarily and intrinsically affect the senses but do by reason of the things' properly perceptible qualities (e.g., surfaces affect the sense of sight by reason of their color).

Nor are things perceptible by several senses by chance perceptible, since they produce different alterations of the senses (e.g., large and small surfaces affect the senses differently), since we call whiteness large or small and so distinguish it by the subject to which it belongs.

A second objection runs as follows: The object of each sense is one set of contraries (e.g., white and black are the objects of the sense of sight). But the sense of touch has many sets of contraries (e.g., hot and cold, wet and dry, and the like). Therefore, there are several senses of touch.

Aquinas replies that the sense of touch is generically one sense and specifically many senses, and different sets of contraries are for this reason the objects of the sense of touch. But different sets of contraries accompany one another throughout the body and are not separate from one another with respect to sense organs, and so there is no apparent distinction between them. (Conversely, the sense of taste accompanies the sense of touch in the tongue, not throughout the body, and so we easily distinguish the sense of taste from the sense of touch.) We could say that each set of contraries of the sense of touch belongs to a proximate genus, and that all of them belong to a common genus, which in its common aspect is the object of the sense of touch. But there is no name for the common genus, nor is there a common name for the proximate genus of hot and cold.

Aquinas, following Aristotle, says that human beings have four internal senses: the common sense, imagination, the cogitative power, and memory. The common sense is necessary to unify the perceptions of different external senses, each of which can only perceive the object proper to it (e.g., sight can perceive only color, not sweetness). The common sense enables individual human beings and animals to perceive that they are both seeing and hearing something. Imagination retains and preserves the forms of perceived things and composes or divides these forms to create new forms (e.g., to compose the image of a gold mountain from the images of gold and mountain). The cogitative power, called particular reason because of its connection with reason, by a process of comparison perceives indices that certain things are beneficial or detrimental, indices that the external senses do not perceive. (In irrational animals, Aristotle and Aquinas call this the estimative power.) Memory preserves and recalls particular indices about past things (Q. 78, A. 4).

Sense Appetites

Aristotle and Aquinas distinguish two kinds of appetite: the concupiscible and the irascible. The concupiscible appetitive power seeks to acquire sensibly agreeable things and to flee from harmful things (e.g., love and hate). The irascible appetitive power concerns useful things that can be obtained only with difficulty and consists of resisting hostile forces that attack suitable things and inflict harms (e.g., fear and anger) (Q. 81, A. 2). These appetites are subject to judgments of reason: to particular reason, that is, reason in conjunction with the cogitative power ("this apple is good for me"), and ultimately to universal reason ("I should eat the apple"). Acts of the appetites are subject to commands of the will regarding execution (e.g., eat the apple) (Q. 81, A. 3).

Aquinas poses the following objection, which gives him the opportunity to make an important distinction regarding reason's control of sense appetites. Nothing resists what it obeys. But the irascible and concupiscible powers resist reason. Therefore, the powers do not obey reason. Aquinas replies that the principle of governance whereby a master rules slaves lacking the capacity to resist his orders is despotic. But the principle of governance whereby a ruler rules free persons subject to the ruler but possessing things of their own to resist the ruler's orders is political and monarchical. The soul rules the body by a despotic principle of governance, and every member of the body subject to voluntary movement is immediately moved at the soul's will. But reason rules the irascible and concupiscible appetites by a political principle of governance, since sense appetites have things of their own whereby they can resist the orders of reason. Sense appetites are constituted not only to be moved by the cogitative power, which universal reason directs, but also to be moved by the power of imagination and the external senses. We perceive or imagine things to be pleasant that reason forbids, or things to be harsh that reason commands, and so the fact that the irascible and concupiscible appetites resist reason in some matters does not preclude them from obeying reason in other matters.

Cognitive Intellectual Powers

A created intellect is related to all intelligible things as potentiality to actuality, and so no created intellect by the fact of its existence is the actuality of intelligible things. The potential intellect is initially like a blank slate (*tabula rasa*) and brought to actual understanding (Q. 79, A. 2). The active intellect makes universal things actually understood by abstracting forms from the particular conditions of matter, namely, sense images (Q. 79, A. 3). The active intellect belongs to each human soul, although a higher intellect, namely, God, needs to help the soul to understand (Q. 79, A. 4). The potential intellect retains the abstracted intelligible forms, and so the intellect has memory (Q. 79, A. 6). The potential intellect can proceed from understanding some things to understanding other things, that is, it can proceed to reason, and some propositions are self-evident, that is, immediately understood to be true when the terms are understood (e.g., every whole is greater than any of its parts) (Q. 79, A. 8). Aristotle and Aquinas call such propositions first principles.

As nature implants in human beings first principles about theoretical things, so it implants in them first principles about practical things (e.g., one should act in accord with right reason). Knowledge of the first principles of practical reason is called *synderesis* (Q. 79, A. 12). Conscience is an act of the intellect whereby human beings judge that they have or have not done something, that they should or should not do something, or that they have or have not done something worthily (Q. 79, A. 13).

How the Soul Understands Material Things

The intellect understands the forms of material substances in an immaterial, universal way (Q. 84, A. 1).

Aquinas poses an objection: Things necessary and always disposed in the same way constitute the object of the intellect. But every material substance can undergo change and is disposed in different ways. Therefore, the soul cannot know material substances intellectually. He replies that every change presupposes something constant, since substances remain constant when qualitative changes occur, and matter remains constant when changes of substantial form occur. Also, constant relationships belong to changeable things (e.g., it is unalterably true that Socrates remains in one place while he is seated even if he is not always sitting). This is why nothing prevents us from having unalterable knowledge about changeable things.

If a created intellect were to know all things by its own essence, its essence would need to possess all things in an immaterial way, which only the essence of God, the cause of all things, does (Q. 84, A. 2). Nor are the intelligible forms of material things implanted by nature in the human soul, since learning or discovery brings human beings from potentiality to actuality, so that they understand (Q. 84, A. 3). Nor do intelligible forms flow into our soul from separate forms, as Plato said, since it is contrary to the nature of sensibly perceptible things that their forms subsist apart from matter (Q. 84, A. 4). The human soul knows material things in their eternal natures (the divine ideas) but only insofar as the eternal natures are the sources of human understanding, not as known objects, since the soul cannot in the present life know things in their eternal natures, that is, in God's essence (Q. 84, A. 5). The sense images are the sources of human understanding, but the active intellect makes the images actually intelligible, since the sense images cannot suffice to affect the potential intellect (Q. 84, A. 6). In this life, the intellect needs to have recourse to sense images to understand anything, since the proper objects of the human intellect are the essences or natures existing in material substances, and it can rise to some knowledge of immaterial things only through knowledge of material things (Q. 84, A. 7).

To the latter Aquinas poses an objection: No sense images belong to immaterial things, since the power of imagination does not transcend time and place. Therefore, if our intellect could not actually understand anything without recourse to sense images, it could not understand anything immaterial. But we understand truth and God and angels. Therefore, our intellect can actually understand things without recourse to sense images. Aquinas replies that we know immaterial things, of which we have no sense images, in relation to sensibly perceptible material substances, of which we do have sense images. For example, we understand truth by considering the things about which we spy out the truth, and we know God as their cause by what surpasses them and by eliminating their defects. And we can in our present life know other immaterial substances only by eliminating defects from, and in relation to, material substances. And so, when we understand things about immaterial substances, we need to have recourse to sense images, although we have no sense images of the immaterial substances themselves.

Moreover, the intellect cannot form perfect judgments if the senses are restrained (e.g., the blind cannot form perfect judgments about visible objects) (Q. 84, A. 8).

Manner and Process of Understanding

Material things are the proper objects of the human intellect, since the intellect is a power of the human soul, and the human soul is the form of the body (Q. 85, A. 1).

Aquinas poses an objection that enables him to distinguish different degrees of abstraction from matter. Material things are things of nature, and matter is included in the definition of such things. But we cannot understand anything apart from what is included in the definition. Therefore, we cannot understand the things apart from matter. But matter is the source of individuation. Therefore, we cannot understand material things by abstracting universals from individual things, that is, by abstracting intelligible forms from sense images.

Aquinas replies that we posit matter in the definitions of things of nature, but there are two kinds of sensibly perceptible matter: the common matter of a species (e.g., flesh and bones), and the particular matter of an individual (e.g., *this* flesh and *these* bones). And so the intellect abstracts the forms of things of nature from individual sensibly perceptible matter but not from common sensibly perceptible matter. For example, the intellect abstracts the form of human being from this particular flesh and these particular bones, which do not belong to the nature of the human species but are parts of the individual human being. And so the intellect can consider the form of human being apart from this flesh and these bones. But the intellect cannot abstract the form of human being from flesh and bones, the common matter of the species.

And our intellect can abstract mathematical forms from both individual and common sensibly perceptible matter and from individual intelligible matter. Intelligible matter is a substance insofar as matter is the subject of extension, and a material substance has extension before it has sensibly perceptible qualities. And so we can consider quantities as numbers, which are units of extension, apart from sensibly perceptible qualities, and this is to abstract quantities from sensibly perceptible matter. But we cannot consider quantities without understanding a substance that is the subject of extension, that is, we cannot abstract quantities from common intelligible matter, although we can consider quantities apart from this or that particular substance.

The intellect first understands material things themselves, not the intelligible forms of the things in the intellect, although it can by reflection understand the forms as the means whereby it understands the things (Q. 85, A. 2). Our intellect has more general knowledge before it has distinct knowledge (e.g., it knows animal in a confused way before it knows the distinction between rational and irrational animals) (Q. 85, A. 3). Different intelligible forms cannot simultaneously actualize the same intellect to understand different things (Q. 85, A. 4).

The essences of things are the first objects of the intellect. Second, the intellect understands properties and accidents of the things. Third, the intellect makes affirmative and negative judgments composing and dividing understood things and advances by reasoning to conclusions (Q. 85, A. 5). The senses cannot err about their proper objects (e.g., sight about color) except in the case of defective sense organs. The senses can be deceived about quantitative things (e.g., size and shape) and accidental characteristics (e.g., mistaking vinegar for honey because of the similar color). The intellect cannot misunderstand the essences of thing but can err when it relates one understood thing to another by affirmative and negative judgments. The intellect cannot err regarding the definition of simple things (e.g., plants, animals, and human beings) or regarding first principles, which are self-evident (Q. 85, A, 6). Understanding is the same for all, but some have a greater power of understanding than others (Q. 85, A. 7).

What the Intellect Knows about Material Things

The intellect directly understands universals by abstracting intelligible forms from individual matter, namely, sense images, but it can know individual things indirectly and reflexively by having recourse to the sense images from which it has abstracted the intelligible forms (Q. 86, A. 1).

Aquinas poses an objection: Our intellect understands itself. But the intellect is something individual. Otherwise, it would have no acts, since acts belong to individual things. Therefore, our intellect knows individual things. He answers that individual things *as such* can be understood, but individual things *as material* cannot be, since we understand only in an immaterial way. And so something immaterial like the intellect can be understood.

The intellect understands one thing after another. Since we could know an infinite number of things only if we were to have considered all of them, the intellect can know an unlimited number of things only potentially (Q. 86, A. 2)

The intellect indirectly understands individual contingent things, that is, things that can exist or not exist, and such things are the objects of some sciences (Q. 86, A. 3). The intellect can know future things only insofar as they will certainly or probably result from given causes, not in themselves (Q. 86, A. 4).

How the Soul Knows Itself, Its Innate Dispositions, and Its Acts

The intellect knows itself by its acts, not by its essence, as the intelligible forms of material things actualize it. It does so in particular as one is conscious that one understands. It does so in general as one contemplates the intellect's nature by considering its activity (Q. 87, A. 1). The intellect knows habits of the soul by perceiving that we produce the acts belonging to the habits or by considering their nature when we inquire into their nature (Q. 87, A. 2). The intellect primarily knows the nature of material things, but it secondarily knows the acts by which it knows material objects, and knows the intellect itself, whose perfection is the act of understanding, by the acts (Q. 87, A. 3). The intellect understands acts of the will both insofar as persons perceive that they are willing, and insofar as persons know the nature of such acts, namely, as intellectual inclinations (Q. 87, A. 4).

How the Soul Knows Superior Things

The intellect in our present life cannot primarily and intrinsically understand immaterial substances, since it is now by nature ordered to the essences of material things, and immaterial substances do not fall within the power of the senses and imagination (Q. 88, A. 1). Nor can the intellect in this life ever arrive at anything as an immaterial substance by the abstraction of essences from matter (Q. 88, A. 2).

Aquinas poses an objection: The human soul belongs to the genus of immaterial substances. But we can understand the human soul by its own activity, the activity whereby it understands material things. Therefore, we can also understand other immaterial substances (e.g., angels) by their effects in material things. He replies that the human soul understands itself by reason of its understanding, that is, by reason of its habitual activity, which perfectly manifests its power and nature. But we cannot know perfectly the power and nature of immaterial substances by such activity, or by anything else in material things, since material things are not commensurate with the powers of immaterial substances. Much less can God be the first thing we know (Q. 88, A. 3).

The Will

Needing to be externally coerced is completely contrary to the will, since the will is the intellectual appetite; however, there is a natural necessity that the will adhere to the ultimate human end: happiness (Q. 82, A. 1). One can be happy without some goods, and so these goods have no necessary connection to happiness nor necessity that the will adhere to them. Although the goods whereby human beings adhere to God have a necessary connection to happiness, the will does not necessarily adhere to them before the vision of God evidences the necessity of such a connection (Q. 82, A. 2).

Aquinas poses an objection: The will tends toward good, not evil. Therefore, the will necessarily tends toward the good proposed to it. He replies that the will can tend toward things only under the aspect of good. But there are many kinds of good. Therefore, the will is not determined necessarily to one of them.

The intellect—as such and absolutely—is higher than the will, but the will inclines to a higher good than the intellect insofar as the will inclines to a good more excellent than the soul itself, namely, God (Q. 82, A. 3). The intellect activates the will insofar as the intellect presents understood goods to the will as objects to be desired, and the will as efficient cause activates all the powers of the soul except the vegetative to their particular acts (Q. 82, A. 4).

Human beings can be moved to desire contrary things, and so they have free choice regarding particular things (Q. 83, A. 1).

Aquinas poses several objections. The first runs as follows: To be free is to cause oneself to act. Therefore, whatever is moved by something else is not free. But God moves the will. Therefore, human beings do not have free choice. Aquinas replies that human beings by free choice move themselves to act. But it does not necessarily belong to freedom that something free should be its own first cause, nor is it required for something to cause something else that the former should be the first cause of the latter. Therefore, God is the first cause that moves both natural and voluntary causes. And as God, by causing the movement of natural causes, does not take away the fact that their actions are from nature, so God, by causing the movement of voluntary causes, does not take away the fact that their actions are voluntary. Rather, God causes the actions' voluntary character, since he acts in each thing according to what is proper to it.

Aquinas poses another objection: Persons have ends as each is constituted. But we do not have the power to be any kind of thing. Rather, this comes from nature. Therefore, it is natural for us to pursue our ends. Therefore, we do not by free choice pursue the end.

Aquinas replies that human beings have two kinds of properties: one kind from nature, and the other kind from something added. But the properties of human beings are from nature either regarding the intellectual part of the soul or regarding the body and powers connected to the body. Therefore, since human beings have the natural power of intellection, they by nature desire their last end, happiness. This appetite is natural and not subject to free choice.

Regarding the body and the powers connected to it, human beings can have natural properties insofar as the body and its powers have dispositions from the imprints of natural causes. But such causes cannot make an imprint on the intellectual part of the soul, since that part is not the actuality of a material substance. Therefore, persons have ends as constituted by material properties inasmuch as such dispositions incline human beings to choose or reject particular things. But these inclinations are subject to the judgment of reason, which the lower appetites obey. And so such inclinations are not prejudicial to freedom of choice.

And there are added properties, such as habits and emotions, that incline individuals to one thing rather than another. But those inclinations are likewise subject to the judgment of reason. The properties are also subject to reason insofar as it lies in our power to acquire them, whether by causing them or disposing ourselves toward them, or to remove them. And so there is nothing regarding the properties inconsistent with freedom of choice.

Free choice is a power, not a habit (Q. 83, A. 2). The source of free choice is the will, but the intellect and the will work together to produce election. Regarding the intellect, there needs to be deliberation, whereby we judge something to be preferred to something else. Regarding the will, there needs to be acceptance of what we judge by deliberation. Election is an act of the will because it chooses means to happiness, and this object has the nature of a useful good. Since good is the object of an appetite, election is chiefly the object of the appetitive power, the will (Q. 83, A. 3).

How the Soul Is Produced

The human soul cannot be part of God's substance, since he, unlike the soul, is pure actuality, receives nothing from anything else, and has no different parts (Q. 90, A. 1). The rational soul is created, since it is a subsistent form and so cannot come to be out of preexisting matter (Q. 90, A. 2). Only God, acting directly, can produce a rational soul, since only the first efficient cause can produce without the existence of something presupposed (Q. 90, A. 3). It would have been improper for the soul to be created before the body, since the soul, as part of human nature, has its natural perfection only insofar as it is united to the body (Q. 90, A. 4).

Semen cannot produce the intellectual soul, since the source of intellection transcends matter, and the body does not share in the activity of the intellect (Q. 118, A. 2).

Aquinas poses an objection that enables him to elaborate on the process of human generation. The nutritive, sensory, and intellectual souls in human beings are essentially one and the same soul. But, as in other animals, semen produces the sensory soul in human beings. And so the animal and the human being are produced successively, the animal with the sensory soul first. Therefore, semen also produces the intellectual soul. He replies that a soul preexists in the embryo: first the nutritive soul, then the sensory soul, and finally the intellectual soul. The previous form passes away when the more advanced form comes, since the coming to be of one thing is always the passing away of another. But the subsequent form possesses whatever the prior form had, and still more. And so both human beings and other animals derive their ultimate substantial form by the coming to be and passing away of several forms. Therefore, God creates the intellectual soul at the end of the process of human generation, a soul that is also sensory and nutritive, at which time the preexisting forms pass away.

The human soul is not the human being, nor is the union of body and soul an accidental union. Since it is natural for the human soul to be united to the body and unnatural for it to be without a body, it was unfitting that God should begin his work with things incomplete and at variance with nature (e.g., God did not make human beings without hands or feet, which are natural parts of human beings). And so God creates souls when they are infused into bodies (Q. 118, A. 3).

ST I-2

5

✧

THE HUMAN END

If there were no ultimate end, nothing would be sought, no activity would reach fruition, and no striving of an efficient cause would come to a state of rest. And so human life has an ultimate end, and that end is happiness, which consists of attaining human perfection. It causes the will's movement and its choice of means to the end (Q. 1, A. 4). Happiness is a perfect good, one that completely satisfies the will, and the object of the will is universal good. And so only God, the uncreated good, can satisfy the will (Q. 2, A. 8). If the human will knows only that God exists, it does not attain knowledge of what God is essentially, and so it is not completely satisfied. Only the vision of God's essence can make human beings completely happy (Q. 3, A. 8).

Aquinas poses an objection to human beings beholding God's essence: A higher perfection belongs to a higher nature. But to behold God's essence is a perfection that belongs to his essence. Therefore, the ultimate perfection of the human intellect does not reach so far and falls short of beholding God's essence. Aquinas replies that we can understand an end in two ways: in one way regarding the thing desired, and then the ends of higher and lower natures are the same; in the second way regarding the attainment of the thing desired, and then the ends of higher and lower things differ according to the natures' different dispositions toward the thing desired. Therefore, the happiness of God, whose intellect beholds his essence comprehensively—with the comprehended object included in the comprehending subject—is superior to the happiness of human beings and angels, who behold his essence but not comprehensively.

Pleasure necessarily accompanies happiness (Q. 4, A. 1), and human beings, being happy, actually possess their end, God (Q. 4, A. 3). A rightly directed will is both antecedently and concomitantly necessary for happiness, that is, the will needs to be directed toward God both in this life and in the vision of God (Q. 4, A. 4). For imperfect happiness in this life, human beings need a body, but for perfect happiness in the next life, which consists of the vision of God, human beings do not (Q. 4, A. 5).

Aquinas poses an objection: Happiness satisfies desire. But the separated soul still desires to be united to the body, and so the soul's desire for happiness is not satisfied. Therefore, the soul cannot be happy when separated from the body. He replies that the separated soul's desire is completely satisfied regarding the *object* of its desire, namely, by possessing what suffices to satisfy its desire, which is the vision of God. But the separated soul's desire is not completely satisfied regarding the *subject* that desires, in that one desiring does not possess the desired good in every way that one would wish to possess it. And so, when human beings regain their bodies, their happiness increases in scope but not in intensity.

Human beings need a good disposition of the body for imperfect happiness in this life, since indisposition of the body can hinder them in every kind of virtuous activity (Q. 4, A. 6). External goods are not necessary for perfect happiness, which is the vision of God, but bodily necessities are necessary for imperfect happiness in this life, which consists of intellectually and morally virtuous activities (Q. 4, A. 7). Human beings need the company of friends in this life in order to act virtuously in both their practical life and their theoretical life, and the company of friends enhances happiness in our heavenly home, although it is not absolutely necessary there (Q. 4, A. 8).

Human beings can attain happiness, since their intellect can apprehend the universal and perfect good, and their will can desire that good (Q. 5, A. 1). Human beings cannot be perfectly happy in this life, since they do not have the beatific vision, and they suffer many evils (Q. 5, A. 3). Human beings cannot by their natural powers attain the ultimate happiness, since the vision of God transcends natural power (Q. 5, A. 5).

Aquinas poses an objection: Nature does not fail to provide necessary things. But nothing is so necessary for human beings as the means whereby they obtain their ultimate end. Therefore, human nature does not lack such means. And so human beings can obtain happiness by their own powers. He replies that nature does not fail to provide necessary things for human beings even though it did not give them any source whereby they could attain perfect happiness. For nature does endow human beings with free choice, which is the means whereby they could direct themselves to God, who would make them happy.

God's wisdom ordains that the perfect happiness of human beings be the reward of their meritorious good deeds (Q. 5, A. 7).

Aquinas poses an objection: Romans 4:6 says that God bestows righteousness on human beings without regard to their deeds. Therefore, no deeds on the part of human beings are necessary in order for them to attain happiness. Aquinas replies that the text is speaking about the righteousness of hope, which we have by the grace that makes us righteous, and such grace is not bestowed upon us because of our previous deeds. For such grace is the starting point of the activity whereby we strive for happiness, not the end point of activity, as happiness is.

6

❖

HUMAN ACTS

The Voluntary and the Involuntary

Things that proceed directly from the will are voluntary (e.g., one studies because one wills to study). Things proceed indirectly from the will when they happen because the will does not do something (e.g., one does not study because one does not will to study) or wills not to do something (e.g., one does not study because one wills not to study). Things proceeding indirectly from the will are voluntary if one has the capacity and the duty to act (Q. 6, A. 3).

Force can prevent the execution of external bodily acts commanded by the will (e.g., walking) but not coerce the will's own acts (Q. 6, A. 4).

Aquinas poses several objections. One is as follows: Anything can be coerced by something more powerful. But something, namely, God, is more powerful than the human will. Therefore, at least God can coerce the human will. Aquinas replies that God is more powerful than the human will and can move it. But if this were to be done by force, no longer would there be an act of the will, nor would the will itself be inclined. Rather, the thing done by force would be something contrary to the will.

A second objection runs as follows: Everything affected by something acting upon it is coerced by the cause. But the will is acted upon, and the cause acting upon it will sometimes move it. Therefore, the will is sometimes coerced. Aquinas replies that movements are only forced if they occur in opposition to the internal inclinations of the things acted upon. Otherwise, all accidental changes and comings-to-be of elementary material substances would be contrary to nature and forced. But accidental changes and comings-to-be of elementary material substances are from nature, since the matter or subjects of changes and comings-to-be have from nature the capacity for such dispositions. Likewise, if desirable things move the will by reason of the will's own inclinations, the movements of the will are voluntary, not forced.

Force causes things externally, and forced things, if contrary to the will, are involuntary (Q. 6, A. 5).

Absolutely speaking, deeds done out of fear are voluntary in the concrete case, that is, as concretely willed (e.g., when a ship's crew jettisons the cargo out of fear of danger during a storm), but they are involuntary if considered apart from the concrete case, that is, in that the will would not will the deed if there were no fear (Q. 6, A. 6).

Concupiscence causes voluntary things if the will wills the objects of lust (Q. 6, A. 7).

Ignorance is related to the will's activity in three ways: (1) as accompanying the will's activity; (2) as a consequence of the will's activity; and (3) as preceding the will's activity. Ignorance accompanies the will's activity when one does not know what one is doing but would do it if one did know (e.g., a hunter, thinking to kill a deer, kills an enemy whom he wishes to kill). Such ignorance does not cause something involuntary, since the deed is not contrary to the will, nor does it cause something voluntary, since one cannot will what one does not know. Ignorance is a consequence of the will's activity if the ignorance is voluntary, either because one wills not to know, or because one is negligent in considering what one can and should consider. Ignorance is antecedent to the will's activity if the ignorance is not voluntary but causes one to will what one otherwise would not will (e.g., if a human being, not knowing that a passerby is in the hunter's line of fire, and after taking adequate precaution, shoots and kills the passerby). Such ignorance causes deeds to be absolutely involuntary (Q. 6, A. 8).

The Will

The will needs to be brought from potentiality to actuality in two ways: one with respect to performing acts (acting or not acting), and the other with respect to specifying acts (doing this or doing that). The end of the will is good in general, and the will activates other powers of the soul to their acts regarding particular goods. The intellect presents its object to the will and activates the will by way of formal causality, that is, by specifying the object of the will's action (Q. 9, A. 1). The disposition of the senses and of emotions render objects desirable and so activate the will regarding the objects (Q. 9, A. 2). The will, by willing the end (object) activates itself to will movement of other powers of the soul as means to the end (Q. 9, A. 3).

Aquinas poses an objection: The intellect moves the will. Therefore, if the will moves itself, then two causes at the same time move the same thing, and this conclusion seems improper. Therefore, the will does not move itself. He replies that the will does not move itself in the same respect that the intellect moves the will. Rather, the intellect moves the will by reason of the will's object, while the will, regarding performance of acts, moves the will by reason of its end.

No external cause other than God can cause the will to will, since the will is a power of the rational soul, which only God by creation causes, and everything besides God, who is universal good, is a particular kind of good, which kind of good does not impart universal inclinations (Q. 9, A. 6).

Aquinas poses an objection: God causes only good things. Therefore, if only God were to move the will of human beings, their will would never be moved to evil, although it is by the will that human beings sin or live righteously. Aquinas replies that as the universal cause of movement, God moves the will of human beings to the universal object of the will, that is, the good, and human beings can will nothing apart from this universal movement. But human beings by their power of reason determine themselves to will this or that, and particular things are real or apparent goods. Nonetheless, God sometimes moves certain individuals specifically to will certain good things, as in the case of those he moves by his grace.

Human beings by nature will the will's end, good in general, and things belonging to powers of the soul—subsistence, life, and the like—which are particular goods regarding the natural human constitution (Q. 10, A. 1).

Since human beings in this life are able not to think about an object, no object now necessarily moves the will to act. Regarding specification of the object of the will's act, the universal good, happiness, necessarily activates the will, but particular goods, since they are not good in every respect, do not (Q. 10, A. 2). Unless emotions completely restrain reason, the will does not necessarily tend to the things to which emotions incline (Q. 10, A. 3). God moves everything according to its condition, and so he moves the will in such a way that its movement remains contingent and only necessary regarding things to which nature moves it (Q. 10, A. 4).

To the latter, Aquinas poses an objection: Irresistible efficient causes necessarily move things. But God, since he has infinite power, cannot be resisted. Therefore, God moves the will in a necessary way. Aquinas replies that God's will extends both to the deeds done by the things he moves, and to the ways in which the deeds are done in accord with the things' nature. And so it would be more contrary to God's causal motion if he were to move the will in a necessary way, which way does not belong to the will's nature, than if he were to move the will in a free way, since free movement belongs to the will's nature.

Intention

The tendency of a thing's movement toward something results from the action of a cause moving the thing. The will moves other powers of the soul, and so intention is an act of the will rather than an act of the intellect (Q. 12, A. 1). Intention always concerns an end, whether the ultimate end or an intermediate end (Q. 12, A. 2). Human beings can simultaneously intend several things, one as the proximate end and another as the ultimate end (e.g., to take medicine to restore health, and heath to be happy). Human beings can also simultaneously intend several unrelated things if one of them is useful for another (Q. 12, A. 3). There are two movements of the will when one is moved to will ends and means separately. There is only one movement of the will when the will wills means for the sake of an end (Q. 12, A. 4).

Choice

Choice is materially and substantially an act of the will, since movements of the soul toward chosen goods make choice effective, although the power of reason after deliberation orders the will to ends and so provides the form of choice (Q. 13, A. 1).

Ends as such (e.g., the health of patients as the end of doctors) are not subject to choice (e.g., a doctor has no choice about the nature and end of practicing medicine). But one end may be the means to another end and in this way subject to choice (e.g., a doctor's exercise of medicine presupposes that health is the final cause of his choice of means, but bodily health is ordered to the soul's good and so subject to choice by those responsible for the soul's health) (Q. 13, A. 3).

Aquinas poses an objection: Virtue causes human beings to choose rightly, and every deed done for the sake of virtue belongs to other powers. But that for the sake of which deeds are done is an end. Therefore, choice concerns ends. He replies that virtuous ends are ordered to happiness as the final end of human beings, and that is why we can choose those ends.

Choice always concerns human actions, either as such or in order to cause or use desired things (Q. 13, A. 4), and so choice concerns only possible things, since one cannot choose to do something impossible (Q. 13, A. 5).

Aquinas poses an objection: Choice is an act of the will. But people sometimes will impossible things. Therefore, there is choice of impossible things. He replies that willing is intermediate between intellectual understanding and external action, since the intellect presents an object to the will, and the will causes external action. Therefore, since the will's movement proceeds from the soul to things, we consider the source of the will's acts in relation to the intellect, which understands things as generally good, and we consider the end or completion of the will's acts in relation to external actions, which are the means whereby human beings strive to attain things. And so we consider the completion of the will's acts insofar as there are good things for human beings to do, and these things are possible. Incomplete willing concerns impossible things, and some call such willing merely wishing, namely, that one would will such things if they were possible.

Choice concerns particular goods, which reason can consider under their good or deficient aspect as suitable or unsuitable means to happiness, and so human beings choose particular goods freely. But human beings necessarily will the perfect good—happiness—and cannot will to be unhappy (Q. 13, A. 6).

Aquinas poses a classic medieval objection to free choice: Human beings are not moved to one thing rather than another if the two things are completely equal (e.g., if hungry persons have within their grasp two separate, equally distant portions of equally appetizing food, they are not moved more to one than to the other). Far less can persons choose things understood to be of less worth than other things. Therefore, if one of several things presented to someone seems to be of greater worth than the others, that one cannot choose any of the others. Therefore, human beings always choose necessarily. Aquinas gives a short and rather formalistic answer: if two things equal in one respect are presented to someone, nothing prevents the person from considering a superior characteristic regarding one of them, or the person's will from tending to that one rather than the other.

Deliberation

There is much uncertainty in practical matters, since human actions deal with contingent particulars, and contingent particulars can vary. And so reason needs to inquire before it judges about what things are to be done, and which things to be chosen (Q. 14, A. 1). We deliberate about doubtful things, contingent things useful for our actions. And so deliberation concerns our actions (Q. 14, A. 3).

Aquinas poses an objection: If human beings were to deliberate only about their own deeds, no one would deliberate about things to be done by others. But this conclusion is false. Therefore, deliberation does not concern only our own deeds. He replies that we seek deliberation about the deeds of others insofar as others are one with us. Bonds of affection unite us to others, as, for example, one is as solicitous about a friend's concerns as about one's own. Or we are united to others in an instrumental way, since the chief cause and an instrumental cause are as if one cause. And so masters deliberate abut what their slaves are to do.

We do not deliberate about things beyond doubt, whether activities requiring fixed skills or activities of no consequence (Q. 14, A. 4.). Deliberation is analytic, beginning with the end we intend to obtain until we reach a decision about what we should do to obtain it (Q. 14, A. 5). Deliberation presupposes the end, knowledge of particulars, and truths of theoretical and practical sciences as sources, and deliberation ceases when a means to the end is chosen (Q. 14, A. 6).

Consent

Consent is an act of the will whereby the will inclines toward something and takes pleasure in it, and so consent is an appetitive act (Q. 15, A. 1). The inclination of the will toward the ultimate human end—happiness—is pure volition, not consent, but inclinations of the will toward particular things, which inclinations are determined by deliberation as means to the end, constitute consent in the proper sense. And so consent in the proper sense concerns only means (Q. 15, A. 3).

Aquinas poses an objection: To desire means is to choose. Therefore, if consent were to concern only means, consent would seem not to differ from choice in any respect. But this is not true. Therefore, consent does not concern only means. He replies that choice adds to consent a relationship regarding the preference of one thing over another, and so there still remains a choice after consent. We may by deliberation discover that several means conduce to an end, and we consent to each when we approve of each, and we in choosing prefer one of the approved means to the others. But if there should be only one means of which we approve, there is only a conceptual and not a real difference between consent and choice. Then there is consent insofar as we approve the means in order to do something, and there is choice insofar as we prefer the approved means to those of which we disapprove.

Acts Commanded by the Will

Commanding is essentially an act of reason, since ordering in a communicative way belongs to reason. But the will is the primary power that causes the movement of other powers of the soul. And so the will is the primary power that causes the very fact that reason commands the movements of other powers of the soul (Q. 17, A. 1).

Reason can order things to be done by commanding human beings to will those things (Q. 17, A. 5).

Aquinas poses several objections. The first runs as follows: The soul sometimes commands itself to will but then doesn't will. Therefore, we do not actually command acts of the will. He replies that the soul wills when it *completely* commands itself to will. But the soul sometimes does not completely command, since different considerations impel reason to command or not to command. And so reason wavers between the two outcomes and does not completely command.

The second objection runs as follows: If some acts of the will are commanded, the same reasoning leads to the conclusion that all of them are. But if every act of the will is commanded, there necessarily results an infinite regression, since an act of the will precedes the act of reason that commands, and if that act of the will is also commanded, another act of reason in turn precedes this act of the will. And so on. But an infinite regress is impossible. Therefore, we do not command acts of the will. Aquinas replies briefly: Because commands are acts of reason, the acts of the will subject to reason are commanded. But the first act of the will is from a natural desire or a higher cause, not from an order of reason. And so there is no need to regress endlessly.

Reason is reflexively conscious of itself, and so it can order and command things related to its own acts. It can always command itself to act, that is, to think. But regarding the objects of its acts, it cannot command the intellect to understand things. Nature orders assent to some understood things, namely, first principles, and assent in such cases is not subject to our command. But other understood things do not compel the intellect to assent (e.g., that

John should marry Joan), and so assent or dissent in such cases is subject to the command of reason (Q. 17, A. 6).

Reason governs the power of imagination, and so acts of sense appetites are in this respect subject to the command of reason. But the condition and disposition of the body is not subject to the command of reason. And so acts of the sense appetites are not totally subject to the command of reason. Also, sense perception and imagination may suddenly arouse movements of sense appetites that are beyond the command of reason (Q. 17, A. 7).

Acts of vegetative powers (e.g., digestion), which are not cognitive natural powers, are not subject to the command of reason (Q. 17, A. 8). Bodily movements by sense powers (e.g., locomotion) are subject to the command of reason, but bodily movements by noncognitive natural powers (e.g., sneezing) are not (Q. 17, A. 9).

Aquinas poses an objection: Sex organs are at times aroused unsuitably and apart from any desire, and they at other times fail to be aroused when there is a desire. Therefore, movements of our bodily members do not obey reason. He replies that mental perceptions arouse our sex organs, namely, as the intellect and imagination represent things that result in emotions of the soul, and the emotions result in movements of these bodily members. But natural changes, namely, those of heat and cold, are necessary for sex organs to be aroused, and natural changes are not subject to the command of reason. And so these bodily members are not aroused at the command of reason. Like the heart, sex organs are a primary source of life, and primary sources of life are potentially the whole living thing. And so these bodily members have their specific movements from nature, since first things need to be from nature.

7

MORAL GOODNESS AND MALICE

Human Acts in General

Human actions are good insofar as they share in proper human existing, and evil inasmuch as they lack the perfection of existing proper to human action (Q. 18, A. 1). The chief good in human action consists of the propriety of the objects of the actions, since objects specify actions, and the chief evil is an improper aspect regarding the objects (Q. 18, A. 2).

Aquinas poses an objection: The goodness of effects depends on their causes, not the converse. But actions cause the objects of active powers. Therefore, human actions are not good or evil by reason of their objects. He replies that the objects of human actions are sometimes not the objects of active powers (e.g., appetitive powers are passive in one respect, since desirable objects move our appetites, although the powers cause human actions). Nor do the objects of active powers always have the nature of effects. They are such only after they have been transformed (e.g., digested food is an effect of the nutritive power, but undigested food is the matter on which the nutritive power acts). And because objects are somehow effects of active powers, the object is the end of a power's action and gives the action its form and species. Moreover, although the goodness of effects does not cause the goodness of actions, actions are good because they are able to produce good effects. And so the very relation of actions to their effects is the reason why the actions are good.

Second, human actions will be evil if they lack any requisite circumstance (e.g., proper place, proper time) (Q. 18, A. 3).

Third, the goodness of human actions depends on the end or purpose of the actions (Q. 18, A. 4).

The objects of some human actions may not comprise anything belonging to the order of reason (e.g., going for a walk), and such human actions are in themselves morally indifferent (Q. 18, A. 8). Human actions individually considered, however, need to have some circumstance, at least an intended end, which causes the actions to be good or evil. Human actions that take place without reflection (e.g., humming to music) are not, properly speaking, human acts (Q. 18, A. 9). Whenever a circumstance concerns a particular order of reason, the circumstance necessarily specifies the moral act as good or evil (e.g., stealing property from a church adds a special contrariety to the order of reason against stealing) (Q. 18, A. 10).

Interior Acts of the Will

Good and evil intrinsically differentiate the will's acts, and so good and evil acts of the will are specifically different acts. But objects specifically differentiate human acts. And so human acts are good or evil by reason of the acts' objects (Q. 19, A. 1).

Aquinas poses an objection: Good alone is the object of the will. Therefore, if the will were good by reason of the will's object, every act of the will would be good, and no act of the will would be evil. He replies that an apparent, not a real, good is sometimes the will's object, and an apparent good does not have the character of good as absolutely suitable. And so acts of the will are sometimes evil.

The will's goodness depends exclusively on the one thing that intrinsically causes the goodness of the will's acts, namely, its object (Q. 19, A. 2). Since reason presents objects to the will, the will's goodness depends on reason, just as the will's goodness depends on its object (Q. 19, A. 3). The fact that human reason rules the human will and measures its goodness derives from the eternal divine law—God's reason (Q. 19, A. 4).

A will that wills contrary to erroneous reason is evil in one respect, since reason happens to understand a good object of the will as evil, and the will inclines to the object as evil (e.g., if a person who believes drinking even a small amount of alcohol is evil chooses to drink a little wine) (Q. 19, A. 5). On the other hand, the will is not necessarily good if it wills in accord with erroneous reason. It does not excuse a person if reason errs voluntarily, whether directly or due to negligence, about one's obligation, since the error springs from ignorance of God's law, which one can and should know (e.g., if a person's reason judges that adultery is permissible). But the will is excused if the error springs from reasonable ignorance of a circumstantial fact (e.g., one takes a coat that one erroneously thinks is one's own) (Q. 19, A. 6).

External Human Acts

External acts have two kinds of moral good or evil. One kind is by reason of the acts' requisite matter and circumstances, and the other kind by reason of the acts' relation to ends. The goodness or malice in the acts' requisite matter and circumstances depends on reason. Integral goodness is required to make things good in every respect, and a single defect suffices to make things evil. But the whole goodness or malice in the relation of external acts to ends depends on the will, although the will's goodness in intending good ends does not suffice to make external acts good. External acts are evil if the will is evil either because it wills evil acts, or because it wills evil ends (Q. 20, A. 2).

Emotions

Emotions are the movements of sense appetites. Aquinas' analysis follows that of Aristotle and rejects the view of the Stoics that emotions as such are evil. Since sense appetites are not rational, their movements in themselves have no moral goodness or evil. But they are morally good or evil insofar as they are subject to the command of reason and to the will, and they will be voluntary and so good or evil if the will commands them, or if the will fails to forbid them (Q. 24, A. 1).

8

⁜

LOVE

Aquinas expounds on natural love relatively briefly, and he substantially follows Aristotle. He will have much more to say in connection with the theological virtue of charity.

Kinds

There are two kinds of love: the love of desire and the love of friendship. One has a love of desire for a good that one wishes for oneself or another. One has a love of friendship for the other for whom one wills a good. The love of friendship—love of another—is love without qualification, and the love of desire—love of good for another—is love with qualification (Q. 26, A. 4).

Aquinas poses an objection: There are three kinds of friendship: the useful, the pleasurable, and the worthy. But there is desire in useful and pleasurable friendships. Therefore, we should not contradistinguish desire from friendship. He replies that in useful and pleasurable friendships, one wills good things for friends, and the character of friendship is in this respect preserved in such friendships. But because that good is additionally related to one's own pleasure or utility, useful and pleasurable friendships are subsumed under love of desire and so lack the true character of friendship in this respect.

Causes

Likeness in possessing the human form, that is, the rational soul, causes a love of friendship. The affection of one person extends to another as the other is one with oneself, and one wills good things for the other just as one does for oneself. Likeness in potentially possessing what another actually possesses causes a love of desire or a friendship of utility or pleasure. Regarding love of desire, one loves oneself more than others (Q. 27, A. 3).

Aquinas poses an objection: Persons love in others what they themselves would not wish to be (e.g., persons who would not wish to be film actors love such persons). But this would not happen if likeness were to be the specific cause of love, since human beings would in that case love in others what they themselves possessed or wished to possess. Therefore, likeness does not cause love. He replies that there is a proportional likeness even in persons loving in another what they do not love in themselves, since the persons are related to what they love in themselves as the other is related to what the persons love in the other. For example, if a good singer loves a good writer, there is a proportional likeness in such love insofar as each possesses what is proportional to the person with respect to the person's skill.

Effects

Love is the efficient cause of the external union of the lover and the beloved, since love moves the lover to desire and seek the company of the beloved as fitting for, and belonging to, the lover. Love is the formal cause of the union of affection, which results when persons conceive others as part of their own well-being (love of desire) and friends as other selves (love of friendship) (Q. 28, A. 1).

Mutual indwelling is an effect of love regarding understanding, since the beloved abides in the understanding of the lover, and the lover strives to discern particulars of the beloved's innermost being. Mutual love is an effect of love regarding desire, since the beloved is in the lover's affection by reason of some satisfaction. The lover is satisfied by pleasure in the beloved or the qualities of the beloved when the beloved is present, or by desire of the beloved when the beloved is absent, or by striving for good things for the beloved with a love of friendship because of deep satisfaction in the beloved. Conversely, the lover is in the beloved by a love of desire, which seeks to possess the beloved completely, and by a love of friendship, which reckons the friend's good or bad fortune and the friend's will as the lover's own.

Thus the lover, reckoning the friend identical with the lover, is in the beloved, and the beloved, reckoning the friend identical with the beloved, is in the lover. The mutual indwelling in a love of friendship is reciprocal, since friends mutually love one another and will and do good things for one another (Q. 28, A. 2).

9

✦

HABITS

In General

Habits are dispositions in some way related to action. They are suitably or unsuitably related to human nature, which is the source of human action, or to the human end, which is either action itself or an effect attained by action. Powers are primarily and intrinsically related to acts, and so habits belonging to powers (e.g., justice to the will) chiefly signify a relation to the powers' acts (e.g., the habit of justice to the will's just acts) (Q. 49, A. 3).

Aquinas poses an objection: Health, leanness, and beauty are sometimes habits. But we do not predicate these things in relation to acts. Therefore, it is not essential that habits be sources of acts. He replies that health is a habit or habitual disposition in relation to a thing's nature. But natures as sources of action consequently signify a relation to acts. And so human beings or their bodily members are healthy when they can perform the actions of healthy human beings. The same is true of other habits of human beings.

The prerequisites of habits are: (1) that the subjects in which habits inhere differ from the objects of habits as potentialities from actualities; (2) that things can be determined in several ways and to different things; and (3) that several things be apportioned to act in concert to dispose a subject to one of the objects for which the subject has potentiality. And so habits are dispositions, and dispositions are arrangements of things with spatial or potential or specific parts. Therefore, habits are necessary, since there are many beings whose natures and actions need several things to act in concert, and these things can be apportioned in different ways (Q. 49, A. 4).

Subjects in Which Habits Inhere

Bodily actions springing from nature (e.g., circulation of the blood) are determined to one thing, and so no habit disposes the body for such actions. Bodily actions springing from the soul by means of the body (e.g., acts of courage) belong chiefly to the soul and secondarily to the body, as the body is disposed to be readily apt for the soul's action. Regarding the disposition of the body as a subject for its form, the soul, the body has habitual dispositions (e.g., health, beauty, and the like), but these dispositions are imperfect habits, since they can be easily altered (Q. 50, A. 1).

Habits inhere in the soul by reason of the soul's powers, since the soul causes actions by its powers (Q. 50, A. 2). Sense powers, insofar as they are subject to the command of reason and to the will, can have habits whereby they are well or ill disposed toward contrary things (Q. 50, A. 3). The potential intellect can have habitual understanding, habitual scientific knowledge, and habitual theoretical wisdom (Q. 50, A. 4). And the will especially needs habits that rightly dispose it regarding its exercise of choice (Q. 50, A. 5).

Causes

As dispositions of subjects to their forms or natures, habits may be natural in two ways: (1) by reason of human nature itself (e.g., the disposition to laugh at witty remarks) and (2) by reason of the bodily nature or constitution of individuals (e.g., John's healthy or sickly constitution). In the former case, all human beings have the dispositions. In the latter case, different individuals may possess different degrees of the dispositions, which may spring entirely from nature (e.g., health from an individual's bodily constitution), or partially from nature and partially from an external source (e.g., health from both the individual's bodily constitution and from the powers of medicine).

As dispositions of subjects of habits toward action, habits belonging to the soul's powers may be natural by reason of human nature itself or by reason of individuals' bodily constitution. But human beings in no way possess these natural habits entirely from nature. Therefore, these habits of human beings spring partially from an external source. The intellect has natural habits only formatively, both by reason of our specific nature (e.g., to understand first principles by means of intelligible forms derived from sense images) and by reason of the sense powers of individuals (e.g., as the particular body organs of some individuals render them more fit to understand well). This is because human beings need cognitive sense powers for intellectual activities. The will has natural habits formatively only as to the source of the habits, not as to their substance (e.g., the first principles of the natural law are the sources of moral virtues but not the moral virtues themselves). The will also has natural habits by reason of the bodily constitution of individuals (e.g., the bodily constitution of some individuals inclines them more to chastity or patience than the bodily constitution of other individuals does) (Q. 51, A. 1).

The intellect and the will are partially passive powers, that is, they are not active until they are acted upon. And so repeated acts produce characteristics in passive powers, and such characteristics are habits (e.g., morally virtuous habits are produced in appetitive sense powers as reason moves the powers, and habits of scientific knowledge are produced in the intellect as first principles move the intellect) (Q. 51, A. 2).

Single acts of reason can produce habits of scientific knowledge (e.g., a self-evident proposition convinces the intellect to give firm assent to a conclusion). But single acts of reason cannot so completely dominate the will that the will strives to act uniformly in accord with human nature, that is, acquires morally virtuous habits. Regarding particular reason, namely, the judgment of the cogitative power in conjunction with memory and imagination that particular things are helpful or harmful, the same acts need to be repeated over and over in order that the things be firmly impressed on memory. For example, one needs repeatedly to watch and wait for the proper traffic signals before crossing streets in order for such an action to be habitual. But powerful single acts may suffice to produce bodily dispositions (e.g., one dose of strong medicine may restore health) (Q. 51, A. 3).

10

✥

VIRTUE

Definition

Aquinas uses Peter Lombard's definition of virtue (*Sentences* II, dist. 27, A. 2) as the point of departure for his treatment of the subject. Virtue is a good characteristic of the mind by which we live rightly, of which no one makes wrong use, and of which God works in us apart from any work of ours. Something belonging to the mind—that is, the rational—constitutes the subject matter, which is the material cause of virtue. Virtue is directed toward good action, and so good action is the end, that is, the final cause, of virtue. God is the efficient cause of infused virtues (e.g., charity), but human beings acquire some virtues (e.g., courage) by their own activity (Q. 55, A. 4).

Intellectual Virtues

There are three kinds of theoretical intellectual virtue. One kind is the habit of theoretical first principles, which disposes the intellect to understand self-evident principles (e.g., the principle of contradiction). The second kind consists of the habit of scientific knowledge (e.g., Aristotelian biology, physics), which disposes the intellect to demonstrate truths about this or that kind of thing. The third kind is the habit of theoretical wisdom proper to theology and philosophy, which disposes the intellect to reason about the first cause of all things, namely, God (Q. 57, A. 2). Theoretical wisdom, because its object is God, is the greatest intellectual virtue (Q. 66, A. 5).

There are two kinds of practical intellectual virtue: skills and practical wisdom. Skills (e.g., shipbuilding) are practical intellectual virtues about rightly *making* external things (Q. 57, A. 3). Practical wisdom, on the other hand, is the practical intellectual virtue about rightly *doing* things, that is, rightly ordered internal desire in producing and using external things. To be practically wise, human beings need to be rightly disposed regarding ends. And since moral virtues produce the right disposition toward properly human ends, human beings need moral virtues, which produce right desire, in order to have practical wisdom (Q. 57, A. 4).

On the distinction between practical wisdom and skills, Aquinas poses an objection: Good deliberation belongs to practical wisdom. But some skills (e.g., military skill, navigational skill, medical skill) involve deliberation. Therefore, practical wisdom is indistinguishable from skill. He replies that practical wisdom deliberates rightly about things belonging to the entire life of human beings and the final goal of human life. But some skills involve deliberation about things that belong to the skills' own ends. And so we call some persons wise commanders or wise ship captains because they deliberate rightly about warfare or seafaring, but we do not call them absolutely wise. Rather, we call absolutely wise only those who deliberate rightly about things of benefit to the entire life of human beings.

Since means to the human end are the object of choice, right choosing requires not only the right disposition toward properly human ends, which the moral virtues produce, but also the virtue of practical wisdom in order to be properly disposed in choosing means to the human end (Q. 57, A. 5).

Aquinas poses an objection: We deliberate rightly by practical wisdom. But human beings can act both by their own counsel and by another's. Therefore, in order to live rightly, human beings do not themselves need to possess practical wisdom. Rather, it suffices for them to follow the counsel of wise persons. He replies that if human beings do good things because the counsel of others moves them, not because of their own reason, their actions are not yet altogether perfect as regards their own reason directing them and as regards their own will moving them to act. And so, although they do good things, they nonetheless do not do them rightly in an absolute sense, and acting rightly in an absolute sense is living rightly.

Moral Virtues

Emotions, as ordered by reason, can coexist with moral virtues (Q. 59, A. 2). Emotions are the object of some moral virtues (e.g., fortitude, temperance), and acts of the will the object of other moral virtues (e.g., justice), which exist apart from emotion (Q. 59, AA. 4 and 5).

Moral virtues are formatively natural to human beings by reason of their specific rational nature, inasmuch as reason by nature knows certain first moral principles (e.g., one should take reasonable means to preserve one's life), and inasmuch as the will has a natural desire for good according to reason. And moral virtues are natural to human beings by reason of their individual bodily constitution, inasmuch as bodily constitutions dispose individuals to particular moral virtues (e.g., meekness) (Q. 63, A. 1).

Repeated human acts governed by reason can produce moral virtues measured by reason, but the acts cannot produce virtues that dispose human beings for the good measured by divine law, not by human reason. Only God's action can produce the latter virtues, which he works in us apart from our action (Q. 63, A. 2).

Aquinas poses an objection: Sin is incompatible with virtue.

But human beings can avoid sin only through God's grace. Therefore, only God's gift, not our repetition of acts, can produce virtues in us. Aquinas replies that divinely infused virtues, especially if considered in their perfection, are incompatible with any mortal sin. But humanly acquired virtues may be compatible with sinful, even mortally sinful, acts. The exercise of habits that we possess is subject to our will, and one sinful act does not destroy the habits of acquired virtues, since bad habits, not bad acts, are directly contrary to good habits. And so, although human beings cannot without grace avoid mortal sin so as never to sin mortally, they are nonetheless not prevented from acquiring virtuous habits, whereby they may abstain for the most part from evil deeds, especially deeds very contrary to reason.

Moral virtues aim at the mean between too much and too little. The mean of some moral virtues (e.g., fortitude, temperance) is a mean of reason, one that reason itself imposes on internal emotions in different ways according to the constitution of each individual. But justice concerns external things, and so the mean of justice is a real mean of external things, one that renders to each what is due to each, neither more nor less (Q.64, A. 2).

There are four cardinal, that is, chief, virtues that are related in various ways to the formative source of moral virtues, namely, the good of reason. Prudence, that is, practical wisdom, consists of the very contemplation of reason. Justice consists of reason controlling human actions. Temperance consists of reason controlling emotions that incite human beings to act contrary to reason. Fortitude consists of reason controlling emotions that incite human beings not to act when reason says that they should. Prudence inheres in reason, justice in the will, temperance in the concupiscible appetite, and fortitude in the irascible appetite (Q. 61, A. 2).

Incomplete virtues are tendencies only to particular kinds of good deeds and so are not interconnected. But complete virtues (e.g., the cardinal virtues) are general tendencies to do good deeds rightly and are interconnected (e.g., fortitude cannot exist as a complete virtue without the restraint of temperance or the right order of justice or the judgment of prudence). No moral virtue is possible without prudence, since moral virtues involve reason choosing the means to proper human ends, nor can human beings possess prudence without possessing moral virtues, since moral virtues dispose human beings to proper ends (Q. 65, A. 1).

Moral virtues, insofar as they result in the good related to the supernatural end of human beings, namely, the vision of God, need to be infused by God and cannot exist without the supernatural virtue of charity. Charity causes prudence to be rightly disposed toward the supernatural end (Q. 65, A. 2).

Justice is the most excellent moral virtue, since it is more closely related to reason than the other moral virtues are, since it inheres in the rational appetite (the will), and since its object concerns human (i.e., rational) actions in relation to oneself and others. Fortitude, which subjects desire to reason in things proper to life, ranks the highest of moral virtues concerning emotions. And temperance, which subjects desire to reason in things ordered to life, namely, food for the life of the individual, and sex for the life of the species, ranks the next highest. These three moral virtues, in conjunction with prudence, are the most worthy virtues (Q. 66, A. 4).

Relation of Moral Virtue to Intellectual Virtue

Human beings need to have the requisite intention of the human end, and moral virtues, which incline the will toward the good befitting reason, accomplish this. But human beings also need to understand the means to the end, and practical reason—prudence—accomplishes this by deliberating, judging, and commanding. And so there can be no moral virtue without practical reason, nor moral virtue without understanding the first principles of practical reason (e.g., one should take reasonable means to maintain one's life) (Q. 58, A. 4).

Aquinas poses an objection: Moral virtues cause human beings to incline to act rightly. But some human beings have such inclinations from nature even without judgments of reason. Therefore, there can be moral virtue without intellectual virtue. He replies that an inclination from nature toward a virtuous good is a virtuous beginning, but not a complete virtue, since the stronger such inclinations are, the more dangerous they may be unless they are united to right reason, which makes right choices of means suitable for the requisite end. Just so, the faster a blind horse runs, the more forcibly it collides with something and inflicts worse injury on itself. And so, although moral virtues do not consist of right reason, they are both in accord with right reason and need to be done with right reason.

Human beings can have theoretical intellectual virtues and practical intellectual skills without having moral virtue. But practical wisdom (prudence) is impossible without moral virtue. Valid arguments about particular things require both universal principles and particular principles, and to be rightly disposed about particular things, one needs habits that cause one to judge rightly about things to be done. And so human beings need moral virtues for right reasoning about things to be done, that is, for practical wisdom (Q. 58, A. 5).

Absolutely speaking, intellectual virtues, which perfect reason, are more excellent than moral virtues, which perfect the will. But in relation to acts, moral virtues, whose function is to activate other powers, is more excellent (Q. 66, A. 3).

II

⁘

LAW

Definition

First, law is an order of reason, since the source of human acts is reason, which rules and measures them by ordering human beings to their end and commanding means to the end (Q. 90, A. 1).

Aquinas poses an objection: Law induces those subject to it to act rightly. But inducing them to act rightly belongs in the strict sense to the will. Therefore, law belongs to the will rather than to reason. He replies that reason has from the will the power to induce activity, since reason commands means because one wills ends. But an act of reason needs to rule the will regarding the means commanded in order for the willing to have the character of law. And the will of the ruler in this way has the force of law. Otherwise, the willing of the ruler would be injustice rather than justice.

Second, the first source of law is the ultimate human end, namely, happiness or blessedness. And so law especially needs to concern the order to happiness in general. Law is such primarily because of its order to the common good, and so every precept regarding particular acts has the character of law only because of its order to that good (Q. 90, A. 2).

Third, lawmaking—that is, ordering things to the common good—belongs to the whole people or to persons acting in the name of the whole people, that is, a public authority that has the care of the community (Q. 90, A. 3).

Aquinas poses an objection: Lawmakers aim to induce human beings to virtue. But any human being can lead others to virtue. Therefore, the reason of any human being is competent to make law. He replies that private persons cannot effectively induce others to virtue, since private persons can only offer advice, and they have no coercive power to compel others if their advice is rejected, which power law should have. But the people or a public authority has such coercive power and the right to inflict punishment. And so it belongs only to the people or a public authority to make law.

Fourth, laws need to be promulgated if they are to impose obligations on those subject to the laws (Q. 90, A. 4).

Aquinas poses an objection: The natural law most has the character of law. But the natural law does not need to be promulgated. Therefore, promulgation is not an essential component of law. He replies briefly: God promulgates the natural law when he implants it in the minds of human beings, so that they know it by nature.

And so law is defined by the four characteristics: law is an order of reason for the common good by one who has the care of the community, and it has been promulgated.

Kinds

God's reason governs the whole community of the universe, and this is the eternal law (Q. 91, A. 1).

Human beings, as rational creatures, share in his providence by their use of reason to provide for themselves, and so they share in the eternal law, whereby they have a natural inclination toward their requisite end and proper activity. This participation in the eternal law is the natural law (Q. 91, A. 2).

Aquinas poses an objection: The freer one is, the less one is subject to law. But human beings have free choice and so are freer than other animals. Therefore, since other animals are not subject to the natural law, neither are human beings. He replies that even irrational animals, like human beings, share in the eternal law in their own way. But because human beings share in the eternal law by using their intellect and reason, their participation in the eternal law is law in the strict sense, since law belongs to reason. But the participation of irrational creatures in the eternal law is only by analogy, since they do not share in the eternal law by the use of reason.

Human reason needs to go beyond the general principles of the natural law to precise regulations, and such regulations devised by reason are human laws (Q. 91, A. 3).

Aquinas poses an objection: The natural law shares in the eternal law. But the eternal law renders all things most orderly. Therefore, the natural law suffices for ordering human affairs. Therefore, there is no need of human laws. He replies that human reason cannot partake of the complete dictates of God's reason but partakes of them in human reason's own way and incompletely. And so, regarding theoretical reason, we by our natural participation in God's wisdom know general principles but do not specifically know every truth, as God's wisdom does. Just so, regarding practical reason, human beings by nature partake of the eternal law in general principles but not as to particular specifications of particular matters, although such specifications belong to the eternal law. And so human reason needs to proceed further to determine the particular prescriptions of human law.

In addition to the natural law and human laws, revealed divine law was necessary to direct human life. Aquinas gives four reasons why. First, human beings are ordered to eternal blessedness, and so God needed to lay down a law superior to the natural law and human laws in order to direct human beings to this end. Second, in order that human beings should know beyond doubt what they should or should not do regarding contingent and particular matters, a divinely revealed law was necessary. Third, divine laws were necessary to supplement human laws in order to regulate hidden internal movements of the soul, which human laws could not reach. Fourth, a divine law forbidding all sins was necessary in order that every evil should be forbidden and punished, although human laws may tolerate some evils to benefit the common good (Q. 91, A. 4).

Aquinas argues that the New Law is superior to the Old Law, as a perfect law to an imperfect law. First, the Old Law was for an earthly common good, the land of the Canaanites (Ex. 3:8–17), but the New Law for a heavenly common good. Second, the New Law surpasses the Old Law in regard to righteousness by ordering internal spiritual acts. Third, the Old Law induced human beings to observe the commandments by fear of punishments, but the New Law does so by love, which God's grace pours into human hearts (Q. 91, A. 5).

Concupiscence consists of sudden movements of sense appetites to act outside the control of, or contrary to, reason. The so-called "law of concupiscence" is only a law inasmuch as it is a just punishment of Adam's sin (Q. 91, A. 6).

Effects

The proper effect of law is to make those subject to the law good. If the aim of the lawmakers is set upon what is not absolutely good but what is useful or desirable for themselves or what is contrary to divine justice, the law makes human beings relatively good, namely, in relation to such a regime. But if the aim of the lawmakers strives for the real common good, which is regulated by divine justice, the law makes human beings absolutely good. This distinction originated with Aristotle (Q. 92, A. 1).

Aquinas poses several objections. One runs as follows: Law is ordered to the common good. But some human beings ill-disposed regarding their individual good are well-disposed regarding what belongs to the common good. Therefore, it does not belong to law to make human beings good. He replies that since every human being is part of a political community, no human being can be good unless rightly related to the common good. Nor can a whole be rightly constituted unless its parts are rightly related to it. And so the common good of a political community will be rightly disposed only if its citizens, at least those to whom its ruling belongs, are virtuous. But it suffices as regards the good of the community that other citizens be virtuous enough to obey the commands of the law. And so the virtue of a ruler and that of a good man are the same, but the virtue of an ordinary citizen and that of a good man are not. This distinction also originated with Aristotle.

A second objection runs as follows: Some laws are tyrannical. But a tyrant strives for his individual good, not the good of his subjects. Therefore, it does not belong to law to make human beings good. Aquinas replies that a tyrannical law, since it is not in accord with reason, is not a law, absolutely speaking. Rather, it is a perversion of law. And yet such a law strives to make citizens good inasmuch as it partakes of the nature of law. It partakes of the nature of law only insofar as it is a dictate for his subjects and strives to make them duly obedient, that is, to make them good in relation to such a regime, not absolutely good.

The Eternal Law

As the plan of divine wisdom has the nature of a type or idea, since all things are created through it, so the plan causing the movement of everything to its requisite end has the character of law (Q. 93, A. 1). All human beings, inasmuch as they are rational, know the plan of divine wisdom in some of its effects, just as one knows the sun in its rays even if one is not looking at the sun. Every known truth is a radiation and participation of the eternal law, which itself is incommunicable. Everyone knows truth to some extent, at least regarding the general principles of the natural law and also regarding other things (Q. 93, A. 2). All human laws, as plans of government subordinate to the supreme ruler and partaking of right reason, are derived from eternal law (Q. 93, A. 3).

Aquinas poses an objection: Nothing evil can come from the eternal law. But some laws are evil. Therefore, not every law comes from the eternal law. He replies that human law has the nature of law insofar as it is in accord with right reason, and then it is derived from the eternal law, but human law is evil insofar as it withdraws from reason, and then it has the nature of brute force, not law. But insofar as some likeness of law is preserved in an evil law because one empowered to make law ordered it, it is also in this respect derived from the eternal law.

Everything belonging to creatures, whether necessary or contingent, belongs to the eternal law, but things belonging to the divine essence are in reality the eternal law itself and not things belonging to the eternal law (Q. 93, A. 4). God imprints on all the things of nature the sources of their activities, and so he in this respect commands the whole of nature, and all movements and actions of nature are subject to the eternal law, although irrational creatures do not understand the commands of God (Q. 93, A. 5).

Aquinas poses an objection: The eternal law is most efficacious. But deficiencies occur in contingent natural things. Therefore, such things are not subject to the eternal law. He replies that deficiencies occurring in natural things, although outside the order of particular causes, are not outside the order of universal causes, especially of the first cause, God, from whose providence nothing can escape. Moreover, because the eternal law is the plan of divine providence, deficiencies of natural things are subject to the eternal law.

Human beings partake of the eternal law in a conscious way, since they know the eternal law in some regard and have an inclination from nature toward things consonant with the eternal law. The virtuous are completely subject to the eternal law, since they always act in accord with it, and the wicked are incompletely subject to the eternal law, since they incompletely act in accord with it. But what their actions lack is proportionately supplemented by suffering the punishment that the eternal law dictates for those who fail to observe it (Q. 93, A. 6).

The Natural Law

Reason habitually possesses knowledge of the first principles of the natural law (Q. 94, A. 1).

The first self-evident precept of the natural law is that one should seek what is good for human beings and shun what is evil for them. All precepts of the natural law are based on that one. Reason by nature and without argument understands that everything for which human beings have a natural inclination is good for human beings and to be actively sought, and everything contrary to a natural inclination is evil for them and to be avoided. First, human beings as substances have a natural inclination to preserve their lives, and so they should use means to do so. Second, human beings as animals have a natural inclination to mate and raise children, and so they should do so. Third, human beings as human have natural inclinations to seek truth and live cooperatively in society, and so they should do so. Note that these natural inclinations are the inclinations of *human*, that is, rational, nature, and so the inclinations are natural only insofar as they are in accord with reason (Q. 94, A. 2).

All virtuous natural acts as such belong to the natural law, since human beings have a natural inclination to act according to reason, that is, virtuously. But some particular virtuous acts (e.g., particular acts of modesty) do not belong to the natural law, since human beings do many things virtuously to which nature at first does not incline them (Q. 94, A. 3).

Aquinas poses an objection: Everyone agrees about things that are in accord with nature. But not everyone agrees about virtuous acts, inasmuch as things that are virtuous for some are vicious for others. Therefore, not all virtuous acts belong to the natural law. He replies that the argument of this objection is valid regarding virtuous acts as such-and-such acts. Then, because of the different conditions or human beings, some acts may be virtuous for some persons, as proportionate and suitable for them, but vicious for other persons, as disproportionate for them.

Truth in practical matters is the same for all human beings only regarding general principles, not regarding particular conclusions from the principles (e.g., one should return goods to their owners, but there are exceptions). Nor do all know particular conclusions (e.g., emotions or bad habits or evil dispositions may pervert the reason of some) (Q. 94, A. 4).

The natural law may vary insofar as divine law or human law adds beneficial things to it. Nothing can be subtracted from the primary precepts of the natural law, and so the natural law is in this respect altogether immutable. As to secondary precepts, namely, proximate conclusions from the first principles, what the natural law prescribes is for the most part completely correct. But the natural law may in relatively few cases vary regarding particular conclusions (e.g., it is a principle of the natural law that one should return goods to their owners, but one should not return firearms to an owner who is homicidal maniac) (Q. 94, A. 5).

Aquinas poses several objections. One runs as follows: Killing innocent human beings, theft, and adultery are contrary to the natural law. But God altered these precepts. For example, God on one occasion commanded Abraham to slay his innocent son (Gen 22:2). On another occasion, God commanded the Jews to steal vessels that the Egyptians had lent them (Ex 12:35). On still another occasion, God commanded Hosea to take a fornicating wife (Hos 1:2). Therefore, the natural law can vary.

Aquinas replies that all human beings, both the innocent and the guilty, die when natural death comes. But God's power inflicts natural death because of original sin. And so, at the command of God, death can without any injustice be inflicted on any human being, whether innocent or guilty. Likewise, adultery is sexual intercourse with another man's wife, whom the law laid down by God allotted to the husband. And so there is no adultery or fornication in having intercourse with any woman at the command of God. The argument is the same regarding theft, which consists of taking another's property. One does not take without the consent of an owner (steal) anything one takes at the command of God, who is the owner of the property. Nor is it only regarding human affairs that every thing God commands is owed to him. Rather, regarding things of nature, everything that God does is also in one respect natural.

A second objection runs as follows: Common possession of all property and equal freedom of all persons belong to the natural law. But human laws have altered these precepts. Therefore, the natural law can vary. Aquinas replies that we speak of things belonging to the natural law in one way because nature inclines us to them (e.g., one should not cause injury to another). We can speak of things belonging to the natural law in a second way because nature did not introduce the contrary (e.g., we could say that it belongs to the natural law that human beings be naked, since nature does not endow them with clothes, which human skills created). It is in this way that we say that the common possession of all property and equal freedom of all persons belong to the natural law: the reason of human beings, not nature, introduced private property and involuntary servitude. And so the natural law in this way varies only by way of addition.

The general principles of the natural law cannot be excised from the hearts of human beings, but the natural law is wiped out regarding particular actions when desires or emotions prevent reason from applying the general principles to the actions. And the natural law can be excised from the hearts of human beings regarding secondary precepts because of wicked opinions or evil customs or corrupt habits (e.g., some did not think robbery a sin, or even sins contrary to nature, to be sinful) (Q. 94, A. 6).

Human Laws

Human beings need instruction and training in order to arrive at complete virtue. Force and fear are necessary to restrain the wicked, at least so that they leave others in peace. And human laws are necessary in order that human beings may live in peace and attain virtue (Q. 95, A. 1).

Human laws impose moral obligation insofar as they are just, and things are just insofar as they are in accord with reason, whose primary rule is the natural law. And so every human law has the character of law insofar as it is from the natural law. Some human laws are conclusions from general precepts of the natural law (e.g., laws prohibiting homicide, which are conclusions from the general principle that one should do no evil to others). Other human laws are further specifications of general principles of the natural law (e.g., laws punishing criminals in specific ways, which are further specifications from the general principle that criminals should be punished) (Q. 95, A. 2).

First, human laws can be distinguished by the way in which they are derived from the natural law: the common law of peoples (the *jus gentium*) as conclusions from it, and the laws of particular commonwealths (e.g., tax laws) as specifications of it. Second, human laws can be distinguished according to the persons affected (e.g., military law for military personnel). Third, human laws can be distinguished according to the regime of the community (e.g., monarchy, aristocracy, democracy). Fourth, human laws can be distinguished by their subject matter (e.g., property law) (Q. 95, A. 4).

Some human laws are framed exclusively in general terms (e.g., criminal laws), some in general terms but concerning particular persons (e.g., laws defining the powers of particular office holders), and some apply general laws to particular cases (administrative and judicial decisions) (Q. 96, A. 1).

Human laws are established for the collectivity of human beings, most of whom have imperfect virtue. And so human laws prohibit only the most serious vices, vices that inflict harm on others (e.g., homicide and theft) (Q. 96, A. 2).

Aquinas poses an objection: Human law is derived from the natural law. But all vices are contrary to the natural law. Therefore, the law ought to prohibit all vices. He replies that the natural law is our participation in the eternal law, but human law falls short of the eternal law, since laws framed for the governance of political communities permit and leave unpunished many things that God's providence punishes. And so human laws could not prohibit everything that the natural law punishes.

There are no virtues regarding whose actions laws could not command, but they do not command every action of every virtue. Rather, they command only things that can be ordered to the common good, whether immediately, as when things are done directly for that good (e.g., maintaining armed forces), or indirectly, as when lawmakers command things belonging to good training for the common good (e.g., education) (Q. 96, A. 3).

Just human laws oblige in conscience. Human laws are just if they are ordered to the common good, if lawmakers are authorized to make the laws, and if the laws impose proportionately equal burdens on citizens. Conversely, human laws are unjust regarding the human good if they are established to benefit the lawmakers rather than the community, if they exceed the authority of the lawmakers, or if they impose disproportionate burdens on citizens. Such laws of themselves do not oblige in conscience, but may do so if obedience is necessary to avoid scandal or civil unrest. One should never obey unjust human laws contrary to the divine good, and one has a duty to disobey them (e.g., laws commanding worship of idols) (Q. 96, A. 4).

Aquinas poses an objection: Lower powers cannot impose laws on the courts of higher powers. But the power of human beings, which establishes human laws, is inferior to God's power. Therefore, human law cannot impose laws on the court of God, that is, the court of conscience. He replies that all human power is from God, and so those who resist human power in matters belonging to its scope resist God's order. And so such persons become guilty in respect to their conscience.

Only those subject to the authority of lawmakers are subject to their laws (e.g., only those subject to U.S. jurisdiction are subject to U.S. laws). The authority of a higher power (such as the U.S. president) overrides the authority of a lower power (such as a U.S. military commander). Rulers with supreme authority are exempt from the coercive power of human laws but should of their own free will subject themselves to the laws (Q. 96, A. 5).

Aquinas poses an objection: Rulers are exempt from the law. But those exempt from the law are not subject to it. Therefore, not everyone is subject to the law. He replies that rulers are exempt from the law regarding its coercive force, since, properly speaking, one is not coerced by oneself, and law has coercive force only from the ruler. Therefore, rulers are exempt from the law because no one can pass sentence on them if they act contrary to the law. But regarding the directive power of law, rulers are subject to the law by their own will. Rulers should follow the law they decree for others. And so regarding God's judgment, rulers are not exempt from the law regarding its directive power, and they should willingly, not by coercion, fulfill the law. Rulers are also above the law insofar as they can, if it be expedient, alter the law and dispense from it at certain times and places.

One should not obey a law in particular circumstances if observance would result in a clear and imminent danger to the community or a component of the common good (e.g., a driver may, with due caution, exceed the legal speed limit in order to bring a severely injured person to a hospital) (Q. 96, A. 6).

Human laws may need to be revised to make them more perfect. They may also need to be revised in order to suit the altered conditions of human beings (e.g., new laws may be needed to prevent terrorist attacks) (Q. 97, A. 1).

Aquinas poses an objection: Human law is derived from the natural law. But the natural law remains immutable. Therefore, human law ought to remain immutable. He replies that the natural law is a participation in the eternal law, and so the natural law remains immutable. The natural law has this immutability from the immutability and perfection of the divine reason that established human nature. But human reason is mutable and imperfect. Moreover, the natural law consists of universal precepts that always abide, while laws established by human beings consist of particular precepts that regard different situations that arise.

But the binding force of law is diminished whenever laws are revised, since custom powerfully influences legal observance (Q. 97, A. 2). Things done repeatedly seem to proceed from the deliberate judgments of reason, and so custom has the force of law, abolishes law, and interprets law (Q. 97, A. 3).

Aquinas poses several objections. One runs as follows: Moral good cannot come out of many wicked acts. But those who first begin to act contrary to a law act wickedly. Therefore, many such acts do not produce anything morally good. But law is something morally good, since law regulates human actions. Therefore, custom cannot abolish laws, so that the customs establish the force of law. He replies that human laws are deficient in particular cases. And so one can sometimes act outside the law, namely, in cases in which the laws are deficient, and the actions will not be morally evil. When such actions are repeated because of alterations regarding human beings, then customs indicate that the laws are no longer useful, just as it would be evident that laws were no longer useful if expressly contrary laws were to be promulgated. But if the same reason for which the original law was useful still persists, the law prevails over the custom, not the custom over the law. One exception may be if the law seems useless simply because it is impossible by reason of a country's customs.

A second objection is important because the response brings out the distinction between self-governing and dependent peoples. The objection runs as follows: Framing laws belongs to public persons, whose business is to govern a community, and so private persons cannot make law. But customs flourish through the acts of private persons. Therefore, customs cannot obtain the force of law so as to abolish laws. Aquinas replies that the people among whom a custom is introduced can be in two conditions. If a people is free, that is, self-governing, the custom of the whole people, which custom indicates, counts more in favor of a particular legal observance than the authority of its ruler, who only has the power to frame laws insofar as the ruler acts in the name of the people. And so the whole people can establish laws, but individual persons cannot. But if the people do not have the free disposition to frame laws for themselves or to abolish laws imposed by a higher power, the customs prevailing in such a population can still obtain the force of law insofar as those who have the power to impose laws on the people tolerate the customs, since rulers thereby seem to approve the customs introduced.

Rulers should dispense subjects from observing human laws when persons or situations warrant it (Q. 97, A. 4).

Aquinas poses an objection: Human law, to be just, needs to be in accord with the natural and divine laws. But no human being can dispense anyone from the divine and natural laws. Therefore, neither can any human being dispense someone from a human law. He replies that the general precepts of the natural law, which are never wanting, cannot be dispensed, although human beings may sometimes be dispensed from other precepts of the natural law, namely, conclusions, as it were, from the general precepts (e.g., rulers may dispense debtors from the obligation to repay loans owed to traitors).

The Moral Precepts of the Old Law

Aquinas distinguishes three kinds of precepts of the Old Law: moral, ceremonial, and judicial. Moral precepts concern good morals, and human acts are morally good if they are in accord with reason. Judgments of practical reason derive from naturally known first principles (e.g., live cooperatively in society), and so the moral precepts of the Old Law necessarily belong to the natural law in some way. Some of these moral precepts (e.g., do not steal) are proximate conclusions that one can easily draw from the first general principles. Other moral precepts (e.g., respect the elderly) are remote conclusions that require greater reflection and instruction by the wise. Still other moral precepts concern divine things (e.g., do not take the name of the Lord thy God in vain), about which human beings need divine instruction (Q. 100, A. 1).

Human laws lay down precepts regarding acts of justice and prescribe other virtuous acts only insofar as the acts take on an aspect of justice. But divine law lays down precepts about everything required for communion with God and so about the acts of every virtue (e.g., precepts governing chastity) (Q. 100, A. 2).

The Decalogue includes moral precepts from God himself, both proximate precepts easily known from the first principles of the natural law and special precepts revealed by God. The first principles themselves are not included in the Decalogue, since they are self-evident to natural reason. Nor are the remote conclusions from the first principles that the wise discover by careful study, and that God communicates by the instruction of the wise (Q. 100, A. 3).

Aquinas poses an objection: We do not trace moral precepts of the Old Law to its ceremonial precepts. Rather, we do the converse. But one of the commandments, namely, to keep holy the Sabbath, is expressly ceremonial. Therefore, we do not trace all the moral precepts of the Old Law to any commandment of the Decalogue. He replies that the commandment to observe the Sabbath is moral in one respect, namely, that human beings devote some time to divine things. But we do not reckon the Sabbath among the moral precepts of the Decalogue as to the appointed day, since the commandment in this respect is ceremonial.

The commandments of the first tablet of the Decalogue (e.g., do not have strange gods before me) direct human beings in relation to God, who is their ultimate end. The commandments of the second tablet (e.g., honor your parents) order the justice to be observed in human society. Both sets of commandments include God's intention that they be observed, and so there can be no dispensations from them (Q. 100, A. 8).

Aquinas poses an objection that gives him an opportunity to make an important qualification: A commandment of the Decalogue prohibits homicide. But human laws seem to dispense human beings from this commandment. Therefore, there can be dispensations from the commandments of the Decalogue. To this, he gives a long reply.

The Decalogue prohibits the killing of human beings insofar as such killing is undeserved, since the commandment thereby includes the nature of justice, and human law cannot make it lawful that human beings be killed undeservedly. But it is not undeserved that criminals and enemies of the commonwealth be killed. And so this is not contrary to the commandment of the Decalogue, nor is such killing murder, which the commandment prohibits.

Likewise, it is not theft or robbery, which another commandment of the Decalogue prohibits, if property is taken from one who ought to relinquish it. And so there was no theft when the children of Israel at the command of God took away the spoils of the Egyptians (Ex 12:35–36), since the spoils were due the Israelites by reason of God's judgment.

Likewise, Abraham, when he agreed to kill his son (Gen 22:1–12), did not consent to murder, since it is proper that Isaac be killed at the command of God, who is the Lord of life and death. God inflicts death on all human beings, just and unjust, for the sin of our first parents, and human beings will not be murderers if they should by divine authority execute judgment, as God is not a murderer.

Likewise, Hosea, having sexual intercourse with a fornicating wife or adulterous woman (Hos 1:2–11), is not an adulterer or fornicator, since he had intercourse with a woman who was his by the command of God, who is the author of the institution of marriage.

Therefore, the commandments of the Decalogue, regarding the nature of justice that they include, cannot be changed. But specifications applying a commandment to particular acts, namely, specifications whether this or that act is murder, theft, or adultery, are variable. The specifications sometimes change only because of divine authority, namely, regarding matters that God alone instituted, such as marriage and the like. The specifications also sometimes change because of human authority, as in matters committed to human jurisdiction, since human beings in this but not every respect take the place of God.

Both God and human lawmakers have power to judge the external acts of human beings, but only God has power to judge internal acts of their will. Neither divine nor human law punishes involuntary deeds. Divine but not human law punishes those who intend to do evil but don't (e.g., those who intend to commit murder but do not). Neither divine nor human law punishes those who observe the law without possessing the corresponding virtue (the habit) to do so (Q. 100, A. 9).

Acts of charity as such fall under precepts of the divine law if the precepts lay down specific commands of charity (e.g., to love God and one's neighbor). But precepts commanding other virtuous acts (e.g., to honor one's parents) can be observed without possession of the virtue of charity (Q. 100, A. 10).

Precepts of the Old Law Regarding Rulers

Aquinas claims that the regime established by Moses to govern the Israelites was (and presumably remains) the best regime. It was best because it mixed the best features of monarchy, aristocracy, and democracy. Moses and his successors, the Judges, ruled as monarchs because of their virtue. Seventy-two elders assisted in governing because of their virtue. The principal virtue in both cases is political wisdom, the special kind of practical wisdom (prudence) involved in governance. Further, Aquinas claims that all citizens should participate in the best regime. Popular participation was desirable because it helped legitimize the regime, thereby insuring domestic peace and broad support for the regime. But contrary to our contemporary democratic standards, the people participated only in the choice of rulers, and the business of government was the sole responsibility of Moses and the elders (Q. 105, A. 1). Aquinas' inclusion of popular participation in governance, however limited, was an important contribution to the development of Western political thought.

ST 2-2

12

⁘

FAITH

The Object

The formal aspect of the object of faith, the means of demonstration by which we know the conclusions of faith, is God himself, since faith assents to something only because God has revealed it. The matter of faith consists of the things to which faith assents, both God and many other things, but the other things only insofar as they have a relation to God, namely, as some effects of God (such as the life and death of Christ and the sacraments of the Church) help human beings to strive to enjoy the vision of God (Q. 1, A. 1).

Although the object of faith in itself is something simple, the human intellect knows the object by affirmative and negative judgments (Q. 1, A. 2). Since God is the formal aspect of faith, nothing false can come under faith (Q. 1, A. 3). Since faith involves the intellect assenting to something because a choice of the will inclines it to one of two alternatives, faith cannot be about things seen, whether by the senses or the intellect (Q. 1, A. 4).

Aquinas poses an objection: Paul says in 1 Cor 13:12 that "we see now through a mirror darkly." But he is speaking about the knowledge of faith. Therefore, we see what we believe. Aquinas replies that we can consider the objects of faith in one way in particular, and then they cannot be simultaneously seen and believed. We can consider them in a second way in general, namely, under the common aspect of credibility, and then the believer has seen them, since one would only believe if one were to "see" the things to be believed, whether because of the evidence of signs or something similar.

All scientific knowledge is through principles that are self-evident and therefore seen. But the same individual cannot see and believe the same thing. And so the same individual cannot know scientifically and believe the same thing. Nonetheless, one individual may believe what another individual sees or knows scientifically (Q. 1, A. 5).

Aquinas poses an objection: Demonstrated things are known scientifically, since demonstration is a syllogism concerning scientific knowledge. But philosophers have demonstrated some of the things included in faith (e.g., that God exists, that there is only one God, and that the human soul is immortal). Therefore, the things belonging to faith can be scientifically known. Aquinas replies that among the things to be believed, we can demonstrate some things not because all human beings, absolutely speaking, believe them, but because they are prerequisite for the things that belong to faith, and because those who have not demonstrated them need to assume them at least by faith.

There is a special article of faith where there is something that is not seen by reason of a particular aspect (e.g., seeing that God suffered poses one aspect, and seeing that he rose from the dead another, and so we distinguish the article on the resurrection from the one on the passion) (Q. 1, A. 6).

Regarding the substance of the articles of faith, there has been no increase over time, since whatever things later Church Fathers believed were implicitly contained in the faith professed by earlier

Church Fathers. But regarding explication of the faith, the number of articles increased, since later generations knew certain things explicitly that prior generations did not (Q. 1, A. 7).

The things whose vision we shall enjoy in eternal life and by which we are led to eternal life belong intrinsically to faith, and two things are proposed for us to see in heaven: what is hidden in divinity, and the mystery of Christ's humanity. And so some articles of faith suitably belong to the majesty of divinity, and some to the mystery of Christ's humanity (Q. 1, A. 8).

A person can believe only if the truth to be believed should be proposed to that person. And so the truth of faith needs to be collected in one creed in order that it could be more easily proposed to all (Q. 1, A. 9).

A new statement of the creed is necessary to avoid errors that arise. It belongs to the authority of the pope to determine definitively the things that belong to faith. The unity of faith could be preserved only if the one who is in charge of the whole Church were to determine questions that arise concerning faith. Therefore, a new statement of the creed belongs only to the authority of the pope, just like all the other things that pertain to the whole Church (e.g., convoking a general council) (Q. 1, A. 10).

The Internal Act of Faith

The act of faith firmly adheres to one alternative, in which clear vision has not yet perfected the believer's knowledge, and so the believer thinks with assent, and the act of faith is distinguished from the other acts of the intellect (understanding, scientific knowledge, and opinion) (Q. 2, A. 1).

Aquinas poses an objection: Believing is an act of the intellect, since the object of belief is truth. But assenting, like consenting, seems to be an act of the will, not an act of the intellect. Therefore, believing is not thinking with assent. He replies that we should say that the will, not reason, determines the intellect of the believer to one thing. And so we understand assent as an act of the intellect insofar as the will determines it to one thing.

Regarding the material object of faith, we consider the act of faith an act of belief *in* God, since nothing is proposed to us to believe except insofar as it pertains to him. Regarding the formal aspect of the object of faith, the means whereby we assent, the act of faith is proposed to us as an act believing God, since the formal object is the first truth, God. And if we consider the object of faith insofar as the will moves the intellect, we consider the act of faith as an act believing the first truth, God, in order to know him, since the first truth is related to the will insofar as God is our end (Q. 2, A. 2).

Aquinas poses an objection: We cannot consider what belongs also to unbelievers an act of faith. But believing that God exists belongs even to unbelievers. Therefore, we should not consider this belief part of the act of faith. He replies that belief in God does not belong to unbelievers under the aspect by which we are considering the act of faith, since they do not believe that God exists under the conditions that faith determines. And so they do not truly believe in God, since, regarding simple things, lack of knowledge consists simply of not attaining them at all.

A rational nature has an immediate ordering to the universal source of being, since it knows the universal aspect of good and being. Therefore, the perfection of a rational creature consists both of what belongs to it by nature and of what is ascribed to it by a supernatural sharing in the divine goodness, the vision of God. Human beings can attain this vision only by way of learning from the divine teacher, and every such learner needs to believe in order to arrive at the complete vision of God (Q. 2, A. 3).

Aquinas poses an objection: For the well-being and perfection of anything, the things that belong to it by nature seem to suffice. But the things belonging to faith surpass a human being's natural reason, since they are unseen things. Therefore, believing does not seem to be necessary for salvation. He replies that as the nature of a human being depends on a higher nature, natural knowledge does not suffice for a human being's perfection. Rather, a supernatural knowledge is required.

Human beings need to accept by faith both things above reason and things known through reason, and this is for several reasons. First, human beings would by reason come to scientific knowledge of God only late in life. Second, many human beings would lack the talent or time to come to knowledge of God through reason. Third, human reason about divine things is very deficient (Q. 2, A. 4).

Aquinas poses an objection: Nothing is superfluous in the works of God. But something else is superfluously assigned to what one thing can accomplish. Therefore, it would be superfluous to accept on faith the things that one can know by natural reason. Aquinas replies that the investigation of natural reason does not suffice for the human race to know divine things, even those things that reason can show. And so it is not superfluous that such things are believed.

The intrinsic object of faith is what makes human beings blessed. All the things contained in the sacred Scripture handed down by God are incidentally or secondarily related to the object of faith (e.g., that David was the son of Jesse). Therefore, a human being is bound to believe explicitly the first things, which are articles of faith. But a human being is bound to believe only implicitly the other things (Q. 2, A. 5).

More expert human beings, to whom instruction of less expert human beings belongs, are bound to have fuller knowledge about the things to be believed and to believe in them more explicitly (Q. 2, A. 6).

It was necessary that all human beings in every age believe in the mystery of Christ's incarnation, although in different ways in different ages and by different persons. But after the time of Christ's coming, both leaders and ordinary people are bound to have explicit faith in the mysteries of Christ, especially regarding the things universally celebrated in the Church and publicly promulgated, such as the creed's articles on the incarnation (Q, 2, A. 7).

Aquinas poses an objection: Many pagans gained salvation by the ministry of the angels. But the pagans had neither explicit nor implicit faith about Christ, since they had no revelation about him. Therefore, it seems that it was not necessary that all believe explicitly in the mystery of Christ. He replies that there was revelation about Christ to many pagans. But if some were saved to whom no revelation was made, they were not saved without faith in the mediator. Although they did not have explicit faith in him, they still had faith in divine providence, believing that God delivers human beings in ways pleasing to him and insofar as he were to have revealed this to those who would know the truth.

One cannot explicitly believe the mystery of Christ's incarnation without faith in the Trinity. And so, in the same way by which leaders believed in the mystery of the incarnation before Christ's coming, and ordinary people believed implicitly and confusedly, so did they believe in the mystery of the Trinity. And so also after the revelation of grace, all human beings are bound to believe explicitly in the mystery of the Trinity (Q. 2, A. 8).

Every act of faith is the result of a free decision in relation to God, and so the act can be meritorious (Q. 2, A. 9).

Aquinas poses an objection: Believing is in between having an opinion and knowing scientifically or considering things scientifically known. But the consideration in science is not meritorious, nor is opinion. Therefore, believing is not meritorious. He replies that the assent of scientific knowledge is not subject to a free decision, since the power of a demonstration forces the knower to assent, and so the assent in scientific knowledge is not meritorious. But actual consideration of the thing known is subject to free decision, and so consideration in scientific knowledge can be meritorious if it is related to the end of charity, that is, the honor of God and the benefit of neighbor. In faith, both the assent and the consideration are subject to a free decision, and so the act of faith can be meritorious regarding both. In opinion, there is only weak assent, which has little merit, but actual consideration can be meritorious.

Human reason antecedently introduced to support the act of faith lessens the merit of faith, since a human being ought to believe the things belonging to faith because of divine authority, not because of human reason. But human reason subsequently introduced to the assent of faith in order to support it is evidence of greater merit (Q. 2, A. 10).

Aquinas poses an objection: Whatever lessens the reckoning of virtue lessens the reckoning of merit, since happiness is the reward of virtue. But human reason seems to weaken the reckoning of the virtue of faith itself, since it belongs to the nature of faith to be about unseen things. And the more reasons are introduced to support something, the less unseen it is. Therefore, human reason introduced to support things belonging to faith lessens the merit of faith. He replies that the reasons introduced to support the authority of faith are not demonstrations that can bring the human intellect to intelligible vision, and so the reasons do not lessen things being unseen. Rather, they remove hindrances to faith, by showing that what is proposed regarding faith is not impossible. And so such reasons do not lessen the merit or the aspect of faith. On the other hand, demonstrative arguments introduced to support the things belonging to faith as preambles to the articles of faith diminish the aspect of faith, since they cause us to see what is proposed to us for belief. But such arguments do not lessen the aspect of charity, which renders the will ready to believe those things even if they were not to be seen. And so the aspect of merit is not lessened.

The External Act of Faith

Profession of the things belonging to faith is specifically ordered to what belongs to faith as its end, since external speech is ordered to signifying what is conceived in the mind. And so, as the internal conception of the things that belong to faith is properly an act of faith, so also is their external profession (Q. 3, A. 1).

Affirmative precepts of the divine law do not oblige under all circumstances. Rather, they oblige according to where, when, and other requisite circumstances that need to circumscribe the human act in order for it to be a virtuous act. Therefore, external profession of the faith is not always or everywhere necessary for salvation but only in a certain place and at a certain time, namely, when omission of such profession would lessen the honor of God and the benefit that one should expend for one's neighbor. For example, profession of the faith would be necessary if a respondent questioned about the faith were to remain silent, and the questioner were thereby led to believe either that the one questioned did not have the faith, or that the faith was untrue, or if others were to be turned away from the faith by the respondent's silence (Q. 3, A. 2).

The Virtue of Faith

Faith is the habit of mind whereby we begin to have eternal life, causing the intellect to assent to unseen things. This distinguishes faith from other things that belong to the intellect. What we call evidence distinguishes faith from opinion, suspicion, and doubt, none of which causes the intellect to adhere firmly to anything. What we call evidence of things to be hoped for distinguishes faith from scientific knowledge and understanding, which cause something to be seen. And what we call the substance of things to be hoped for distinguishes the virtue of faith from faith as generally understood, which is not ordered to the blessedness hoped for (Q. 4, A. 1).

Aquinas poses an objection: Evidence manifests the truth of that for which the evidence is introduced. But something is seen whose truth has been manifested. Therefore, contradiction seems to be implied in the phrase *the evidence of things unseen.*

He replies that evidence taken from something's own sources causes a thing to be seen. But evidence taken on divine authority does not cause the thing in itself to be seen. And such evidence is proposed in the definition of faith.

Belief is directly an act of the intellect, since the object of the act is truth, which properly belongs to the intellect. And so the virtue of faith, which is the proper source of the act of faith, necessarily resides in the intellect as its source (Q. 4, A. 2).

The act of faith is ordered to the object of the will, that is, the good, as its end, and the good that is the end of faith, namely, the divine good, is the proper object of charity. And so we call charity the form of faith, inasmuch as charity perfects and gives form to the act of faith (Q. 4, A. 3).

What intrinsically belongs to a habit distinguishes the habit. Faith is a perfection of the intellect. And so what belongs to the intellect belongs intrinsically to faith, and what belongs to the will, namely, charity, does not. And so formed faith—faith with charity—and unformed faith—faith without charity—are not different habits (Q. 4, A. 4).

Formed faith is a virtue, since, by reason of faith itself, the intellect is always borne to truth, and, by reason of charity, the will is unerringly ordered to the good end, love of God and love of neighbor. But unformed faith is not a virtue, since, although faith has the requisite perfection of an act of faith regarding the intellect, it does not have the requisite perfection regarding the will (Q. 4, A. 5).

If we should understand faith as the habit by which we believe, then faith is specifically the same habit in all believers but numerically different habits in different human beings. If we should understand faith to mean what we believe, there is also one faith, since all believe the same thing (Q. 4, A. 6).

The theological virtues (faith, hope, and charity), whose object is our final end, are necessarily prior to other virtues. But the final end itself is necessarily in the intellect before it is in the will, since the will is borne to something only as the thing is apprehended in the intellect. And so, since the final end is in the intellect by faith and in the will by hope and charity, faith is necessarily the first of all the virtues. But a particular virtue by removing obstacles to faith may be incidentally prior to it (Q. 4, A. 7).

Faith surpasses the intellectual virtues of prudence and skills because of its matter, since it concerns eternal things, while prudence and skills concern contingent things. Since faith relies on divine truth, it is more certain than theoretical wisdom, scientific knowledge, and understanding, which rely on human reason. But faith is less certain in that the things belonging to faith are above the human intellect, while the things that belong to theoretical wisdom, scientific knowledge, and understanding are not (Q. 4, A. 8).

Those Who Have Faith

Adam and the angels were created with the gift of grace and so received a beginning of the blessedness hoped for, which begins in the intellect with faith. And so the angels before their confirmation, and Adam before his sin, had faith and had clear knowledge of some of the divine mysteries that we now know only by faith (Q. 5, A. 1).

The devils have faith but in a significantly different way than Christian believers do. The will of true believers, ordered to the good, commands their intellect to assent to things unseen, but the intellect of devils, without a will ordered to the good, perceives clear indications whereby they know that the teaching of the Church is from God, although they do not see the very things that the Church teaches (e.g., that God is triune) (Q. 5, A. 2).

The specific essence of any habit depends on the formal aspect of the object, without which the specific essence cannot abide. But the formal object of faith is the first truth insofar as it is manifested in sacred Scripture and the teaching of the Church. And so whoever does not adhere to the teaching of the Church, which proceeds from the first truth, does not have the habit of faith (Q. 5, A. 3).

Faith is specifically one and the same in all believers, but one individual can have greater explicitness of faith, greater in one way regarding the intellect, because of greater certitude and firmness, and in another way regarding the will, because of greater readiness, devotion, or confidence (Q.5, A. 4).

The Cause of Faith

The things that belong to faith surpass human reason and so do not fall within a human being's knowledge unless God reveals them, either directly or indirectly through preachers of the faith. Regarding the assent of a human being to the things that belong to faith, one cause is external (e.g., witnessing a miracle), but no such cause is sufficient, since some who witness a miracle do not believe. And so we need to posit an internal cause. This must be a supernatural cause, since human beings assenting to the things that belong to faith are elevated above their nature. And so faith regarding assent is from God, who moves human beings interiorly by grace (Q. 6, A. 1).

Lack of form (charity) does not belong to the specific essence of faith itself, since faith is unformed because of the lack of an external form. And so what causes faith, absolutely speaking, causes unformed faith. But this is God. And so unformed faith is a gift from God (Q. 6, A. 2).

Unbelief

Unbelief in the proper sense consists of resisting hearing about the faith or of contemning it, and this is a sin. But unbelief as simple ignorance of the faith is not itself a sin but a punishment, since such ignorance of divine things resulted from the sin of Adam (Q. 10, A. 1).

Unbelief, like faith, belongs to the intellect as its proximate subject, but to the will as the first cause of its movement (Q. 10, A. 2).

Unbelief most distances a human being from God, since an unbeliever lacks true knowledge about God and draws further away from him by false knowledge. And so the sin of unbelief is worse than moral sins (Q. 10, A. 3).

Unbelievers clearly cannot perform the good works that are the works of grace, namely, meritorious works, but they can to a degree perform the good works for which human nature suffices. And so unbelievers do not necessarily sin in everything that they do (Q. 10, A. 4).

There are different species of unbelief. First, there is the unbelief consisting of resistance to the faith never before accepted (e.g., the unbelief of pagans and gentiles). Second, there is the unbelief consisting of resistance to the previously accepted Christian faith, whether accepted in a type (as in the unbelief of Jews), or accepted in the revealed truth itself (as in the unbelief of heretics) (Q. 10, A. 5).

Regarding the relation of unbelief to faith, heretics, who resist the faith they previously accepted, sin more seriously against it than Jews and pagans, who never accepted the faith. But Jews, who accepted a type of the faith in the Old Law, sin more seriously against the faith than the pagans, who never did. Regarding corruption of things belonging to faith, however, pagans err more than Jews, and Jews more than heretics, although some heretics (e.g., Manicheans) err more than pagans (Q. 10, A. 6).

It is praiseworthy to engage in public debate about faith in order to refute errors but not to test its truth by arguments. When unbelievers are disturbing the faith of ordinary people, public debate about faith with them is advisable, provided that there are capable discussants for it (Q. 10, A.7).

Jews and pagans should in no way be compelled to embrace the faith, since faith belongs to the will of each person, but believers should compel them, if possible, not to hinder the faith. On the other hand, heretics should be compelled, even physically, to fulfill what they promised and to hold what they once accepted (Q. 10, A. 8).

Believers may communicate with pagans and Jews but not with heretics or apostates, since the Church has punished them with excommunication. Only those who are firm in the faith should communicate with pagan and Jewish unbelievers (Q. 10, A. 9).

The Church in no way permits unbelievers to acquire power over the faithful or to rule over them in any way in any office, since this would lead to danger to the faith. But the distinction between believer and unbelievers does not take away the already-established power of unbelievers over believers, since the divine law does not take away human law. But the ordinance of the Church, which has divine authority, can justly take away such a right to power or authority, since unbelievers because of their unbelief deserve to lose their power over the faithful (Q. 10, A. 10).

Although unbelievers sin in their rites, the rites can be tolerated either because some good comes from them, or because some evil is avoided. Jewish rites represent the faith as a type, and so the rites should be tolerated. But the rites of other unbelievers, which convey no truth or benefit, are not in any way to be tolerated, except to avoid civic strife or for some other reason (Q. 10, A. 11).

The children of Jews and pagans should not be baptized against the wishes of their parents. Aquinas appeals to the tradition of the Church and the reasons for it. The first reason is the danger to the faith, since parents could later, when the children reached maturity, easily induce them to abandon the faith the children unknowingly accepted. But the principal reason is that the practice would be contrary to natural justice, namely, that children are under the care of their parents until they reach maturity. The child can then be brought to the faith by persuasion, not coercion, even against the wishes of the parents (Q. 10, A. 12).

Heresy

Those who correctly have the Christian faith voluntarily assent to Christ in things that truly belong to his teaching. One can deviate from the Christian faith in two ways. The first way is that one does not wish to assent to Christ himself, and this way has a bad will regarding the end itself, which is the species of unbelief of pagans and Jews. The second way is that one intends to assent to Christ but falls short in choosing the things whereby one assents to Christ, since one chooses things that one's own mind suggests, not those that Christ truly handed down (Q. 11, A. 1).

It belongs to the corruption of Christian faith when one has a false opinion regarding the things that belong to the faith. Things belong to faith either directly and chiefly (e.g., articles of faith) or indirectly and secondarily (e.g., things that corrupt the faith). Heresy regards both (Q. 11, A. 2).

Regarding heretics themselves, they by their sin merit to be excommunicated by the Church and justly executed. Regarding the Church, it should be merciful in order to convert the heretics, and so it does not, without a first and second admonition, excommunicate them and hand them over to the secular arm for execution (Q. 11, A. 3). (For comment, see Introduction, p. 27.)

Aquinas poses an objection: The master commanded his servants to allow the cockle to grow until the harvest (Mt 13:30), that is, the end of time. But the cockle signifies heretics. Therefore, we should tolerate heretics. He replies that excommunication is one thing, and eradication another, since one is excommunicated in order that one's spirit be saved in the day of the Lord (1 Cor 5:5). But even if death should completely eradicate heretics, this is not contrary to the Lord's command, which we should understand to be about when we cannot uproot the cockle without uprooting the wheat as well.

The Church extends charity to all, and charity regards a neighbor's spiritual good, namely, salvation, and the neighbor's temporal welfare, such as bodily life, earthly possessions, good reputation, and honors. Regarding the spiritual good, the Church receives repenting heretics, howsoever often they have relapsed, and this opens the way of their salvation. Regarding temporal goods, if heretics' possession of them would hinder the salvation of others, charity requires that heretics not retain them (Q. 11, A. 4).

Apostasy

Apostasy is the total renunciation of the Christian faith in general and the Catholic faith in particular (Q. 12, A. 1). It does not belong to the Church to punish the unbelief of those who have never accepted the faith, but it can by judicial sentence punish the unbelief of those who accepted the faith. And so, as soon as the Church by judicial sentence excommunicates a ruler for apostasy, the subjects are thereby ipso facto absolved from the ruler's authority and their oath of allegiance to him (Q. 12, A. 2).

The excommunication itself, of course, is a spiritual punishment that falls under the jurisdiction of the Church and is consistent with the freedom of religion in democratic theory. But the claim that the Church had the right to depose automatically an apostate ruler is inconsistent with the separation of Church and State in democratic political philosophy and current Catholic theology. (The Declaration on Religious Freedom of Vatican II renounced any power to depose rulers.) Again, the position of Aquinas on the subject reflects the widely held view of medieval theologians that organized political society should be professedly Christian and Catholic.

Blasphemy

Whoever denies something about God that belongs to him or asserts about him what does not belong to him derogates from the divine goodness, and this constitutes blasphemy. If the derogation is only in thought, it is mental blasphemy. If the derogation is external in speech, it is verbal blasphemy (Q. 13, A. 1).

Blasphemy is by its nature a mortal sin, since it derogates from the divine goodness, and the divine goodness is the object of charity (Q. 13, A. 2)

Aquinas poses an objection: Sins committed without deliberation are not mortal. Therefore, first movements toward sinning are not mortal sins, since they precede the deliberation of reason. But blasphemy sometimes proceeds without deliberation. Therefore, blasphemy is not always a mortal sin. He replies that blasphemy can happen suddenly without deliberation in one way when one is unaware that what one is saying is blasphemy (e.g., when one out of emotion bursts into figurative language without considering its meaning). This is a venial sin and does not have the nature of blasphemy. Blasphemy without deliberation happens in a second way when one is aware that what one is saying is blasphemy, conscious of the meaning of one's words. This is a mortal sin.

13

✤

HOPE

Hope in Itself

The object of hope is a difficult future good that is possible to obtain, and the act of hope about which we are now speaking concerns God, since we hope for something as possible for us through his help. And so hope is a virtue, since it makes a human being's act of hope good and concerns the requisite measure (Q. 17, A. 1).

The good that we ought properly and chiefly to hope for from God is an infinite good, one proportioned to the power of God helping us, since it belongs to infinite power to produce an infinite good. But this good is eternal life, which consists of the enjoyment of God himself. And so the proper and chief object of hope is eternal blessedness (Q. 17, A. 2).

If we presuppose a union of love with another, then one can desire and hope for something for the other, as one can for oneself, and one can accordingly hope for eternal life for another, since one is united to the other by love (Q. 17, A. 3).

One is permitted to hope for blessedness from a human being or a creature as a secondary and instrumental cause, a cause that helps one to obtain goods subordinate to the ultimate end of blessedness. And we turn to the saints in this way and even seek things from living human beings (Q. 17, A. 4).

The chief object of hope is God, and since the nature of a theological virtue consists of the fact that it has God as its object, hope is a theological virtue (Q. 17, A. 5). Faith makes a human being adhere to God inasmuch as he is for us the source of knowing the truth, and hope makes a human being adhere to God as he is for us a source of perfect goodness, namely, inasmuch as we through hope rely on divine help to obtain blessedness (Q. 17, A. 6). Faith precedes hope, since it is necessary that the object of hope be proposed to one as possible, and faith makes known that we can arrive at eternal life, and that divine help has been prepared for attaining this object (Q. 17, A. 7). In the order of coming to be, hope is prior to charity, but in the order of perfection, charity is prior to hope. The love of God, which adheres to God as such, is perfect love and belongs to charity, but hope is imperfect love and belongs to the love of desire, since one who hopes strives to obtain something for oneself (Q. 17, A. 8).

The Subject in Which Hope Resides

An act of the virtue of hope cannot belong to the sense appetite, since the good that is the chief object of the virtue is a divine good, not a sensibly perceptible good. And so hope resides in the rational appetite, the will, as its subject (Q. 18, A. 1).

A possible difficult good falls under the nature of hope only insofar as it is a future good, and so the virtue of hope cannot exist when blessedness is already present. And so hope, just like faith, is void in heaven (Q. 18, A. 2). It belongs to the condition of wretchedness of the damned that they know that they can in no way escape damnation and arrive at blessedness. And so neither the blessed nor the damned have hope, but wayfarers, whether in this life or in purgatory, can have hope, since they understand blessedness as a future possible good (Q. 18, A. 3). Hope tends unerringly to its end, as sharing in the certitude from faith, which certitude belongs to the intellect (Q. 18, A. 4).

Despair

The true judgment of the intellect about God is that the salvation of human beings comes from him, and that he grants pardon to sinners. The false opinion is that he denies pardon to a repentant sinner, or that he does not convert sinners to himself through justifying grace. And so the movement of hope, which is in conformity with a true judgment, is virtuous, and the contrary movement of despair, which is in conformity with a false judgment about God, is vicious and a sin (Q. 20, A. 1).

One who retains the true judgment of the faith regarding the universal, namely, that there is remission of sins in the Church, can still undergo a movement of despair regarding the particular, namely, that the one in such a condition should not hope for pardon (Q. 20, A. 2).

Unbelief, which is contrary to faith, and hatred of God, which is contrary to charity, are contrary to God as such, while despair is contrary to God insofar as we share in his goodness. And so it is a greater sin, absolutely speaking, not to believe God's truth or to hold God in hatred than not to hope to obtain glory from him. But if we compare despair to the two other sins regarding us, then despair is more dangerous, since hope recalls us from evil things and induces us to seek good things (Q. 20, A. 3).

Hope of obtaining happiness can be deficient either because one does not consider happiness a difficult good to obtain, or because one does not consider it a good possible to obtain, whether through oneself or another. Out of desire for bodily pleasures, especially sexual lust, a human being may loathe spiritual goods and not hope for them as being difficult to obtain. Excessive depression causes one not to consider a difficult good as possible, and when this dominates one's emotions, it seems to such a one that the person can never be elevated to any good. Because spiritual apathy is a depressing sadness of the spirit, it generates despair in this way (Q. 20, A. 4).

Presumption

Presumption signifies immoderate hope. Regarding the hope whereby one trusts in one's own power, there will be presumption if one strives for something exceeding one's capacity. Regarding the hope whereby one adheres to divine power, there can be presumption if one strives for some impossible good (e.g., pardon without repentance, or glory without merit) (Q. 21, A. 1).

Every movement of the will in conformity with a false judgment is evil and sinful. But the movement of presumption is in conformity with a false judgment, namely, that God grants pardon to those who persevere in sin and bestows glory on those who cease to perform good deeds. And so presumption is a sin but a lesser sin than despair, since it is more proper to God to have mercy and spare than to punish (Q. 21, A. 2)

If one presumes to rely on one's own power beyond one's capacity, such presumption clearly proceeds out of vainglory. If one relies inordinately on divine mercy or power, whereby one hopes to obtain glory without merit and pardon without repentance, such presumption arises directly out of pride, as if one thinks oneself of such great worth that God would not punish the person who sins or exclude such a one from glory (Q. 21, A. 4).

14

⁜

CHARITY

Charity in Itself

The love of benevolence, namely, when we so love someone as to wish good for the other, has the character of friendship. But benevolence by one person is not enough for friendship, since friendship requires mutual love, and mutual benevolence is founded on sharing. A friendship with God is based on human beings sharing with God insofar as he shares blessedness with us. The love of friendship based on this sharing is charity (Q. 23, A. 1).

It is necessary that the Holy Spirit so move the human will to the act of love that the human will itself also wills the act. But an active power perfectly produces an act only if the act should be innate to the power by a form that is the source of the action. And so God, who moves all things to their proper ends, has endowed individual things with the forms whereby they are inclined to the ends prescribed by God. But an act of charity clearly exceeds the nature of the power of the will. And so it is necessary that, for an act of charity, there be in us a habitual form added to a natural power that inclines the power to acts of charity and makes it act readily and pleasurably (Q. 23, A. 2).

Human virtue, which is the source of good acts, consists of being connected with the rule of human acts. The rule is twofold: human reason and God himself. Moral virtue consists of being in accord with right reason, and theological virtue consists of being connected with God. And so, because charity unites us with God, it is a virtue (Q. 23, A. 3). The divine good, as the object of blessedness, has a special aspect of good, and so the love of charity, which is love of this good, is a special love, and charity a special virtue (Q. 23, A. 4). There is only one end of charity, namely, the divine goodness, and only one sharing of the eternal blessedness on which this friendship is based. And so charity is absolutely one virtue (Q. 23, A. 5).

Since the object of theological virtues is God, they are more excellent than the moral and intellectual virtues, which consist of being connected with human reason. But faith and hope are connected with God insofar as knowledge of the true and possession of the good come to us from him, but charity is connected with God himself as he exists in himself, not as something comes to us from him. And so charity is more excellent than faith and hope, and consequently more excellent than all the other virtues (Q. 23, A. 6).

True virtue, absolutely speaking, is ordered to the chief good of human beings, which is to enjoy God. But charity does this. And so no true virtue can exist without charity. But we can call virtue without charity a virtue insofar as it is ordered to a particular good (Q. 23, A. 7). Charity orders the acts of all the other virtues to the ultimate end and in this respect gives form to the acts of all the other virtues (Q. 23, A. 8).

The Subject in Which Charity Exists

The object of charity is the divine good, which we know only intellectually. And so the subject in which charity inheres is the intellectual appetite, the will, and not the sense appetite (Q. 24, A. 1).

Charity is the friendship of a human being with God based on a sharing of eternal blessedness. This sharing surpasses the power of nature. But what surpasses the power of nature cannot be natural or acquired by natural powers. And so the Holy Spirit, who is the love of the Father and Son, infuses charity in us, the sharing of which in us is created charity itself (Q. 24, A. 2). The quantity of charity depends only on the will of the Holy Spirit, who distributes his gifts as he wishes, not on the condition or capacity of the recipient's nature (Q. 24, A. 3).

We as wayfarers can increase charity in this life (Q. 24, A. 4). Charity is increased by it being extended in the subject, that is, increased substantially, not that one charity is added to another (Q. 24, A. 5). Not every act of charity actually increases charity, but it does dispose one for an increase of charity, since an act of charity renders a human being more ready to act again according to charity and with a more fervent act of love. Then charity is actually increased (Q. 24, A. 6). There is no fixed limit to the potential increase of charity in this life, and this is for three reasons. First, it is sharing in infinite charity, namely, the Holy Spirit. Second, the cause increasing charity, God, has infinite power. Third, regarding the subject, the capacity for further increase always increases with increasing charity (Q. 24, A. 7).

One has perfect charity when one habitually directs one's whole mind on God, that is, when one does not desire or will anything contrary to the love of God. This perfect charity is common to all who have charity (Q. 24, S. 8). There are three grades of charity: the beginning, in which one turns away from sin; progress, in which one strives to increase charity; and perfection, in which one chiefly strives to adhere to God and to enjoy him (Q. 24, A. 9).

Mortal sin does not lessen charity but rather destroys it, nor can venial sin lessen charity, since venial sin is a disorder regarding means to the ultimate end rather than the ultimate end (Q. 24, A. 10). Charity in heaven cannot be lost, but charity in this life, in which we do not see the very essence of God, can be lost through mortal sin (Q. 24, A. 11). Any single mortal sin places an obstacle to the infusion of charity from God, and so the habit is lost (Q. 24, A. 12).

The Object of Charity

God is the reason for loving one's neighbor, since we ought to love in our neighbor that our neighbor belongs to God. And so the act by which one loves God and the act by which one loves one's neighbor are specifically the same. And so the habit of charity extends to both love of God and love of neighbor (Q. 25, A. 1). Love can reflect on itself, and so one, because one loves, loves the fact that one does (Q. 25, A. 2). We cannot love irrational animals as friends for whom we wish good things, since one can only wish good in the proper sense for a rational creature, but we can, out of charity, love irrational creatures as good things that we wish for others, namely, as we wish to preserve them for the honor of God and the benefit of human beings (Q. 25, A. 3).

One does not have friendship in the proper sense with oneself but something greater: unity. Among other things that one loves out of charity as things belonging to God, one also loves oneself out of charity (Q. 25, A. 4). Out of the love of charity whereby we love God, we ought also to love our body but not the taint of sin and the corruption of punishment in our body (Q. 25, A. 5).

We should, out of charity, love sinners regarding their human nature, which is capable of blessedness. But we should hate sinners regarding their sin, whereby they are enemies of God (Q. 25, A. 6). All human beings, good and wicked, love themselves, since they love their own preservation. But the wicked esteem their sensory and material nature as the chief thing in them, and so, not rightly knowing themselves, do not truly love themselves (Q. 25, A. 7). We cannot love enemies as enemies, since this is to love the evil in another. But loving one's enemies in a general way as to their humanity necessarily belongs to charity, and it necessarily belongs to charity to love an enemy in particular by preparing one's spirit to do so if a need were to arise. And apart from a case of necessity, actually carrying out love of an enemy on God's account belongs to perfect charity (Q. 25, A. 8). To show the signs and benefits of love that one shows to neighbors in general belongs to the precept to love one's enemies. But to show the other signs and benefits that one shows to particular persons does not necessarily belong to salvation except that one should be prepared to help them in case of necessity. To bestow such benefits on enemies aside from a case of necessity belongs to perfect charity (Q. 25, A. 9).

The friendship of charity also extends to angels, since we share with them in eternal blessedness (Q. 25, A. 10). We cannot have the friendship of charity with devils, since it belongs to friendship that one will good for one's friends, and we cannot will the good of eternal life for those spirits eternally damned by God, since this would be contrary to the charity of God. But we can out of charity love the angelic nature of devils, namely, inasmuch as we wish those spirits to be preserved in their natural properties for the glory of God (Q. 25, A. 11).

The Order of Charity

We necessarily note an order in the things that one loves out of charity by their relation to the first source of this love, namely, God (Q. 26, A. 1). The friendship of charity is based on sharing in blessedness, which consists essentially of God as its primary source, from which it flows into all those capable of it. And so we should chiefly and most of all love God out of charity, since we love him as the cause of our blessedness, and the neighbor as one sharing with us in the blessedness from him (Q. 26, A. 2). Out of charity one ought to love God, who is the common good of all, more than oneself, since blessedness belongs to God as the universal and overflowing source of it for all who can share in it (Q. 26, A. 3).

The fact that a human being shares in the divine good is a more important reason for loving that human being than if one is associated with the other in that sharing. And so a human being ought, out of charity, to love self more than one's neighbor (Q. 26, A. 4). We ought to love our neighbor, regarding salvation of the neighbor's soul, more than our own body (Q. 26, A. 5).

It is necessary that, even regarding affection, one love one neighbor more than another, since there is necessarily greater affection of love according to the other's greater closeness to God or to the one loving (Q. 26, A. 6). It belongs to a species of charity to wish that the justice of God, whereby those who are better share more perfectly in blessedness. But we should note the strength of love by its relation to the human being who loves. Accordingly, one loves those who are closer to oneself with stronger love for the good for which one loves them than one loves those who are better for a greater good. One can, out of charity, wish that one who is united to that one be better than another and so can arrive at a greater grade of blessedness. Out of charity, we love more those connected to us in many ways (e.g., as relatives, associates, or fellow citizens) (Q. 26, A. 7).

The strength of love is from the connection of the beloved to the lover. The friendship of blood relatives is based on the connection of natural origin, the friendship of fellow citizens on civic sharing, and the friendship of fellow soldiers on sharing in warfare. And so we should love blood relatives more in things belonging to nature, fellow citizens more in things belonging to civic intercourse, and fellow soldiers more in things of war. Relatively speaking, the connection of natural origin is prior and more invariable, and the other connections additional and removable (Q. 26, A. 8).

Regarding the object of love, one should love one's father more than one's son, since a father is the source of the son, which is a higher good. Regarding the one loving, however, one should love one's son more than one's father, since a son is in a sense part of a father, and a father is not part of a son (Q. 26, A. 9). Absolutely speaking, one should love one's father more than one's mother, since a father is the active source of a son, and a mother the passive source (Q. 26, A. 10). By reason of the object of love, we should love parents more than wives, since we love parents under the aspect of source and a higher good, but, by reason of the connection, one should love one's wife more, since a wife is joined to her husband as one flesh. And so one should love one's wife more strongly but show greater reverence for one's parents (Q. 26, A. 11).

Regarding higher good, one should love a benefactor more, since a benefactor is the source of good in the beneficiary, but regarding greater connection, one should, for various reasons, love a beneficiary more (Q. 26, A. 12).

The order of charity necessarily abides in heaven regarding love of God above all things, but we should distinguish about the order of oneself to others. One will love those who are better more than oneself, and those who are less good less than oneself, since each of the blessed will have what is due to that one in divine justice. But regarding strength of love, one will love oneself more than one's neighbor, even one who is better. Regarding the order of neighbors to one another, absolutely speaking, one will love more one who is better (Q. 26, A. 13).

The Chief Act of Charity: Love

Loving belongs to charity as such, since charity, as a virtue, essentially has an inclination to its own act, which consists of loving (Q. 27, A. 1). Love in the intellectual appetite, the will, differs from goodwill, since love signifies a union by the affection of a lover for the beloved, namely, inasmuch as the lover esteems the beloved as somehow one with the lover. But goodwill is a simple act of the will whereby one wishes good for someone, even without presupposing a union of affection toward that one (Q. 27, A. 2).

In three regards, one should love God because of himself, not because of something else. First, we should love him because he is our final cause. Second, we should love him because his essence is his goodness. Third, we should love him because he causes the goodness of all other things. But we can love him because of some other things (e.g., the benefits received from him or the rewards hoped for from him or the punishments to be avoided through him) dispose us to progress in loving him (Q. 27, A. 3).

Love tends first toward God even in our present condition and comes to other things by means of him (Q. 27, A. 4). God, whose goodness is infinite, is infinitely lovable, but no creature can love God infinitely, since every power of a creature, whether natural or infused, is finite (Q. 27, A. 5). There can be no excess in loving God, and so the more one loves God the better (Q. 27, A. 6). Regarding the neighbor who is loved, the love of a friend is superior to the love of an enemy, but regarding the reason for loving an enemy, love of an enemy is superior to love of a friend (Q. 27, A. 7). If we understand love of God and love of neighbor separately, there is no doubt that love of God is more meritorious, but if we understand the love of neighbor to include the love of God, and the love of God not to include love of neighbor, the love of neighbor is superior (Q. 27, A. 8).

Joy

Charity is love of God, and he by being loved is in the one loving by the most excellent of his effects. And so charity causes spiritual joy (Q. 28, A. 1). The joy proper to charity, namely, the joy whereby we rejoice in the divine good as such allows no mixture of sadness, but the joy of charity whereby one rejoices in the divine good as it is shared in us, which sharing something contrary can hinder, can have a mixture of sadness regarding what is repugnant to the sharing (Q. 28, A. 2). When we have arrived at perfect blessedness, nothing will remain for us to desire, and so the joy of the blessed is completely full (Q. 28, A. 3). Joy is an actuality or effect of charity, not a virtue distinct from love (Q. 28, A. 4).

Peace

Harmony signifies the mutual union of the appetites of different persons, but peace, in addition, signifies the union of the sense and rational appetites of one person desiring (Q. 29, A. 1). Everything that seeks something necessarily seeks peace, namely, seeks to arrive quietly and without hindrance at what it seeks (Q. 29, A. 2). Charity causes one to direct one's desires to one thing, the union whereby we love God wholeheartedly, and to unite one's desire with the desire of another, the union whereby one loves a neighbor as oneself (Q. 29, A. 3). Since the charity of the love of God and neighbor by its nature causes peace, peace is not a virtue other than charity but rather its proper actuality (Q. 29, A. 4).

Mercy

Mercy is compassion for another's misery. The motive for mercy is something contrary to the natural appetite of the one willing, namely, sorrowful evils, whose contraries human beings by nature desire. Second, such evils evoke mercy more if they should be contrary to what one hoped for. Third, evils are still more wretched if they are contrary to good things that one has striven for (Q. 30, A. 1). A want is always the reason for having pity, either inasmuch as one thinks of the deficiency of another as one's own because of a union of love, or because of the possibility of suffering the like (Q. 30, A. 2). Mercy is a movement of the will insofar as the evil befalling another displeases one, and reason can govern it. Therefore, mercy is a virtue, since the nature of human virtue consists of the movement of the spirit governed by reason (Q. 30, A. 3). Mercy as such is the greatest virtue, since it overflows to another, but regarding the possessor, mercy is the greatest virtue only if the possessor is the greatest, having no one above self and all under self. And so charity, which unites one to God, who is superior, is more important for a human being than mercy, but mercy is the most important of all the virtues that pertain to one's neighbor (Q. 30, A. 4).

Kindness

Kindness, according to its general nature, is an act of friendship and love. But if we should understand the good that one does for another under a special aspect of good, kindness will take on a special aspect and belong to a special virtue (Q. 31, A. 1). The love of charity extends to all, and so kindness should also extend to all, but at the proper place and time (Q. 31, A. 2). We need to benefit more those closer to us, but we note the closeness of one human being to another by different things in which they share with one another (e.g., blood relatives by natural sharing), and there are different favors to be dispensed according to different conditions (e.g., aid to a stranger in extreme necessity rather than to a father in no great need) (Q. 31, A. 3). Kindness is an act of charity, not a different virtue than charity (Q. 31, A. 4).

Works of Mercy

Doing a work of mercy is an act of charity (Q. 32, A. 1). Some works of mercy concern the soul, which we call spiritual works of mercy, and some concern the body, which call corporal works of mercy. The corporal works of mercy are: feed the hungry, give drink to the thirsty, clothe the naked, receive the stranger, visit the sick, ransom the captive, and bury the dead. The spiritual works of mercy are: pray for others, instruct, counsel, console, reprove, forgive, and bear with the sinner (Q. 32, A. 2). Absolutely speaking, the spiritual works of mercy are superior but a corporal work of mercy may in particular circumstances be superior to a spiritual work (e.g., one should feed another dying of hunger rather than instruct the other) (Q. 32, A. 3). A corporal work of mercy essentially has only a material effect. But regarding its cause, love of God and neighbor, and regarding its effect, as the assisted neighbor may be moved to pray for the benefactor, it bears spiritual fruit (Q. 32, A. 4).

Giving alms out of superfluities regarding both the benefactor and those under the benefactor's care and to one in extreme need is under precept, but otherwise giving alms is under a counsel (Q. 32, A. 5). As a general rule, one should not at all give alms out of what is necessary for oneself and one's own. It is also good to give alms out of things necessary for maintaining a life suitable to one's position, but it falls under a counsel, not a precept (Q. 32, A. 6). One may not give alms from goods belonging to another. One ought to give away as alms goods illicitly but not unjustly acquired. For prostitutes to receive payment for services is not illegal, and so they may retain the receipts and give alms if they wish (Q. 32, A. 7). An inferior should give alms according to instructions of the superior (Q. 32, A. 8). One should give alms to one much holier in greater need and to one more useful for the common good rather than to a person more closely connected, especially one not very connected (Q. 32, A. 9). Regarding the giver, it is praiseworthy to give abundantly, but it is not praiseworthy to give alms abundantly if they abound to superfluity, since it is better to give to many needy (Q. 32, A. 10).

Fraternal Correction

Fraternal correction in the proper sense is ordered to the improvement of a sinner, but removing an evil from someone is the same as procuring good for someone. And so fraternal correction is also an act of charity. Another kind of correction is a remedy of a wrongdoer's sin insofar as the sin causes evil for others, and especially harm of the common good, and such correction is an act of justice preserving the rectitude of justice of one person to another (Q. 33, A. 1).

Fraternal correction of a sinner is an affirmative, not a negative, precept. Negative precepts of the law prohibit sinful acts. But sinful acts as such are never to be done. And so negative precepts oblige always and in all circumstances. But fraternal charity is an affirmative precept regarding the improvement of a brother, and affirmative precepts induce human beings to perform virtuous acts. And so fraternal correction falls under precept insofar as it is necessary for improving a brother, not so that one corrects an erring brother at any time or place (Q. 33, A. 2). As an act of charity, fraternal correction of a brother by a simple admonition is proper to anyone who has charity, whether a subject or a religious superior. As an act of justice, fraternal correction belongs only to religious superiors (Q. 33, A. 3). As an act of charity, subjects may admonish religious superiors but should do so mildly and with reverence (Q. 33, A. 4). If a sinner should reprove a wrongdoer with humility, the sinner does not sin or acquire any new condemnation of self (Q. 33, A. 5). As an act of justice, religious superiors may use coercion for the common good. As an act of charity, one should give only a simple admonition and may refrain from doing so if it is inadvisable (Q. 33, A. 6).

Public sins should be publicly denounced, both for improving the wrongdoer and to avoid scandal. Secret sins should be publicly denounced if they threaten immediate harm to others or the common good. One should privately admonish a sinner whose sinful acts affect only you or are known only by you, for the sake of the sinner's good reputation, and it is necessarily of precept that private admonition should precede public denunciation (Q. 33, A. 7). After an admonition, one should indicate the sin of a brother to a few, who can assist the correction, so that the brother is improved in this way without public defamation (Q. 33, A. 8).

Hate

No one who sees God essentially can hate him. Some effects of his (e.g., existing, living, understanding) cannot be contrary to the human will and are desirable and lovable to all. And insofar as one apprehends God as the cause of these effects, one cannot hate him. But one can hate God as the cause of effects contrary to one's disordered will (e.g., hate him for prohibiting sins and inflicting punishments) (Q. 34, A. 1). Hatred of God is more serious than other sins, since it intrinsically signifies turning away from God, while in other sins (e.g., fornication), the will is not as such turned away from him. Rather, it is turned away from him by something else (e.g., sexual pleasure) (Q. 34, A. 2).

It is lawful to hate sin in a brother and everything that belongs to a lack of divine justice, but one cannot hate the very nature and grace of the brother without committing sin (Q. 34, A. 3). Hate is a greater sin than external acts against neighbor insofar as the will of the sinner is disordered. But regarding the harm inflicted on a neighbor, external sins are worse than internal hatred (Q. 34, A. 4).

The first and most natural thing is the last virtuous thing to be destroyed. But the first and most natural thing is for a human being to love the good, especially the divine good and the good of one's neighbor. And so hate, which is contrary to this love, is the last thing in the destruction of virtue. But a capital sin is one from which other sins more often arise. Therefore, hate is not a capital sin (Q. 34, A. 5).

As pleasure causes love, so sadness causes hate. But envy is sadness about the good of another. And so the good of the neighbor is rendered hateful to us, and hate springs from envy (Q. 34, A. 6).

Spiritual Apathy

Spiritual apathy designates sadness about a spiritual good. It is evil as such because it concerns something truly good, and even sadness about what is truly evil is evil by reason of its effect if it so weighs down a human being that one completely withdraws from good works (Q. 35, A. 1). Being saddened over the divine good, about which charity rejoices, belongs to the special sin we call spiritual apathy (Q. 35, A. 2). Spiritual apathy by its kind of sin, namely, sadness about the divine good, is a mortal sin, but only if there is the complete consent of reason (Q. 35, A. 3). Many sins readily arise from sadness, and spiritual apathy is a capital sin (Q. 35, A. 4).

Envy

Envy is sadness at the good of another inasmuch as the latter lessens one's own standing or excellence (Q. 36, A. 1). Envy is properly sadness about the goods of another inasmuch as the other surpasses one in goods. This is always evil, since one grieves over that about which one should rejoice, namely, the good of one's neighbor (Q. 36, A. 2). Envy is by its genus a mortal sin, since it is contrary to charity, but only if there is complete consent of reason (Q. 36, A. 3). Envy is a capital sin, since it readily impels human beings to other sins (Q. 36, A. 4).

Discord

Discord is contrary to peace. One is intrinsically in discord with one's neighbor when one knowingly and intentionally opposes the divine good or the good of one's neighbor. This is by its genus a mortal sin because of its contrariety to charity, provided that it is with the complete consent of reason. When some intend a good that belongs to the honor of God or the benefit of neighbor, but it is disputable whether the particular thing is good, the discord is incidentally, not intentionally, contrary to the divine good or the good of neighbor. Such discord is neither a sin nor contrary to charity unless it is accompanied by moral error or undue obstinacy. Discord is sometimes the sin of only one person and sometimes the sin of both, as when each is opposed to the good of the other (Q. 37, A. 1). Discord, in which each one follows one's own opinion and turns away from the opinion of another, is the daughter of vainglory (Q. 37, A. 2).

Contention

Contention signifies a contrariety in speech. If contention signifies fighting against truth in an inordinate manner, then it is a mortal sin. If contention signifies fighting against falsehood with only a due measure of vehemence, then it is praiseworthy. And if contention signifies fighting against falsehood in an inordinate manner, then it is a venial sin, unless there is so much disorder as to cause scandal to others, in which case it is a mortal sin (Q. 38, A. 1). People are contentious because each defends in words what seems to each to be the case, and so contention, like discord, is the daughter of vainglory (Q. 38, A. 2).

Schism

Charity unites members of the Church in spiritual unity in their connection with one another, that is, their communion, and in their being under one head, who is Christ himself and his vicar on earth, the pope. Schismatics are those who willfully and intentionally separate themselves from the unity of the Church, that is, those who refuse to be subject to the pope or in communion with the members and subjects of the Church. And so schism is a special sin against charity (Q. 39, A. 1). Unbelief is a more serious sin than schism, since unbelief is a sin against a greater good, God himself, while schism is a sin against a lesser good, the unity of the Church (Q. 39, A. 2).

Consecrated schismatic ministers have sacramental power, since they thereby act only as instruments of God, but they do not have jurisdictional power, that is, legal authority, since that power comes from appointment by a human being (Q. 39, A. 3). The spiritual power fittingly excommunicates schismatics for separating themselves from the Church, and the temporal power fittingly compels them to be subject to the head of the Church (Q. 39, A. 4).

War

Three things are required for a war to be just. First, it belongs only to the authority of rulers to initiate war. Second, just war requires a just cause, namely, that those warred against deserve to be because of some wrong. Third, war requires that those waging war have a right intention, namely, that they intend only to promote good or avoid evil (Q. 40, A. 1). Warfare is contrary to the duties of bishops and clerics, who are bound to contemplation of divine things and the ministry of the altar, and so it is not at all lawful for them to wage war (Q. 40, A. 2). No one ought to deceive an enemy by saying something false or by not keeping one's promises, but one may deceive an enemy by not revealing one's purpose or plans to the enemy. Such concealment belongs to the essence of ambushes, and they are lawful to lay in just wars (Q. 40, A. 3). It is lawful to wage just war on feast days, provided it is necessary to defend the commonwealth thereby (Q. 40, A. 4).

Strife

Strife is a confrontation in deeds between private persons, and so strife always signifies sin and is a mortal sin in the one who unjustly attacks the other. But it can be without sin or with venial sin or with mortal sin in the one who defends self, according to the different movements of the defender's spirit and the different ways of defending oneself (Q. 41, A. 1). Strife signifies an intention to wound another with the other knowing this and resisting. This properly belongs to anger, which is the desire of vengeance (Q. 41, A. 2).

Sedition

Sedition belongs with war and strife in signifying a confrontation but differs from them because sedition may not signify actual fighting but only preparation for it, and because sedition is between factions of one community, while war is against foreign enemies, and strife is a conflict between one or a few persons and one or a few other persons. And so sedition, since it has a special good contrary to the unity and peace of the people, is a special sin (Q. 42, A. 1).

Sedition is contrary to the unity of the legally constituted people of a city or kingdom, and so sedition is contrary to both justice and the common good, and a mortal sin by its genus. The sin belongs chiefly to those who procure it and secondarily to those who follow the leaders (Q. 42, A. 2).

Aquinas poses an objection that gives him the opportunity to make an important distinction. The objection runs as follows: We praise those who deliver a people from the power of a tyrant. But this cannot be done without a popular insurrection if some of the people strive to maintain the tyrant, and others try to unseat him. Therefore, there can be sedition without sin. Aquinas replies that tyrannical governance is unjust, since it is ordered to the private good of the ruler, not the common good. And so disturbance of such governance does not have the character of sedition, except, perhaps, in cases where the tyrant's governance is so inordinately disturbed that the subjected people suffer greater harm from the resulting disturbance than from the tyrant's governance. Rather, tyrants, who by seeking greater domination incite discontent and sedition in the people subject to them, are the rebels. For governance is tyrannical when ordered to the ruler's own good, to the detriment of the people.

Scandal

In moving along the spiritual path, the word or deed of another may dispose one to fall down spiritually, namely, inasmuch as the other by advice, inducement, or example draws one into sin. And so scandal is something improperly said or done that occasions another's spiritual downfall (Q. 43, A. 1). Active scandal is in the one whose word or deed is the occasion for another's spiritual downfall, and passive scandal is in the one whose spiritual downfall is occasioned. Passive scandal is always a sin, since the one scandalized rushes to the person's own spiritual downfall. But there can be passive scandal without sin on the part of the one whose word or deed occasions the other's spiritual downfall (e.g., when one is scandalized by the things that another has said or done rightly). Active scandal is always a sin, since either the very deed one does is sinful, or one should out of charity for neighbor abandon a deed with the appearance of sin (Q. 43, A. 2). Passive scandal cannot be a special sin, since one can fall into any kind of sin from the word or deed of another. Only intrinsic active sandal, that is, when one by one's disordered work or deed intends to draw another into sin, is a sin (Q. 43, A. 3).

Passive scandal can sometimes be a venial sin if the disordered word or deed of another leads one to sin venially, and it can be a mortal sin if the disordered word or deed of another leads one to sin mortally. Active scandal, if it is not intentional, can be a venial sin if one commits a venially sinful act or an act that as such is not a sin but has the appearance of evil. Such active scandal can be a mortal sin either because one commits a mortally sinful act, or because one does not omit a deed in order to preserve the welfare of neighbor. If active scandal is intentional, and one intends to induce another to sin mortally, it is a mortal sin. It is likewise a mortal sin if one should intend by a mortally sinful act to induce another to sin venially. But if one should by a venial sin intend to induce a neighbor to sin venially, it is a venial sin (Q, 43, A. 4).

There is no passive scandal in those who adhere completely to God by love (Q. 43, A. 5). Perfect human beings do not fall so short of perfection as to withdraw greatly from the order of reason, and so they cannot actively cause scandal (Q. 43, A. 6).

One should not omit things necessary for salvation in order to avoid giving scandal. One should conceal or defer spiritual deeds not necessary for salvation to avoid giving scandal to the weak-minded and ignorant until an explanation can be provided. One should not forego any spiritual deeds because of fear of malicious scandal (Q. 43, A. 7). One should not forego temporal goods committed to one's care for the benefit of others, but one should at times forego temporal goods that one owns to avoid giving scandal, and at other times not, if explanation will avoid scandal. One should never forego temporal goods to avoid malicious scandal (Q. 43, A. 8).

The Precepts of Charity

The end of the spiritual life is that a human being be united with God, which charity does, and all the things belonging to the spiritual life are directed to this as their end. All virtues, regarding the acts about which precepts are given, are directed to purifying the heart from the turmoil of emotions (e.g., the virtue of temperance) or at least having a good conscience regarding actions (e.g., the virtue of justice) or having right faith (e.g., the things belonging to divine worship). These three things are required for loving God, since an impure heart is withdrawn from the love of God, a bad conscience makes one abhor divine justice, and false faith draws one's affection to what one imagines about God rather than the true God. But what is intrinsic is more important than what is a means for something else. Therefore, the greatest precept is charity (Q. 44, A. 1).

Love of God is the end of charity, to which the love of neighbor is ordered. And so it is necessary that a precept be given about both love of God and love of neighbor for the sake of those less capable, who would not easily consider that the second precept is contained in the first (Q. 44, A. 2). The two precepts suffice, since the first induces us to God as our end, and the second induces us to love our neighbor for the sake of God as our end (Q. 44, A. 3). We should love God as our ultimate end, to which all things should be related, and so the precept of love of God signifies the totality of things signified (Q. 44, A. 4). One will fully and perfectly fulfill the precept of love of God only in heaven, but one imperfectly fulfills the precept in this life (Q. 44, A. 6).

The second precept says that one should love one's neighbor as oneself. The word *neighbor* indicates that we should love others out of charity because they are closest to us, both by reason of their natural image of God and by reason of their capacity for glory. The words *as oneself* indicate the mode of love. First, it indicates the mode regarding the end, namely, that one loves one's neighbor because of God, so that the love of one's neighbor is holy. Second, it indicates the mode regarding the rule of love, namely, that one gives way to a neighbor only in good things, not any evil, just as one ought to satisfy one's own will only in good things, so that the love of one's neighbor is righteous. Third, it indicates the mode regarding the reason for loving, namely, that one loves one's neighbor because one wishes good for one's neighbor as one wishes good for oneself, not for one's own benefit or pleasure, and so the love of neighbor is true love (Q. 44, A. 7). The order of charity belongs to the virtue by the proportion of love to the thing loved. And so the order of charity should fall under the precept (Q. 44, A. 8).

15

PRUDENCE

Prudence in Itself

Prudence is an intellectual cognitive power that deliberates about means to ends (Q. 47, A. 1). But practical, not theoretical, reason deliberates about things to be done for the sake of an end. Therefore, prudence consists solely of practical reason (Q. 47, A. 2). Actions regard individual things, and so a prudent person needs to know both the universal principles of reason and the individual things that are the objects of human actions (Q. 47, A. 3).

Aquinas poses an objection that gives him the opportunity to explain how the human intellect knows individual things. The objection runs as follows: Prudence belongs to reason. But universal things are the objects of reason. Therefore, prudence knows only universal things. He replies that universal things are first and chiefly the object of reason, but reason can apply universal considerations to particular things. It can because the intellect can reach the matter of particular things by returning to the sensory sources of the intellect's activity.

Since one applies right reason to action only if one has right desire, prudence shares the character of virtue that moral virtues (e.g., justice, fortitude, temperance) have (Q. 47, A. 4). But prudence and moral virtues reside in different subjects (prudence in the intellect, moral virtues in the will), and this formally distinguishes prudence from them. Prudence differs materially from other intellectual virtues by their respective objects. Theoretical wisdom, scientific knowledge, and understanding regard necessary things, while skills and prudence regard contingent things. Skills in turn differ materially from prudence by their respective objects: skills concern making things (e.g., houses and tools), namely, things constituted in external matter, while prudence concerns doing things, namely, things constituted in the one who acts (Q. 47, A. 5).

Self-evident principles regarding the ends of moral virtues (e.g., just, brave, moderate actions) preexist in practical reason, and prudence does not prescribe those ends. But prudence, applying universal principles to particular conclusions about things to be done, concerns means to the ends (Q. 47, A. 6).

Aquinas poses an objection: It belongs to the virtue or skill or power to which an end belongs to command other virtues or skills as means to the end. But prudence disposes regarding other, moral virtues and commands them. Therefore, it prescribes their ends. He replies that ends do not belong to moral virtues as if the latter prescribe their own ends, but because they tend toward the ends prescribed by natural reason. But prudence, which prepares the way for them, helps them by disposing means to the ends. And so we conclude that prudence is more excellent than moral virtues and causes them. And *synderesis* (the innate habitual understanding of the first principles governing human action) causes prudence, just as understanding of the first principles governing theoretical knowledge causes scientific knowledge.

Being conformed to right reason is itself the proper end of any moral virtue, and natural reason prescribes the ends of moral virtues. But it belongs to the disposition of prudence how and by what things human beings attain the mean of reason in their actions, the mean between too much and too little (e.g., between temerity and timidity in the virtue of fortitude) (Q. 47, A. 7).

Prudence is right reason about things to be done, regarding which there are three acts. The first act of reason is to deliberate, and this belongs to discovery, since to deliberate is to inquire. The second act is to judge about the things discovered, and this consists of theoretical reason. But practical reason, which is ordered to action, goes further, and the third act of reason is to command that something should or should not be done, and this consists of applying the objects of our deliberation and judgment to our actions. This act, because it is closer to the end of practical reason, is the chief act of practical reason and so of prudence. To indicate this point, Aquinas notes that we consider that one who errs intentionally in the chief act of prudence (i.e., commanding what one should or should not do), is more imprudent than one who errs unintentionally (Q. 47, A. 8). This is the converse of how we judge about one who errs in skills.

Solicitude is shrewdness of mind and quickness to do the things that one ought to do. But this belongs to prudence, whose chief act concerns commanding what to do. And so one needs to deliberate slowly but act quickly (Q. 47, A. 9).

Prudence regards both the private good of the individual and the common good of the community, since it belongs to prudence to deliberate, judge, and command rightly regarding the means to our requisite end, which includes our life in a community (Q. 47, A. 10).

Aquinas poses several objections. One runs as follows: The prudent seem to seek their own good and act for themselves. But those who seek common goods often neglect their own. Therefore, those who seek common goods are not prudent. He replies that those who seek the common good of a community thereby also seek their own good. This is true for two reasons. First, it is true because there cannot be a good of one's own apart from the common good, whether of a family or a city or a kingdom. Second, it is true because human beings, since they are parts of households and political communities, need to consider what is good for them by what is prudent regarding the good of these communities. For we understand the right disposition of the parts by their relation to the whole.

A second objection runs as follows: Prudence, temperance, and fortitude belong to the same genus of virtues related to human action. But we speak of temperance and fortitude only in relation to one's own good. Therefore, we should speak in the same way about prudence. Aquinas replies that we can relate even temperance and fortitude to the common good. Accordingly, precepts of the law are laid down regarding acts of temperance and fortitude. But prudence and justice, which belong to the rational part of the soul, relate more to the common good, and universal things belong directly to that part of the soul, just as individual things belong to the sensory part of the soul.

There are three specifically different kinds of prudence. One kind, prudence in the absolute sense, is ordered to one's individual good. The second kind, domestic prudence, is ordered to the common good of a household or family. The third kind, political prudence, is ordered to the common good of a city or kingdom (Q. 47, A. 11).

Aquinas poses an objection: The virtue of a good person and that of a ruler are the same. But political prudence belongs particularly to the ruler, in whom it is like the skill of a master builder. Therefore, since prudence is the virtue of a good person, it seems that prudence and political prudence are the same characteristic disposition. He replies that the ability to rule well and the ability to be ruled well belong to the same person. Therefore, the virtue of a ruler is included in the virtue of a good person. But the virtue of a ruler and that of a subject differ specifically, as does the virtue of a man from the virtue of a woman.

Being ruled and governed, not ruling and governing, belongs to a subject as such. But, since human beings, as rational, share in governance by their rational decisions, it belongs to them to have prudence to that degree. And so it is evident that prudence belongs to a ruler like a master builder's skill and to subjects like a manual worker's skill (Q. 47, A. 12).

False prudence disposes fitting ways to achieve an evil end (e.g., the means to be a successful robber), and this kind of prudence belongs only to sinners. True but imperfect prudence disposes fitting ways to achieve a good end but is imperfect if the good end is that of a special occupation (to be a good businessman), or if the command of prudence is ineffective, and this kind of prudence is common to the good and the wicked, particularly in the case of seeking the good of a special occupation. True and perfect prudence rightly deliberates, judges, and commands in relation to the good end of life as a whole. This kind of prudence is prudence in an absolute sense and cannot belong to sinners (Q. 47, A. 13).

Virtues are necessarily connected: those who have one of them have all of them. But one who has grace has charity. And so anyone with charity necessarily has the others. But prudence is a virtue. And so one with grace necessarily has prudence (Q. 47, A. 14).

All human beings by nature know the universal first principles of prudence, and these are more connatural to us than the first principles of theoretical wisdom. We derive secondary universal principles by discovery through experience or instruction, not by nature. The right ends of human life are fixed, and so there can be a natural inclination toward them and right judgment about them. But the means to the ends are not fixed. Rather, they differ in many ways because persons and occupations differ. And so such knowledge of particulars cannot be in human beings by nature. Therefore prudence, which concerns means, not ends, is not in us by nature (Q. 47, A. 15).

Prudence consists not only of knowledge but also of desire,

since the chief act of prudence commands, that is, applies the knowledge possessed to desiring and acting. And so forgetfulness does not directly take away prudence. Rather, emotions destroy it. Nonetheless, forgetfulness can hinder prudence, since the command of prudence is the product of some knowledge, which forgetfulness can take away (Q. 47, A. 16).

The Parts of Prudence

The integral parts of prudence are the constitutive parts of its perfect acts. Five of these belong to prudence as cognitive: memory, understanding, disposition to learn, keenness, and reason. Three belong to reason as commanding: providence, circumspection, and caution.

If we should understand prudence broadly, insofar as it includes theoretical knowledge, then we also posit physics, probable reasoning, and rhetoric as parts of prudence according to the three ways of proceeding scientifically. The first way causes sure knowledge by demonstrative syllogisms, and this belongs to physics, under which we may understand all demonstrative sciences. The second way causes probable knowledge from probable premises, and this belongs to probable reasoning. The third way uses certain conjectures to introduce hypothetical propositions or in some way to persuade, and this belongs to rhetoric.

The subjective parts of prudence are its different species. One species is the prudence by which one governs oneself, and the other is the prudence by which one governs many people. The latter is subdivided according to the different kinds of multitude governed: military prudence in commanders, who govern armies for the special task of defending the commonwealth against enemies; domestic prudence in the heads of households, who govern households or families for life as a whole; kingly prudence in rulers, who govern political communities; and political prudence in subjects, who obey their rulers.

The potential parts of a chief virtue are connected virtues relating to secondary acts or subject matters, which do not possess the whole power of the chief virtue. The potential parts of prudence are good deliberation, judgment about things that happen regularly, and higher judgment about things regarding which one sometimes needs to depart from the general law (Q. 48, A. 1).

The Integral Parts
Memory

Prudence concerns contingent things to be done. But human beings need to consider by experience what is true in most cases. And so experience and time generate and increase intellectual power. But experience comes from memory of many things. And so memory of many things is required for prudence, and we appropriately posit memory as a part of prudence (Q. 49, A. 1).

Aquinas poses an objection that gives him the opportunity to show how skill and diligence enhance memory. The objection runs as follows: We acquire and perfect memory by practice, but we have memory from nature. Therefore, memory is not part of prudence. He replies that there are four things whereby human beings progress in remembering well. First, they need to appropriate suitable but unusual images of the things that they wish to remember. Second, they need to consider and dispose in an orderly way the things they wish to remember. Third, they need to be solicitous and determined about the things they wish to remember. Fourth, they need to think often of the things they wish to remember.

Understanding

Every deduction of reason comes from certain things that we understand as first principles. But prudence is right reasoning about things to be done. And so every act of prudence needs to derive from understanding (Q. 49, A. 2).

Aquinas poses an objection: One contrary is not included in the other. But understanding and prudence are contraries. Therefore, understanding is not part of prudence. He replies that prudence arrives at a conclusion about a particular thing to be done. But a syllogism reaches a particular conclusion from a universal proposition and a particular proposition. And so the reasoning of prudence comes from two kinds of understanding. One kind knows universal things, and this belongs to intellectual understanding, since we by nature know both universal theoretical principles and universal practical principles (e.g., do evil to no one). The other kind knows the first particular and contingent thing to be done, namely, the minor premise in a prudential syllogism. But the first particular thing to be done is a particular end. And so the understanding we posit as part of prudence is the right estimation of a particular end.

Disposition to Learn

Prudence concerns particular things to be done. But one human being cannot sufficiently consider the almost infinite variety of things or consider them in a short span of time. And so human beings especially need to learn from others and especially from elders, who have sound understanding of the ends of things to be done. And so we appropriately posit the disposition to learn as part of prudence (Q. 49, A. 3).

Keenness

It belongs to a prudent person to estimate rightly about things to be done, and we acquire right estimation by discovering it on our own and by learning it from someone else. Keenness belongs to human beings who are well disposed to acquire right estimation on their own. Keenness is the easy and ready estimation about discovering the middle term, and so keenness is the habit produced by quickly discovering what is fitting (Q. 49, A. 4).

Reason

A prudent person needs to deliberate well. But deliberation is an inquiry progressing from some known things to other known things, and this is the work of reason. And so it is necessary for prudence that human beings should reason well, and this is an integral part of prudence (Q. 49, A. 5).

Aquinas poses an objection: We should not posit something common to many things as part of any one of them, or if we should, we ought to posit the common thing as part of that to which it most belongs. But reason is necessary in all the intellectual powers and chiefly in theoretical wisdom and scientific knowledge, which use demonstrative reason. Therefore, we ought not posit reason as part of prudence.

Aquinas replies that the certitude of reason is from the intellect, but the need for reason is from the deficiency of the intellect, since beings in which intellectual power is completely active do not need reason. Rather, such things (e.g., God and angels) understand truth by pure intuition. But particular things to be done, regarding which prudence directs, are very remote from the condition of intelligibility, and the less certain or fixed they are, the more remote they are from intelligibility. For example, things proper to skills, although particular, are nonetheless fixed and certain, and so there is no deliberation about most of the things proper to skills, since they are certain. And so, although there is more certain reason in other intellectual virtues than in prudence, human beings need especially to reason well about what they should do or not do, so that they can rightly apply universal principles to particular things, which are various and uncertain.

Providence

Prudence concerns means to an end. Although some things necessary for the sake of an end are subject to divine providence, only contingent practical things that human beings do for the sake of an end are subject to human providence. Future contingent things, insofar as human beings order them to the end of human life, belong to prudence. And the word *providence* signifies both of these things, since providence signifies foresight of something remote, to which present things should be ordered. And so providence is part of prudence (Q. 49, A. 6).

Circumspection

One directs something to an end rightly only if the end is good, and the means suitable to the end. But particular circumstances may render something as such good and suitable for an end either evil or unsuitable for the end. For example, showing signs of love for another, insofar as they are that, seems to be suitable to draw the other's soul to love, but if there should be pride or suspicion of flattery in the process, showing the signs of love will not be suitable to the end. And so circumspection is necessary for prudence, so that human beings also relate the means to circumstances (Q. 49, A. 7).

Caution

Prudence concerns contingent practical things regarding which evil can be mixed with good. This is because of the complexity of such things, in which evil things often appear to be good. And so caution is necessary for prudence, so that we undertake good things in such a way that we avoid evil things (Q. 49, A. 8).

The Subjective Parts

Ruling and commanding belong to prudence, and so there is a special character of prudence in which there is a special character of governance and command in human actions. But there is a special and perfect character of governance in those empowered to rule both themselves and the perfect community of a city or a kingdom. And so prudence in its special and most perfect character belongs to kings, who have authority to rule a city or kingdom. And so we posit kingly prudence as a species of prudence (Q. 50, A. 1).

Aquinas poses an objection: A kingdom is one of six kinds of regime. But we do not understand species of prudence in the other five kinds of regimes, namely, aristocracy, polity (also called timocracy), tyranny, oligarchy, and democracy. Therefore, neither should we understand the kingly prudence of a kingdom as a species of prudence. He replies that a kingdom is the best regime, and so we should designate a species of prudence from kingdoms rather than the other regimes. But we should include under kingly prudence all the other good regimes, though not the bad ones, which are contrary to virtue and do not belong to prudence.

Masters by their commands cause their slaves to act, and rulers by their commands cause their subjects to act, but in a different way than causes induce irrational and inanimate things to act. Other things cause inanimate and irrational things to act without the latter causing themselves to act, since they do not have mastery of their actions by free choice. And so their right governance resides only in the things causing their actions, not in themselves. But the commands of other human beings cause slaves or subjects to act in such a way that the slaves or subjects by free choice cause themselves to act. And so they need to have right governance whereby they direct themselves to obey those who govern them. And the species we call political prudence belongs to them (Q. 50, A. 2).

Aquinas poses several objections. One runs as follows: Kingly prudence is part of political prudence. But we should not distinguish parts from the whole genus of which they are parts. Therefore, we should not posit political prudence as another species of prudence. He replies that kingly prudence is the most perfect species of prudence, and so the prudence of subjects, which falls short of kingly prudence, keeps the general name *political*. Just so, in logic, convertible terms that do not signify the essence of something keep the general name *property*.

A second objection runs as follows: Different objects distinguish different species of habits. But rulers command and subjects execute the same things. Therefore, we should not posit political prudence, insofar as it belongs to subjects, as a species of prudence different from kingly prudence. Aquinas replies that different aspects of the objects of habits specifically distinguish the habits. But a king, while considering the same things to be done, regards an aspect more universal than the aspect that subjects, who obey the king, do, since many subjects obey the king in different tasks. And so we relate kingly prudence to the political prudence about which we are speaking as we relate the skill of a master builder to the skills of manual workers.

Different universal and particular, or whole and partial, aspects of an object distinguish skills and virtues, by which difference one skill or virtue is chief in relation to another. But a household is clearly in between an individual person and a city or kingdom. As an individual person is part of a household, so a household is part of a city or kingdom. And so, as we distinguish prudence in general—which governs an individual—from political prudence, so we need to distinguish domestic prudence from both (Q. 50, A. 3).

Aquinas poses an objection: Prudence is ordered to living well in general. But domestic prudence is directed to a particular end, namely, wealth. Therefore, domestic prudence is not a species of prudence. He replies that wealth is related to domestic prudence as a means, not as its ultimate end. And the ultimate end of domestic prudence is living well in general with respect to life in the household.

There should be not only political prudence, which suitably disposes things proper to the common good, but also military prudence, which repels hostile attacks (Q. 50, A. 4).

Aquinas poses an objection: As the military occupation is included in the political, so also are many other occupations (e.g. those of merchant, craftsman, and the like). But we do not understand the other occupations in a political community as species of prudence. Therefore, neither should we understand the military occupation as a species of prudence. He replies that other occupations in the political community are directed to particular benefits, but the military occupation is directed to preserving the entire common good.

The Potential Parts

GOOD DELIBERATION Deliberation signifies an inquiry of reason about things to be done. But human life consists of such practical things, since a purely contemplative life is beyond human beings. And so good deliberation is a human virtue (Q. 51, A. 1).

Aquinas poses an objection: Virtue is perfection. But right deliberation signifies doubt and inquiry, both of which belong to imperfection. Therefore, good deliberation is not a virtue. He replies that although virtue is essentially perfection, not everything that is the subject matter of a virtue needs to signify perfection. Virtues need to perfect all human things, in regard to both acts of reason (including deliberation) and the emotions of sense appetites, which are much more imperfect. Or we can say that a human virtue is a perfection in the manner of human beings, who cannot with certitude understand the truth about things by pure intuition, especially in practical matters, which are contingent.

Different kinds of acts need to distinguish virtues, especially if a different kind of goodness should belong to the acts. But different acts of reason are directed to action and they do not have the same kind of goodness. Different things cause human beings to deliberate well, judge well, and command well. And so there needs to be one virtue of good deliberation, by which human beings deliberate, and another virtue of prudence, by which human beings command. As deliberating is directed to commanding as the chief thing, so good deliberation is directed to prudence as the chief virtue, without which there would be no virtue (Q. 51, A. 2).

Aquinas poses an objection: Ends, to which human virtues are directed, specify human acts. But good deliberation and prudence are directed to the same end, that is, the general end of one's whole life, not each to a particular end. Therefore, good deliberation is not a virtue distinct from prudence. He replies that different kinds of acts are directed to the ultimate end, namely, living well in general, in a certain order. Deliberation is first, judgment is second, and command is third. The latter is immediately related to the ultimate end, while the other two acts are remotely related to it. But the other two acts have proximate ends: deliberation aims at the discovery of things, and judgment aims at certainty. And so good deliberation is subordinate to prudence as a secondary virtue to the chief one and is not the same virtue as prudence.

RIGHT JUDGMENT Goodness of deliberation and goodness of judgment are not traceable to the same cause, since many who deliberate well do not have common sense, that is, good judgment. Some who deliberate well do not have good judgment, and this is due to a defect in their intellect, which especially results from the wrong disposition of their unifying sense. And so there needs to be the virtue of judging well in addition to good deliberation (Q. 51, A. 3).

Aquinas poses an objection: Virtues are not innate in us. But right judgment is innate in some persons. Therefore, right judgment is not a virtue. He replies that right judgment consists of the intellect understanding things as they are in themselves. This comes form the right disposition of the intellect. Just so, the true forms of material things are accurately impressed on a well-constructed mirror, but images on a poorly constructed mirror appear distorted and warped. That the intellect is well disposed to receive things as they are results radically from nature but perfectly from practice or the gift of grace. Such perfect disposition of the intellect results in two ways. First, it results directly with the intellect itself (e.g., by imbuing the intellect with true, not false, concepts), and this belongs to right judgment as a special virtue. Second, it results indirectly from the good disposition of the will, as a result of which human beings judge rightly about desirable things. And so good judgment about virtue results from the habits of moral virtues, but such judgment concerns the ends of the moral virtues, while right judgment concerns the means to the ends.

JUDGMENT ABOUT EXCEPTIONS TO GENERAL RULES It sometimes happens that one should do something outside the general rules about things that human beings should do or not do (e.g., when one should return something on deposit to the enemy of one's country). And it happens that one needs to judge about such things by principles higher than the general rules of right judgment. Therefore, one needs a higher power of judgment, which means discernment of judgment (Q. 51, A. 4).

Aquinas poses an objection: Right judgment means that one judges well. But we cannot say that one judges well unless one judges well in all things. Therefore, right judgment extends to all things. Thus, there is no other virtue of judging well called the higher power of judgment. He replies that right judgment judges truly about all things done according to general rules. But there are other things that one should judge outside the general rules.

Sins against Prudence: Imprudence and Negligence

We can understand imprudence as a privation insofar as one lacks the prudence with which nature has endowed human beings, and that they ought to have. This imprudence is a sin because one is negligent in applying oneself earnestly to possess prudence.

We can understand imprudence as a contrary insofar as reason acts in a way contrary to prudence (such as spurning deliberation or caution). Such imprudence is a sin directly against prudence and a mortal sin if this happens by turning away from God's laws (Q. 53, A. 1).

Imprudence is a general sin in a qualified sense in relation to the genus of sin because it includes many species of sin in the genus. First, different species of sin belong to imprudence as contrary to the subjective parts of prudence (e.g., individual prudence, political prudence). Second, different species of sin belong to imprudence regarding the potential parts of prudence (deliberation, judgment, command). Regarding lack of deliberation, there is the sin of precipitous action, or temerity. Regarding deficiency of judgment, there is the sin of lack of reflection. And regarding command itself, which is the chief act of prudence, there are the sins of inconstancy and negligence. Third, different species of sin belong to imprudence regarding the integral parts of prudence. But because all of the integral parts are directed to the aforementioned three acts of reason, we trace all contrary sins to precipitous action, lack of reflection, inconstancy, and negligence. Lack of caution and lack of circumspection are included in lack of reflection. Lack of disposition to learn, defective memory, and defective reason belong to hastiness. Lack of providence, defective understanding, and defective solicitude belong to negligence and inconstancy (Q. 53, A. 2).

One should descend from the summit of the soul, reason, to the base of activity performed by the body by a series of steps in an orderly way. But if, without such steps being taken, an impulse of the will or an emotion moves one to act, there will be precipitous action, and this sin will be a species of imprudence (Q. 53, A. 3).

Failure to judge rightly belongs to the sin of failure to reflect, namely, one contemns or neglects paying attention to things leading to right judgment (Q. 53, A. 4).

Inconstancy signifies retreating from a definite good purpose. This retreat is achieved through a failure of reason, which mistakenly rejects what it had rightly accepted. If reason should fail to resist an emotional impulse, this is due to the weakness of reason, which does not hold firmly to the good it has conceived. Inconstancy concerns the command, since one is inconstant because reason fails to command the things that one deliberates about and judges (Q. 53, A. 5).

Pleasure most corrupts the evaluation of prudence, and chiefly sexual pleasure, which absorbs the whole soul and draws human beings to it. But the perfection of prudence and any intellectual virtue consists of drawing one away from sensibly perceptible things. And so the sins of imprudence arise most from sexual lust (Q. 53, A. 6).

Negligence signifies lack of due solicitude. But every lack of a required act is sinful. And so negligence is sinful. It is a special sin because it concerns a special kind of act that covers every kind of subject matter, not because it concerns a special subject matter (Q. 54, A. 1).

Negligence is directly contrary to solicitude. But solicitude belongs to reason, and right solicitude to prudence. And so negligence belongs to imprudence. Negligence concerns the act of commanding but in a different way than inconstancy does. One who is inconstant fails in commanding by something preventing it (an emotional impulse), but one who is negligent fails by lacking a ready will (Q. 54, A. 2)

Negligence comes from the will being remiss, in reason not being solicitous to command the things that it ought to command or in the way that it ought to command. Therefore, negligence may be a mortal sin in two ways. It may be in one way regarding what is omitted through negligence. It will be if it concerns something necessary for salvation, whether an act or a circumstance. It may be a mortal sin in a second way if the will should be so remiss about things that belong to God that it totally falls away from love of him, which chiefly results from contempt. Otherwise, negligence is a venial sin (Q. 54, A. 3).

Sins Contrary to Prudence but Resembling It

Prudence of the flesh in the proper sense means that one considers goods of the flesh to be the ultimate end of one's life. But this is a sin, since one is thereby disordered regarding one's ultimate end. Therefore, prudence of the flesh is a sin (Q. 55, A. 1).

If we understand prudence of the flesh absolutely, namely that one makes care of the flesh the ultimate end of one's life as a whole, then prudence of the flesh is a mortal sin, since one thereby turns away from God as one's end. If we understand prudence of the flesh as a particular prudence like the prudence of a businessman, then prudence of the flesh is a venial sin, since one may sometimes be inordinately drawn to a pleasure of the flesh without being turned away from God by mortal sin. But it is not prudence of the flesh if one should relate care of the flesh to a worthy end (e.g., taking food to sustain one's body), since one then uses care of the flesh as a means to that end (Q. 55, A. 2).

A sin resembling prudence can be contrary to it because reason's desire is directed to an apparent but not truly good end, and this sin belongs to prudence of the flesh. A sin resembling prudence can also be contrary to it because one, in order to gain an end (whether a good or an evil end), employs counterfeit and illusory, not true, means, and this belongs to the sin of craftiness (Q. 55, A. 3). Devising counterfeit and illusory means to attain an end belongs to craftiness, but execution of the planned action belongs to guile (Q. 55, A. 4). Guile seems to belong generally to executing craftiness, whether by word or deeds, but fraud belongs more properly to executing craftiness by deeds (Q. 55, A. 5).

Solicitude about temporal things can be unlawful regarding the matter about which one is solicitous, namely, if we should seek temporal things as our end. Second, solicitude about temporal things can be unlawful if one strives to procure temporal things to the detriment of striving for spiritual things, to which one should be chiefly devoted. Third, solicitude about temporal things can be unlawful regarding excessive fear, namely, when human beings fear lest they, by doing what they ought to do, lack necessary things. Matthew 6:25–33 advises us to have solicitude chiefly about spiritual goods and hope that temporal goods will come to us according to our needs if we have done what we ought to do (Q. 55, A. 6).

Aquinas poses an objection: One is solicitous about the end for which one labors. But it is lawful for human beings to labor for temporal things, with which they sustain their life. Therefore, it is lawful for them to be solicitous about temporal things. He replies briefly: The solicitousness of those who acquire their livelihoods by labor is moderate, not excessive.

An act can be virtuous only in the proper circumstances, one of which is the proper time. To each time there belongs a proper solicitude (e.g., solicitude about harvesting grain is proper in summer, and solicitude about harvesting grapes is proper in autumn). Therefore, if one were to be solicitous about harvesting grapes in summer, one would unnecessarily anticipate the solicitude proper to a later time (Q. 55, A. 7).

Aquinas poses an objection: Solicitude belongs to prudence. But prudence chiefly concerns future things, since its chief part is providence about future things. Therefore, it is virtuous to be solicitous about future things. He replies that requisite providence about future things belongs to prudence. But there would be inordinate providence or solicitude about future things if one were to seek past or future temporal things as ends, or if one were to seek superfluous things beyond the needs of one's present life, or if one were to anticipate the time to be solicitous.

The use of right reason is most evident in the moral virtue of justice, which belongs to the rational appetite, the will. The improper use is also most evident in sins contrary to justice. But covetousness is most contrary to justice. Therefore, the aforementioned sins arise most from covetousness (Q. 55, A. 8).

16

❖

JUSTICE

Right

Right is the object of justice. Other moral virtues (such as fortitude and temperance) perfect human beings only in relation to themselves, and so the acts of those virtues are right only in relation to the human beings who perform the acts (e.g., acts of sobriety perfect the human being who practices the virtue). But justice directs human beings in their relations to other human beings, and so the acts of justice are right if they are rightly related to other human beings, that is, if the acts observe the right objective order of human relations (Q. 57, A. 1).

Natural right order consists of things equivalent by their nature (e.g., the quid pro quo in exchanges). Positive right order consists of things equivalent by private or public agreement (e.g., the terms of a contract and the use of money as a medium of exchange). Divine right order consists of the decrees promulgated by God (Q. 57, A. 2). (Since law establishes right, the two terms are correlative: the natural law corresponds to natural right, positive law to positive right, and divine law to divine right.)

Aquinas poses several objections. One runs as follows: We call things proceeding from the human will positive. But nothing is just simply because it proceeds from a human will; otherwise, the will of a human being could not be unjust. Therefore, since just is the same as right, it seems that there is no positive right. He replies that the human will can, by common agreement, make something just in the case of things intrinsically compatible with natural justice, and positive right plays a role in such things. But if something should be in intrinsically incompatible with natural justice, the human will cannot make it just (e.g., if positive laws decree that it is lawful to steal or commit adultery).

Another objection runs as follows: Divine right is not natural right, since divine right surpasses human nature. Likewise, divine right is not positive right, since divine right depends on divine, not human, authority. Therefore, divine right is not divided into natural right and positive right. Aquinas replies that decrees promulgated by God are divine right, and divine right partially concerns things that are naturally just, although their justice is concealed from human beings, and partially concerns things that are just by divine institution. And so also we can distinguish divine law by these two kinds of things. The divine law commands some things because they are good, and prohibits some things because they are evil, while other things are good because divine law commands them, or evil because divine law prohibits them.

The common right of peoples (the *jus gentium*) consists of things equivalent to other things when natural reason considers consequences and dictates a common policy. For example, there is no intrinsic reason why a plot of land should belong to one individual rather than another. But if we should consider the plot as to its suitable cultivation and peaceful use, the plot belongs commensurately to one person rather than another. And so all peoples protect what natural reason establishes among human beings, and we call this the common right order of peoples (Q. 57, A. 3).

Paternal right order and master–slave right order consist of things equivalent to other things insofar as some persons belong to other persons, namely, children to parents and slaves to masters (Q. 57, A. 4).

Aquinas poses an objection: Law is a plan of justice. But law concerns the common good of a city or kingdom, not the private good of one person or one family. Therefore, there ought to be no special right order, whether master–slave or parental, since masters and fathers belong to households. He replies that children as such belong to their fathers, and slaves as such to their masters. But both children and slaves, considered as particular human beings, are intrinsically subsistent and distinct from other human beings. And so, insofar as they are human beings, there is justice in some respect in relation to them. And it is also for this reason that there are particular laws about the relations of fathers to their children and of masters to their slaves. But insofar as children and slaves belong to others, the relations lack the perfect character of justice and right.

Justice in Itself

Justice is the constant and enduring will to render to others what is due to each (Q. 58, A. 1). Its name signifies equality, and so it is always in relation to other human beings (Q. 58, A. 2). Human virtues make human acts and human beings themselves good, and justice rightly orders human actions and makes them good. Thus justice is a virtue (Q. 58, A. 3). The power whose acts a virtue aims to direct rightly is the subject of the virtue. But the proper source of doing things rightly is an appetitive power, and consideration of the relation of one thing to another belongs to reason. And so justice inheres in the rational appetite, the will, as its subject (Q. 58, A. 4).

Justice directs human beings in relation to others considered individually, but it also directs human beings in relation to others considered in general, namely, as those serving a community serve all the human beings in the community. But all in a community are related to the community as parts to a whole, and the parts belong to the whole. And so any good of the part can be directed to the good of the whole. Therefore, we can relate the good of any virtue to the common good, and the acts of all the virtues can in this respect belong to justice as it directs human beings to the common good. In this sense, justice is virtue in general. And since it belongs to law to order human beings to the common good, we call justice in general legal justice. We do so because human beings, by observing justice in the aforementioned way, are in accord with the law, which orders the acts of all the virtues to the common good (Q. 58, A. 5)

We speak of things being general by predication (e.g., animal is something generic in human beings and horses). Something general in this sense needs to be essentially the same as the things in relation to which it is generic, since genera belong to the essence of species and are part of the species' definition. We call something general in a second way by its power (e.g., a universal cause is general in relation to all its effects, as the sun is in relation to all the material substances its power illumines or affects). And something general in this sense does not need to be essentially the same as the things in relation to which it is general, since the essences of such a cause and its effects differ.

It is in the latter sense that we call legal justice virtue in general, namely, insofar as legal justice directs the acts of other virtues to its end, that is, causes them by commanding them. Legal justice is virtue in general insofar as it directs the acts of all the virtues to the common good. And legal justice in this sense is a special virtue residing chiefly and architectonically in rulers and secondarily and instrumentally in subjects (Q. 58, A. 6).

Besides legal justice, there need to be other virtues that direct human beings immediately regarding particular goods. These virtues are either in relation to self (e.g., temperance and fortitude) or in relation to another individual person. And so there needs to be particular justice, which directs human beings about things in relation to other individual persons (Q. 58, A. 7). Particular justice does not concern the whole subject matter of moral virtue but only external actions and things by a special formal aspect, namely, as the actions and things relate one human being to another (Q. 58, A. 8). Justice does not concern emotions for two reasons. First, justice inheres in the rational appetite, the will, not the sense appetites, but only the movements of sense appetites are emotions. Second, justice concerns things that are in relation to other things, but emotions do not immediately direct us in relation to other things (Q. 58, A. 9).

Aquinas poses an objection: Justice rightly directs actions in relation to others. But we can direct such actions rightly only if we rightly direct our emotions, since disordered actions in relation to others result from disordered emotions (e.g., adultery results from sexual lust, and theft from excessive love of money). Therefore, justice needs to concern emotions.

He replies that external actions are in between external things —which are the subject matter of external actions—and internal emotions—which are the sources of external actions. But there may sometimes be a defect in one of these without a defect in the other (e.g., one may steal the property of another out of a desire to harm the other rather than to possess the property, or, conversely, one may desire the property of another without wanting to steal it). Therefore, it belongs to justice to direct actions rightly insofar as external things are the objects of the actions, but it belongs to other moral virtues, which concern emotions, to direct actions rightly insofar as the actions result from emotions. And so justice prohibits stealing the property of another insofar as this is contrary to the equality that should be established regarding external things, while generosity prohibits stealing out of excessive desire of riches. But internal emotions do not specify external actions. Rather, the external things that are the objects of the actions do.

Therefore, properly speaking, external actions are the subject matter of justice rather than the subject matter of other moral virtues.

We understand the mean of virtues concerning emotions only in relation to the virtuous persons, not by the relation of one thing to another. And so there is in those virtues only a mean determined by reason in relation to ourselves. But the matter of justice consists of external actions insofar as they or the things used have the proper relation to other persons. And so the mean of justice consists of a proportional equality of the external thing to an external person. But equality is a real mean between greater and lesser. And so justice has a real mean (Q. 58, A. 10).

Aquinas poses several objections. One runs as follows: All the species of a genus contain the nature of the genus. But moral virtues are habits of choosing the mean determined by reason in relation to oneself. Therefore, the mean in justice is also one of reason, not a real mean. He replies very succinctly that a real mean is also the mean of reason, and so justice retains the nature of moral virtue.

Another objection runs as follows: There is nothing too much or too little in things absolutely good, and so there is no real mean. But justice concerns absolutely good things. Therefore, there is no real mean in justice. Aquinas replies that we call something absolutely good in one way because it is good in every respect, as virtues are, and so there cannot be too much or too little in absolutely good things. But we call something absolutely good in a second way because it is good by its nature, although it could become evil by misuse (e.g., riches and honors). We can understand too much, too little, and the mean in such things in relation to human beings, who can use them for good or ill, and justice concerns absolutely good things in this sense.

Justice directs us regarding external actions insofar as they or the things we use through them are related to other persons. But what is in equal proportion due other persons belongs to them.

And so the proper act of justice consists only of rendering to others what is due them (Q. 58, A. 11).

As legal justice, justice is the most important moral virtue, since the common good surpasses the good of a single person. As particular justice, justice is for two reasons also the most important moral virtue. First, justice inheres in the most excellent part of the soul, the rational appetite, while the other moral virtues inhere in the sense appetites. Second, unlike other moral virtues, we praise justice insofar as virtuous persons are related to others, and so justice is in one respect the good of others (Q. 58, A. 12).

Injustice

One kind of injustice is contrary to legal justice, and this injustice is a special sin insofar as it concerns a special object: the common good. Regarding its extension, it is a general sin, since contempt of the common good can lead human beings to all kinds of sin. The other kind of injustice is by an inequality in relation to others, namely, as human beings wish to have more goods (e.g., riches and honors) and less evils (e.g., hardships and losses). And then injustice has special matter and is a particular sin contrary to particular justice (Q. 59, A. 1).

Aquinas poses an objection: Special sins are contrary to special virtues (e.g., adultery is contrary to chastity, homicide to meekness, and so forth). But injustice is contrary to all the virtues. Therefore, injustice is not a special sin. He replies that even particular justice is indirectly contrary to all the virtues insofar as external acts belong both to justice and to other moral virtues, albeit in different ways.

As the object of justice is equality in external things, so also the object of injustice is an inequality in those things, namely, as more or less is allotted to someone than belongs to the person. But the habit of injustice is disposed toward its object by the habit's characteristic act, that is, unjust action. Therefore, it may happen in two ways that one who does something unjust may not be an unjust person. It happens in one way because an action is unrelated to its proper object, and the action's intrinsic object specifies and designates the action. In the case of things done to achieve an end, the things one does intentionally are intrinsic objects of an action, and resulting things one does not intend to do are incidental objects of an action. And so, if one should do something unjust without intending to (as when one does something in ignorance, not thinking that one has done anything unjust), then one does something unjust only incidentally and materially but nothing unjust intrinsically and formally. In a second way, unjust action may be unrelated to the habit of justice. Unjust action can sometimes arise from an emotion (e.g., anger or desire). But it can also sometimes arise by choice, namely, when the unjust action itself as such is agreeable, and then it arises strictly from the habit of injustice (Q. 59, A. 2).

The things causing action and the things undergoing action cannot be the same thing in the same respect. But the proper source of action in human beings is the will. And so human beings in the proper sense and intrinsically do what they do willingly, and conversely, human beings in the proper sense undergo what they undergo unwillingly. The source of action is from oneself insofar as one wills the action, and so one is active, not passive, insofar as one acts willingly. Therefore, as such and formally, one can do something unjust only willingly, and one can suffer something unjust only unwillingly. But incidentally and materially, one can do something of itself unjust unwillingly, as when one does something unintentionally, or suffer something of itself unjust willingly, as when one willingly gives to another more than one owes the other (Q. 59, A. 3).

Aquinas poses an objection: One does something unjust only to one who suffers the injustice. But one may do something to one who is willing (e.g., if one should sell something to a willing person for more than it is worth). Therefore, one may willingly suffer something unjust. He replies that undergoing something is the effect of an external action. But in doing and suffering something unjust, we note the matter by what is done externally, considered absolutely. And we note what is formal and intrinsic in the matter by the will of the efficient cause and the recipient. Therefore, we should say that the one doing something unjust and the one suffering something unjust, materially speaking, always accompany each other. But if we should be speaking formally, one can intentionally do something unjust without the other suffering something unjust, since the other willingly undergoes it. And conversely, one may suffer something unjust if one should suffer the injustice unwillingly. But one who unknowingly does something unjust will do something materially but not formally unjust.

Anything contrary to charity is a mortal sin. But any harm that one causes another is of itself contrary to charity, which moves us to will the good of others. And so, since injustice always consists of harm to another, doing anything unjust is generically a mortal sin (Q. 59, A. 4).

Aquinas poses several objections that give him an opportunity to qualify his position. One runs as follows: Venial sin is contrary to mortal sin. But doing something unjust is sometimes a venial sin, since the unjust things one does in ignorance and as a result of it are venial sins. Therefore, not everyone who does something unjust sins mortally. He replies that ignorance of fact (i.e., of particular circumstances) deserves pardon, but ignorance of the law does not excuse. And one who unknowingly does something unjust does it only accidentally.

A second objection runs as follows: One who commits injustice in a small matter deviates little from the mean. But this seems to be tolerable and should be counted among the least evils. Therefore, not everyone who does something unjust sins mortally. He replies that one who commits injustice in small matters lacks the full character of doing something unjust, since we can consider such injustice not to be completely contrary to the will of the one who suffers it (e.g., if one should take an apple from another, and the other is probably neither hurt thereby nor displeased about it).

Judicial Judgment

Judgment in the proper sense designates the act of a judge as such. But a judge declares right order, and right order is the object of justice. Thus the word *judgment* primarily signifies the definition or determination of justice or right. But to define something rightly regarding virtuous actions results from habitual virtue. Therefore, judgment, which signifies the right determination of what is just, belongs to justice (Q. 60, A. 1).

Aquinas poses an objection: Right judgment regarding the proper subject matter of a virtue belongs to that virtue, since the virtuous person is the rule and measure in particular things. Therefore, right judgment does not belong more to justice than to other moral virtues. He replies that other moral virtues direct human beings in relation to themselves, and justice orders them in relation to one another. But human beings are the masters of things that belong to them but not of things that belong to others. And so, in things regarding other virtues, only the judgment of the virtuous person is required, understanding judgment in a broad sense. But regarding things that belong to justice, the further judgment of a superior, who can reprove and has authority over both parties, is required. And so a more particular kind of judgment, judicial judgment, belongs to justice than to any other virtue.

Just judicial judgment requires three things. First, the judgment should result from the desire for justice. Second, one vested with public authority should issue the judgment. Third, right prudential reason should produce the judgment. The judgment will be unjust and sinful if it is contrary to the rectitude of justice, or if the judge has no authority, or if the judge lacks reasonable certitude, namely, lacks solid evidence (Q. 60, A. 2).

Suspicion signifies an opinion of evil based on slight evidence. This happens in one way because one is conscious of one's own wickedness and so easily thinks evil of others. It happens in a second way because one is biased against another. It happens in a third way because of long experience of the defects of others. The first two causes of suspicion belong to wicked desires, but the third cause may lessen the suspicion being unfounded. And so suspicion signifies a sin, and the further one's suspicion reaches, the more sinful it is.

There are three grades of suspicion. The first grade is that one begins to doubt the goodness of another on the basis of slight evidence, and this is a venial sin. The second grade is that one on the basis of slight evidence thinks that the wickedness of another is certain, and this is a mortal sin if it should concern something serious. The third grade is that a judge proceeds to condemn someone on the basis of suspicion, and this belongs directly to injustice and so is a mortal sin (Q. 60, A. 3).

Aquinas poses an objection: Since injustice is generically a mortal sin, a judgment based on suspicion would always be a mortal sin if it were to be unlawful. But we cannot avoid having suspicion of others. Therefore, a judgment based on suspicion does not seem to be unlawful. He replies that since justice and injustice concern external acts, a judgment based on suspicion directly belongs to injustice when it proceeds to an external act, and then it is a mortal sin. The internal judgment belongs to justice insofar as it is related to the external judgment, as internal act to external act, as, for example, lustful desire is to fornication, and anger to homicide.

One who has a bad opinion of another without sufficient cause harms and contemns the other. But no one should contemn or harm another without a compelling reason. And so, where there is no clear evidence of the wickedness of another, we ought to consider the other good and interpret in a favorable light whatever is doubtful (Q. 60, A. 4).

Something is just in one way by the very nature of the things, and this is natural right. Something is just in a second way by an agreement among human beings, and this is positive right. Laws are written to declare both kinds of right but in different ways. Written law contains but does not establish natural right, since natural right gets its force from nature, and written law both contains and establishes positive right, since positive right gets its force from such law. And so judicial judgment needs to be rendered according to the written law. Otherwise, judgment would lack both natural and positive right (Q. 60, A. 5).

Aquinas poses several objections. One runs as follows: Unjust punishment should always be avoided. But written laws sometimes contain injustice. Therefore, one should not always judge according to written laws. He replies that as written law does not give force to natural right, so neither can it lessen or take away the force of natural right, since the will of human beings cannot change nature. Therefore, a written law, if it should contain anything contrary to natural right, is unjust and has no obligatory force, since there is room for positive right only over things in which it does not matter, regarding natural right, whether something is done in this way or that. And so unjust laws are corruptions of law rather than written laws, and one should not judge according to them.

Another objection runs as follows: Judgment should concern individual events. But no written law can comprehend all individual situations. Therefore, it seems that one should not always judge according to written laws. He replies that as unjust laws as such are either always or for the most part contrary to natural right, so also laws rightly laid down are defective in some cases in which it would be contrary to natural right if they were observed. And so one should not judge in such cases by the letter of the law but have recourse to equity, which is the intention of the lawmaker. Even the lawmaker would judge otherwise than the letter of the law in such cases and would have so determined the matter by law if the lawmaker were to have considered it.

Judges, in interpreting written laws, apply the words to particular cases. As only public authority can establish law, so also only public authority can render judicial judgments. And so it is unjust for someone to force another to submit to judicial judgments not sanctioned by public authority (Q. 60, A. 6).

Aquinas poses an objection that gives him an opportunity to comment on the relation of the spiritual power of the Church to the earthly secular power. Spiritual power is different from earthly power. But religious superiors, who have spiritual power, sometimes interpose themselves regarding matters that belong to the secular power. Therefore, usurped power is not unlawful. He replies that the secular power is subject to the spiritual power as the body is subject to the soul. And so judicial judgment is not usurped if a spiritual superior interposes himself about earthly affairs regarding matters in which the secular power is subject to him, or which the secular power relinquishes to him.

The Subjective Parts

There are two species of particular justice: commutative justice and distributive justice. Commutative justice consists of mutual exchanges between individual persons and directs the relation of one individual person to another. Distributive justice directs the distribution of common goods to individual persons (Q. 61, A. 1).

Aquinas poses an objection that gives him the opportunity to highlight the difference between legal justice and distributive justice. Distributive justice concerns common goods. But common goods pertain to legal justice. Therefore, distributive justice is a species of legal justice, not of particular justice. He replies that movements take their species from their goals. And so directing things that belong to private persons to the common good belongs to legal justice, but, conversely, distributing common goods to particular persons belongs to particular justice.

The mean in commutative justice is arithmetic, that is, a quantitatively exact quid pro quo (e.g., the wages paid to a laborer should be quantitatively equal to the value of the work performed). The mean in distributive justice is geometric, that is, a proportional quid pro quo whereby each member of the community receives common goods in proportion to the services each renders to the community (e.g., one who contributes twice as much to the common good than another should receive twice as much of the common goods as the other). Different regimes gauge the importance of contributions by different standards (e.g., aristocratic regimes by the standard of virtue, oligarchic regimes by the standard of wealth, and democratic regimes by the standard of freedom) (Q. 61, A. 2).

Aquinas poses an objection: Both distributive justice and commutative justice are included in particular justice. But the mean in every part of temperance and fortitude are the same. Therefore, the mean in distributive and commutative justice should be the same. He replies that in other moral virtues, we understand the mean as one of reason, not a real mean. But we understand the mean in justice as a real mean and so understand the mean of justice in different ways by real differences.

Justice concerns external actions, and these actions involve treatment of particular things, persons, or deeds. Actions concern the treatment of things when one takes away from, or restores to, another the other's property. Actions concern the treatment of persons when one does an injustice to the very person of a human being (e.g., by striking or insulting a person). Actions concern the treatment of deeds when one justly requires a deed from, or renders a service to, another. The subject matter of the chief actions differs in distributive justice and commutative justice, since distributive justice directs distributions of common goods, and commutative justice directs exchanges between two individuals, and the exchanges may be involuntary or voluntary.

Exchanges are involuntary when one deals with the property or person or deeds of another against the other's will. This sometimes happens secretly, by fraud, and sometimes openly, by coercion. In either case, the offense can be against the property, the proper person, or a closely associated person of another.

In the case of offenses against the property or another, it is theft if one should take the property secretly, and robbery if one should take the property openly. In the case of offenses against the proper person of another, the offense may regard the very substance or reputation of the other.

If the offense regards the substance of another, then one harms the other secretly by killing, striking, or poisoning the other covertly, and one harms the other openly by killing or imprisoning or maiming the other publicly. If the offense regards the reputation of another, one harms the other secretly by false witnesses or detraction or the like, and one harms the other openly by bringing charges in courts of law against, or by shouting insults at, the other.

And if the offense regards the closely associated person of another, one harms the other in the other's wife by adultery, usually in secret, and in the other's slaves when one induces them to leave their master (slavery was legal in Western society until recent centuries). One can also do these things openly. The same argument applies to other closely associated persons, and one can commit offenses against them in all the ways that one can against the chief person. But adultery and inducing slaves to leave their masters are, strictly speaking, offenses against the persons, although inducing slaves to leave their master is related to theft, since slaves are a form of property.

Exchanges are voluntary when one transfers one's property to another, and if one should alienate property to another without the other incurring debt, as in the case of gifts, this is an act of generosity, not justice. But voluntary transfers of property belong to justice insofar as they partake of the nature of debt.

This happens in one way when one alienates one's property to another in exchange for other property, as in buying and selling.

It happens in a second way when one grants the use of one's property to another, and the other is obliged to return it. If one grants the use of one's property without compensation, the transfer regards productive property, or simply borrowing and lending in the case of nonproductive property (e.g., money, dining utensils, and the like). If one grants the use of one's property in return for compensation, the transfer is leasing or renting.

It happens in a third way when one transfers property to another in order to safeguard it, as in the case of entrusted goods or in connection with an obligation, as when one pledges one's property as security for oneself or another.

All such actions, whether voluntary or involuntary, have the same mean of equal recompense. And so all of these actions belong to the same species of justice, namely, commutative justice (Q. 61, A. 3).

Retaliation signifies the equal recompense of suffering on someone who has caused harm to someone else. It concerns the wrongful suffering caused by harming the person or property of one's neighbor and voluntary exchanges (e.g., contracts), in which both parties inflict and suffer harm. The suffering repaid should be equal to the action inflicting harm. But the suffering would not always be equal if one were to suffer specifically the same thing that one caused, for three reasons: First, the one wrongfully harmed may be a greater person (e.g., a king) than the offender (a citizen), and so the recompense by the offender should be greater. Second, the offender should be obliged to make restitution several times over because he would suffer no loss of his own property were only the victim's property taken away from him. Third, the suffering repaid would not always be equal if the offender were to give his own property in return, since his victim's property might be worth more than the offender's property, and money was invented to provide a proportionate common measure.

Retaliation has no place in distributive justice, since the equality in distributive justice consists of the proportion of things to persons, not things to things (Q. 61, A. 4).

Aquinas poses several objections. One runs as follows: In distributive justice, something is given to someone in relation to the worthiness of the person, which we seem most to note by the services that the person has rendered to the community. In commutative justice, something is given to someone in relation to the thing in which one suffered loss. But in each kind of equality, one is repaid according to one's deeds. Therefore, it seems that all justice is absolutely the same as retaliation. He replies that if something were paid to someone for services that the person had rendered to the community, this would belong to commutative, not distributive, justice. In distributive justice, we consider the equality of what one person receives to what another person receives in relation to each person, not the equality of what one person receives to what that person expends.

Another objection runs as follows: Because of the difference between the voluntary and the involuntary, it especially seems that one need not receive as much retribution as the harm one caused, since one who has involuntarily caused a wrong is punished less severely than one who has done so willfully. But we do not distinguish the mean of justice, which is a real mean and not one in relation to ourselves, by the voluntary and the involuntary, which is understood in relation to ourselves. Therefore, justice seems to be absolutely the same as retaliation. He replies that the wrong is greater when the wrongful action is voluntary, and so we understand the wrong as something greater. And so a greater punishment needs to be repaid to the offender because of a real difference, not because of a difference in relation to us.

Restitution

One is obliged in commutative justice to restore another's property to the other, whether the property was unjustly taken by robbery or theft, or held in trust, or lent (Q. 62, A. 1).

An objection argues that one cannot restore what has passed away and no longer exists (e.g., the reputation or uninjured body of a neighbor). Aquinas replies that restitution also includes recompense for any harm caused to the body or reputation of another, although neither the body nor the reputation of the other can be restored.

Restitution is an act of commutative justice. Making restitution signifies returning the very thing unjustly taken, and so this is necessary for salvation (Q. 62, A. 2).

Aquinas poses several objections. One runs as follows: Nothing impossible is necessary for salvation. But it is sometimes impossible to restore what one has taken (e.g., a life or a limb). Therefore, it is not always necessary to return what one has taken from another. He replies that regarding things for which one cannot repay anything equivalent (e.g., the honor due one's parents), it suffices to repay what one can. And so, when one cannot recompense something taken with something equivalent, one should make restitution as far as one can (e.g., a person who has severed another's limb should recompense the victim in money or some honor, according to the judgment of a good person.

Another objection runs as follows: One cannot undo what has been done. But one sometimes takes away the personal honor of another by unjustly insulting the other. Therefore, one cannot restore to the other what one has taken away, and so it is then not necessary for salvation to restore what one has taken away. He replies that insults cannot be undone. But showing respect can undo the action's effect, namely, the lowering of the other's personal honor in public opinion.

Regarding the inequality produced by injustice, restitution applies the remedy, since it suffices that one restore as much as one has of something belonging to another, but regarding the wrongdoing of injustice, punishment applies the remedy, and inflicting punishment belongs to a judge. And so one is bound to pay punitive damages if a judge imposes such a sentence (Q. 62, A. 3).

One may inflict loss on another by preventing the other from obtaining what the other was in the process of obtaining, and one need not recompense such loss with something equivalent, since potential loss is not the same as actual loss. Nevertheless, one is bound to make some recompense according to the circumstances of persons and occupations (Q. 62, A. 4).

Commutative justice consists of equating one thing to another, and one could not do so unless one restores to another what is owed to the other. And so one needs to make restitution to the person from whom one has taken something (Q. 62, A. 5).

Aquinas poses several objections that elicit important replies. One objection runs as follows: We should harm no one. But it would sometimes be to the harm of the person from whom one has taken something, or of others, if one were to return the thing taken to its owner (e.g., if one were to return a sword to a madman). Therefore, one should not always return something to the person from whom one took it. He replies that one should not return something to its owner when the thing returned is likely to be seriously harmful to the owner or another, since restitution is directed to the benefit of the person to whom it is returned, and all possessions fall within the category of the useful. But one who holds the property of another should not appropriate it. Rather, such a person should either keep it in order to return it at a suitable time or deposit it elsewhere in order for it to be more safely preserved.

Another objection runs as follows: A person who unlawfully gave something does not deserve to recover it. But a person sometimes gives what another also unlawfully receives (e.g., a seller and buyer in the practice of simony). Therefore, one should not always make restitution to the person from whom one has received something. Aquinas replies that a person gives something unlawfully in one way when the very giving is unlawful (e.g., in simony). Such a person deserves to lose what the person gave, and so no restitution should be made to that person regarding those things. A person gives something unlawfully in a second way for the sake of something illicit, although the giving itself is lawful (e.g., legal payment to a prostitute for fornication). And so also the woman can keep the money for herself, but she would be bound to make restitution to the customer if she were to have extorted any payment by fraud or guile.

A third objection runs as follows: No one is bound to do the impossible. But it is sometimes impossible to make restitution to the person from whom one has taken something, whether because the person is dead, or because the person is too far away, or because the person is unknown. Therefore, one need not always make restitution to the person from whom one took something. Aquinas replies that if the person to whom one is obliged to make restitution should be completely unknown, one should give back insofar as one can, namely, by giving alms for the salvation of the person, whether the person be living or dead, but only after a diligent search for the person. If the person should be dead, one ought to make restitution to the person's heir. And if the person should be very far away, one ought to transmit to the person what is owed to the person, and especially if the property should be of great value and could be easily sent. Otherwise, one should deposit the property in a safe place to keep it for the person and notify the owner.

A fourth objection runs as follows: One should more recompense a person from whom one received a greater favor. But human beings received more benefits from some (e.g., their parents) than from those who lend things to them or entrust things with them. Therefore, human beings should sometimes assist another person rather than make restitution to the person from whom they received something. Aquinas replies that one should, out of one's own possessions, recompense one's parents or those from whom one received greater favors. But one should not recompense a benefactor out of another's property, which would be the case if one were to recompense someone with what one owes to another. There is perhaps an exception in the case of extreme necessity, in which case one could and should even take away the property of another in order to assist one's father.

Regarding property taken from another, one is bound to return it as long as one has it in one's possession. Regarding the wrongful taking of property by theft or robbery, one is bound to make restitution both by reason of the property taken and of the wrongful action, even if the property no longer remains in the taker's possession, and the thief or robber should be further punished for the wrong inflicted. If one takes the property of another for one's own benefit without wrong (e.g., borrowing a book), one is bound to make restitution both by reason of the property taken and the taking. This is so even if the person has lost the property. If one takes the property of another without wrong but not for one's own benefit (e.g., entrusted goods), one is in no way bound to make restitution by reason of the taking but is bound to do so by reason of the property taken if the property were lost through gross negligence (Q. 62, A. 6).

Aquinas poses several objections that elicit important replies. One runs as follows: Restitution restores the equality of justice. But sometimes the person who has taken property from another no longer has it, and it comes into the possession of a third party. Therefore, the one who now has the property is the one bound to make restitution. Aquinas replies that the chief aim of restitution is that the person who has less than the person ought to have should be compensated. And so, in things that one can take from another without loss to the other, there is no room for restitution (e.g., taking light from the candle of another). And so, although the person who took the property transferred it to another and no longer has it, the victim is nonetheless deprived of the property. And so both the one who took the property, by reason of wrongfully taking the property, and the one who now has the property, by reason of the property itself, are bound to make restitution to the victim.

Another objection runs as follows: One is not obliged to reveal one's crime. But in making restitution, one sometimes reveals one's crime (e.g. in returning stolen goods). Therefore, one who took property is not always obliged to make restitution. Aquinas replies, making the useful suggestion that the thief use an intermediary. Although one is not obliged to reveal one's crime to human beings, one is obliged to reveal one's crime to God in confession. And so the thief can make restitution of property to another through a confessor.

A third objection runs as follows: Restitution of the same property should not be made several times over. But many in concert sometimes steal property, and one of them makes entire restitution of it. Therefore, someone who took the property is not always bound to make restitution. Aquinas replies that the chief aim of restitution is to remove the loss of one from whom something has been unjustly taken. Therefore, after one thief has made adequate restitution to the victim, the other thieves are not bound to make further restitution to the victim, Rather, they are bound to reimburse the thief who made the restitution, although that thief may forgive the debt of the others.

Whoever causes unjust taking of property is bound to make restitution. Some accomplices are always obliged. These include: those commanding the theft or robbery, those consenting to it where their consent is necessary, those giving shelter and protection to thieves or robbers, those participating in the crimes, and those with responsibility to resist who fail to do so. In other cases (e.g., counseling or encouraging), the accomplice is obliged to make restitution only if the person can reasonably calculate that the unjust taking resulted from such a cause (Q. 62, A. 7).

It is also a sin to retain property unjustly taken, and so everyone is bound to make immediate restitution or to seek delay of restitution from the one who owns the property (Q. 62, A. 8).

Aquinas poses an objection that gives him an opportunity to qualify his position. No one is bound to do the impossible. But one sometimes cannot make immediate restitution. Therefore, one sometimes is not bound to make immediate restitution. He replies that when one cannot make immediate restitution, the impossibility itself absolves one from making immediate restitution, just as one is completely absolved from making restitution if one is completely unable to do so. But one, either by oneself or through another, should seek remission or delay from the person to whom one owes restitution.

Preferential Treatment of Persons

Distributive justice requires that common goods be distributed according to the recipient's deserts. But giving preferential treatment to persons because of who they are rather than what they are is not proportional to the persons' worthiness, and so such treatment is a violation of distributive justice. But one may favor one's relatives in certain things (e.g., devising one's property to one's relatives) (Q. 63, A. 1), and worldly considerations may make less holy persons more worthy of spiritual preferment that holier persons (Q. 63, A. 2). One may and should show honor and respect to temporal and spiritual officeholders in spite of their moral defects (Q. 63, A. 3). Preferential treatment of persons should have no place in judicial judgments (Q. 63, A. 4).

Homicide

Animals use plants for food, and human beings use animals for food, and this cannot be done without killing plants and animals. Thus, it is lawful by God's order of things to kill plants for the use of animals and animals for the use of human beings (Q. 64, A. 1).

Aquinas poses an objection that gives him the opportunity to explain the reason why. Homicide is a sin because it deprives a human being of life. But life is common to all animals and plants. Therefore, it is likewise a sin to kill irrational animals and plants. He replies that irrational animals and plants do not have rational life, by means of which they would act on themselves. Rather, something else, a natural impulse, always acts on them. This is a sign that they are by nature at the service of, and suitable for, the use of other things.

Any individual person is related to the whole community as part of the whole. And so, if any human being is dangerous to the community and corrupting it because of some sin, it is praiseworthy and beneficial to kill the human being in order to safeguard the common good (Q. 64, A. 2).

Aquinas poses an objection: It is unlawful to do anything intrinsically evil for any good end. But killing a human being is intrinsically evil, since we ought to have charity toward all human beings. Therefore, it is never lawful to kill a sinner. He replies that human beings by sinning withdraw from the order of reason and so fall from human dignity, that is, human beings, who are by nature free and exist for their own sakes, by sinning fall into the slave status of irrational animals. And so such human beings are subordinate to other things insofar as they are useful to those things. Therefore, although killing a human being who maintains human dignity is intrinsically evil, it can nonetheless be good to kill a sinner, just as it can be good to kill an irrational animal, since an evil human being is worse than an irrational animal and causes more harm.

It is lawful to kill an evildoer insofar as the killing is directed to the well-being of the whole community. And so killing an evildoer belongs only to the one to whom the care of preserving the community is committed, as it belongs to a doctor to amputate a gangrenous limb when care of the whole body has been committed to the doctor. But the care of the common good has been committed to rulers having public authority. Therefore, it is lawful only for them, and not for private persons, to kill evildoers (Q. 64, A. 3).

Aquinas poses an objection: We compare sinful human beings to irrational animals. But it is lawful for a private person to kill wild animals, especially dangerous ones. Therefore, it is lawful for a private person to kill a sinner. He replies that irrational animals are by nature different from human beings, and so no judicial judgment is necessary to decide whether a wild animal should be killed. If the animal is domestic, judicial judgment will be necessary because of the loss to the owner, not because of the animal itself. But a sinful human being is not by nature different from the just. Therefore, there needs to be a public judicial judgment to decide whether the sinful human being should be killed for the sake of the common well-being.

It is altogether unlawful to kill oneself, and this is so for three reasons: First, each thing by nature loves itself, and it belongs to this self-love that each thing should naturally preserve itself in existence and resist destructive things as much as it can. Suicide is contrary to the inclination of nature and to charity, which requires that one love oneself. Second, each human being is part of the community, and whoever kills oneself causes injury to the community. Third, those who deprive themselves of life sin against God, to whom judgment over life and death exclusively belongs (Q. 64, A. 5).

Aquinas poses an objection that elicits a long reply. It is lawful for one voluntarily to undergo a lesser danger to avoid a greater one (e.g., to amputate a gangrenous limb in order to save the whole body). But by killing oneself, one sometimes avoids a greater evil, whether an unhappy life or disgrace. Therefore, it is lawful for one to kill oneself. He makes five points in reply: First, human beings can lawfully make dispositions about themselves regarding things that belong to this life, but passage from this life to the next life is subject to the power of God, not the free choice of human beings. Second, death is the most terrible evil of this life, and to bring death on oneself in order to escape other miseries of this life would take on the greater evil in order to avoid the lesser one. Third, it is not lawful to kill oneself because of some sin, since one thereby most harms oneself by taking away the time needed for repentance, and only judicial judgment by public authority can rightfully kill an evildoer. Fourth, avoidance of rape is no excuse for suicide, since rape is a lesser crime than suicide, which harms oneself, to whom one owes the greatest love. Fifth, avoidance of consent to sin is no excuse for suicide, since one should not do evil things in order to avoid evil things, especially less, and less certain, evils.

Considering a human being as such, it is unlawful to kill anyone, since we should love in all human beings, even sinners, their nature, which God made, and which killing destroys, although killing a sinner is lawful in relation to the common good. And so it is never lawful to kill an innocent human being (Q. 64, A. 6).

Nothing prevents one action from having two effects, only one of which is intended, and the other of which is unintended. But what one intends specifies moral acts, not what one does not intend does not, since the latter result is only incidental. Therefore, one's killing action in self-defense can result in two effects: one, saving one's life, the other, slaying the aggressor. Therefore, such an action, since one intends to preserve one's life, does not have the character of being unlawful, since it is natural to preserve oneself in existence as long as one can. But an act proceeding from a good intention can be rendered unlawful if the act is disproportionate to the end. And so if one should use more force to defend one's own life than is necessary, this will be unlawful, but if one should resist force moderately, this will be lawful self-defense. Nor is it necessary for salvation that one omit acts of moderate self-defense in order to avoid killing another, since one is more bound to safeguard one's own life than the life of another.

But since it is only lawful for the public authority to kill a human being for the sake of the common good, it is unlawful that human beings other than those vested with public authority intend to kill another in self-defense. And those vested with public authority who intentionally kill a human being in self-defense relate such killing to the common good (e.g., soldiers warring against enemies, and police resisting robbers, although even these would sin if they should be motivated by private animosity) (Q. 64, A. 7).

Things happening by chance are not sins. But what one does not actually and as such will or intend may be accidentally willed and intended, as removing something that prevents an effect is an accidental cause of the effect. And so one who does not, when one should, remove things that result in homicide will be in some way guilty of voluntary homicide. This happens in one way when a person engaged in unlawful things incurs the guilt of homicide. It happens in another way when a person does not use due care. And so, if a person should engage in unlawful things or not use due care in the course of lawful activity, the person will not escape the guilt of homicide if the activity results in the death of a human being (Q. 64, A. 8).

Note that Aquinas considers culpable homicide without regard to technical legal categories (e.g., murder in the first or second degree, voluntary and involuntary manslaughter, felony murder).

Other Injuries against the Person

Bodily members are for the sake of the whole human body. They are intrinsically useful for the good of the whole human body, but they may by accident become harmful to the whole body (e.g., when a gangrenous limb is infecting the body). Therefore, individuals may have diseased limbs amputated by doctors for the good of the whole body, but it is otherwise unlawful.

The whole human being is directed to the end of the whole community of which the human being is a part. And so, as it is lawful for the public authority totally to deprive individuals of life because of greater sins, so also it is lawful for the public authority to deprive individuals of a bodily member because of lesser sins. But this is not lawful for a private person, since it injures the community, to which the individual and all the individual's parts belong (Q. 65, A. 1).

Striking someone inflicts harm on the body of the one struck, although it only inflicts pain on the senses. But it is lawful to inflict harm on someone only by way of punishment because of justice. And so it is lawful only for a person who has authority over the one who is struck. But children are subject to the authority of their parents, and slaves to the authority of their masters. Therefore, parents may lawfully strike their children, and masters their slaves, for the sake of correction and discipline (Q. 65, A. 2).

Aquinas poses an objection that allows him to qualify his position. Parents should not provoke their children to anger, nor masters their slaves. But some children or slaves are provoked to anger on account of being struck. Therefore, parents should not strike their children, nor masters their slaves. He replies that anger, since it is the desire for retribution, is chiefly incited when one thinks oneself unjustly hurt. And so parents are permitted to strike their children for the sake of discipline but prohibited from inflicting blows on them immoderately.

Imprisoning or in any way restraining someone is unlawful unless it should be according to justice, either as punishment or as a precaution to avoid some evil (Q. 65, A. 3).

Aquinas poses an objection that gives him the opportunity to expand on the permissiveness of temporarily restraining someone.

A person should be restrained only from an evil deed, and anyone can lawfully prevent another from such. Therefore, if imprisoning a person in order to restrain the person from an evil deed were lawful, it would be lawful for anyone to imprison someone. But that conclusion is false. Therefore, it is unlawful to imprison someone. He replies that it is lawful for anyone to restrain a person for a brief time from an unlawful deed that the person is imminently about to commit (e.g., from jumping off a cliff or killing another). But holding another absolutely in custody or bondage belongs only to one who has the right to dispose universally about the actions and life of the other.

When one inflicts injury on a person who is in some way closely associated with another person, the injury belongs to two persons. And so, other things being equal, a sin is more serious by that very fact. But a sin against a person not closely associated with any other may in some circumstances be more serious because of the dignity of the person or the magnitude of the harm (Q. 65, A. 4).

Aquinas poses an objection: Injuries inflicted on people closely associated with other people have the character of sin insofar as one inflicts harm on another against the other's will. But the evil inflicted on another's own person is more contrary to that person's will than the evil inflicted on the other's close associate. Therefore, the injury inflicted on the closely associated person is lesser. He replies that an injury inflicted on a closely associated person harms the chief person less than if the injury were directly inflicted on the chief person, and the injury inflicted on the closely associated person is in this regard a lesser sin. But all of what belongs to the injury against the chief person is added to the sin that one incurs because one wounds another person as such.

Theft and Robbery

Regarding the use of external things, human beings have a national dominion over them, since human beings can by their reason and will use them for human benefit, as things made for their sake (Q. 66, A. 1).

Aquinas poses an objection: No one should assign to oneself what belongs to God. But dominion over all creatures belongs strictly to God. Therefore, possession of things is not natural to human beings. He replies that God has the chief dominion over all things. But he has by his providence ordained certain things for the material sustenance of human beings, and human beings for that reason have a natural dominion over things regarding the power to use them.

Private ownership of property is preferable to common ownership for several reasons. First, private owners take better care of property. Second, private ownership provides greater precision about the duties of each person regarding property. Third, private ownership has less potential for conflict. But regarding the use of property, owners should possess property as common, that is, they should be ready to share it with those in need (Q. 66, A. 2).

Aquinas poses an objection: Everything contrary to natural right is unlawful. But all things are common by natural right, and individual ownership is contrary to common possession. Therefore, it is unlawful for individual human beings to appropriate external things for themselves. He replies that common possession of things is natural because natural right does not determine who owns what, not because natural right dictates that all things should be possessed in common, and nothing as one's own. Rather, human agreement, which belongs to positive law, determines who owns what. And so individual ownership of property is not contrary to natural right but supplements it through the inventiveness of human reason.

Theft and robbery are sins contrary to justice. Theft is the secret taking of the property of another (Q. 66, A. 3). Robbery is the taking of the property of another openly by the use of force (Q. 66, A. 4). Every theft is a sin by reason of two aspects: it is contrary to justice, and it is done deceitfully, that is, fraudulently (Q. 66, A. 5).

Aquinas poses an objection that gives him the opportunity to distinguish the case of things found. Those who find and keep things that are not their own seem to commit theft. But this seems to be lawful according to natural justice. Therefore, it seems that theft is not always a sin. He replies that some found things were never in the possession of anyone (e.g., precious stones and jewels found on the sea shore), and finders are allowed to keep such things. The argument is the same regarding long-buried treasures, which belong to no one, except that civil laws require finders to give half to the owner of the field if the treasures are found in someone else's field. Some found things have been found close to the goods of another, and then one does not commit theft if one takes them with the intention of returning them to their owner, who has not abandoned them. Likewise, finders do not commit theft in keeping things for themselves if the found things may be considered abandoned, and the finders should so believe. In all other cases, finders who keep things commit the sin of theft.

By theft, human beings inflict harm on their neighbor in the neighbor's property, and human society would perish if human beings were to steal from one another at will. And so theft, being contrary to charity, is a mortal sin (Q. 66, A. 6).

Aquinas poses an objection that gives him an opportunity to make an important distinction. One can commit theft in small as well as large matters. But it seems inappropriate that one should be punished by eternal death for the theft of a small thing (e.g., a needle or a pen). Therefore, theft is not a mortal sin. He replies that reason understands something slight as if it were nothing. And so, regarding very little things, human beings do not think that they suffer harm, and those who take such things can presume that this is not contrary to the will of the owner. And persons can be excused from mortal sin insofar as they take such very little things secretly. But if they should intend to steal and inflict harm on their neighbor, there can be mortal sin even regarding such very little things.

The natural order instituted by divine providence has ordained inferior things for the alleviation of human beings' need. And so the division and appropriation of things, which derive from human law, do not preclude that property should be used to alleviate human beings' need. And so natural right requires that excess possessions of particular persons be used for the sustenance of the poor. But since many suffer need, and the same things cannot assist everyone, dispensing one's goods to help those in need is left to the discretion of each individual. If one's need is so pressing and evident that there is an immediate need to be met out of things at hand (e.g., when personal danger threatens, and there is no other way to alleviate it), one can lawfully use the goods of another, whether taken openly or secretly. Strictly speaking, this does not have the character of theft or robbery (Q. 66, A. 7).

Aquinas poses an objection: Human beings should love their neighbor as they love themselves. But it is not lawful for one to steal in order to assist one's neighbors by giving alms. Therefore, it is also unlawful to steal from them to alleviate one's own need. He replies that one can also, in the case of necessity, secretly take the property of another in order to assist one's neighbor in need.

No one can exercise coercion in society except by the public authority. And so private persons who forcibly take things from others without public authorization act unlawfully and commit robbery. But public authority is committed to rulers in order that they safeguard justice. And so it is only lawful for them to use force and coercion in the course of justice, whether in wars against enemies or in punishment of civilian criminals. Property taken by such force does not have the character of robbery, since the taking is not contrary to justice. On the other hand, if some in the exercise of public authority act contrary to justice in forcibly taking the property of others, they act unlawfully, commit robbery, and are bound to make restitution (Q. 66, A. 8).

Aquinas poses several objections. One concerns the question of the traditional spoils of war. Warriors take spoils by force of arms, and this seems to have the character of robbery. But it is lawful in wars to take spoils from enemies. Therefore, robbery is in some cases lawful. He replies that we should distinguish about the spoils of war. If those who despoil the enemy wage just war, property forcibly acquired in the war becomes theirs, and this does not have the character of robbery, and so there is no obligation to make restitution. Nonetheless, those taking spoils in just wars could sin by covetousness or wicked intention, namely, to wage war chiefly for the spoils and not for the sake of justice. But those who take spoils in an unjust war commit robbery and are bound to make restitution.

Another objection echoes a typical taxpayer's complaint. Earthly rulers forcibly extort many things from their subjects, and this belongs to robbery. But it is hard to say that they sin in this, since then almost all rulers would be condemned. Therefore, robbery is lawful in some cases. He replies that if rulers exact from their subjects what is proper according to justice in order to serve the common good, this is not robbery. But if rulers unduly extort things by force, this is robbery. And so they are also obliged to make restitution. And the more dangerously and generally those constituted the guardians of public justice act against it, the more grievously they sin than robbers do.

Robbery is a more serious sin than theft for two reasons: First, taking property through the use of force is more against the will of the victim than taking property through the victim's ignorance. Second, robbery insults the victim's person as well as takes the person's property (Q, 66, A. 9).

Injustice by Judges

Those vested with public authority can judge other persons only if they have jurisdiction over the persons (Q. 67, A. 1). Judges should judge only on the basis of the evidence submitted, not on the basis of their knowledge as private persons (Q. 67, A. 2). They should judge only if accusers bring charges (Q. 67, A. 3). There are two reasons why judges should not absolve convicted criminals from punishment. First, the accuser has a right to justice if the accused has been found guilty. Second, it belongs to the good of the commonwealth that criminals be punished. But if the victim should wish to remit the punishment, the ruler could lawfully do so if this would not be harmful to the public benefit (Q. 67, A. 4).

Unjust Criminal Charges

In medieval Western Europe, private citizens were the chief prosecutors of crime. According to Aquinas, a private person is obliged to bring a criminal charge if the crime involves material or spiritual detriment to the community, and if the person can adduce sufficient proof (Q. 68, A. 1).

Aquinas poses an objection: No one is obliged to act against the trust that one owes to a friend, since one should not do to another what one does not wish to be done to oneself. But bringing a criminal charge against someone is sometimes contrary to the trust that one owes a friend. Therefore, a human being is not then obliged to bring a criminal charge. He replies that revealing secrets to a person's detriment is contrary to the trust one owes the person, but not if one reveals the secrets for the sake of the common good, which one should always prefer to the private good. And so it is not lawful to keep any secret contrary to the common good. Nor is anything that enough witnesses can substantiate altogether secret.

Since the judge should have as much certitude as possible, it has been established that the criminal charges, as well as other things transacted in court, should be put in writing (Q. 68, A. 2).

There is injustice if the accuser brings false charges against the accused, if the accuser colludes with the accused to undermine the case (presumably because of bribery or coercion), or if the accuser without good reason withdraws the charge (Q. 68, A. 3).

Those who deliberately bring false charges should be punished as much as the punishment they sought to inflict on the accused (Q. 68, A. 4).

Injustice by Defendants

The defendant is obliged to answer the judge's questions if they are in accord with legal process and about matters over which the judge has jurisdiction, and the defendant would commit mortal sin if he were to deny the truth of his guilt (Q. 69, A. 1).

Aquinas poses an objection that considers the right against self-incrimination. One is not obliged to reveal oneself in public or incriminate oneself before others. But if the defendant were to confess the truth in court, the defendant would reveal and incriminate himself. Therefore, the defendant is not obliged to tell the truth, and the defendant does not commit mortal sin if he lies in court. In reply, Aquinas denies that answering the judge truthfully involves self-incrimination. When a judge interrogates a person in accord with the legal process, the person by responding does not reveal himself. Rather, the judge reveals the person, since the judge, whom the person is obliged to obey, imposes the necessity to answer.

It is lawful for the accused not to say anything about the truth beyond that about which the judge rightfully inquires, but it is not lawful for the accused to tell lies, hide the truth that the accused is obliged to admit, or to use fraud or guile, which are the same as lying and misrepresentation of the truth (Q. 69, A. 2).

The defendant may appeal the judge's adverse decision if and only if the defendant is innocent (Q. 69, A. 3).

Only those condemned to death unjustly may resist the ruler, and then only when resistance would not risk serious public disturbance (Q. 69, A. 4).

Aquinas poses several objections. One reads almost as if the objector were Thomas Hobbes. That to which nature always inclines is always lawful, being of natural right. But human beings, animals, and plants have a natural inclination to resist things that threaten their destruction. Therefore, it is lawful for the condemned criminal to resist, if possible, in order not to be handed over to death. Aquinas replies that reason is given to human beings so that things to which nature inclines be followed according to the order of reason, not indiscriminately. And so a defense with due moderation—not any defense—is lawful.

Another objection reads as follows: As a person avoids a death sentence by resistance, so also does a person by flight. But it seems lawful that one free oneself from death by flight. Therefore, it is also lawful to resist. Aquinas replies that one is condemned to suffer death, not to inflict death on oneself, and so one is not obliged to do anything that results in one's own death, such as remaining in the place from which one is brought to execution. Nevertheless, a person is obliged not to resist the executioner in order not to suffer what is just for the person to suffer. So also, if a person is condemned to die of hunger, the person does not sin by eating food secretly provided, since not to eat food would be to kill oneself.

Injustice by Witnesses

Individuals are obliged to testify when a superior with authority over them demands it regarding public matters and the prior report of a crime. Even if a superior with no authority to command individuals to testify should require the individuals' testimony, they are obliged to do so if such testimony is required to deliver those accused from unjust punishment, false accusation, or unjust loss. Individuals are obliged to testify about matters incriminating someone only if a superior requires it according to legal form (Q. 70, A. 1).

Aquinas poses an objection regarding confessional secrecy and other committed secrets. No one is obliged to act deceitfully. But a person who does not keep the secrets a friend has committed to the person acts deceitfully. Therefore, a person is not always obliged to testify, especially about matters a friend commits to the person under secrecy.

He replies that a priest should never testify about matters committed to him under secrecy in confession, since the priest knows such things as God's minister, not as a human being, and the sacramental bond is greater than any human precept. But we should distinguish about things otherwise committed to a person under secrecy. Things are sometimes such that a person is obliged to manifest them as soon as the person knows them (e.g., making public things involving spiritual or material harm of the community, or the grave injury of a person, by testifying in court or giving a warning). The commitment of a secret to a person cannot oblige the person contrary to this duty, since the person would thereby break the fidelity the person owes to another. But things committed to a person under secrecy are sometimes such that the person is not obliged to divulge them. And so a person can be obliged not to divulge these things because they are committed to the person under secrecy. Then one is obliged not to divulge them even at the command of a superior, since keeping faith belongs to natural right, and human beings cannot be commanded to do anything contrary to what concerns natural right.

We cannot have demonstrable certitude about human acts, about which we make judgments and are required to give testimony, since human acts are contingent and variable. And so probable certitude, which attains truth for the most part, although it falls short in rather few cases, suffices regarding human acts. But the testimony of many witnesses is more likely to be true than the testimony of one person. And so, when the defendant denies a crime, and many witnesses affirm what the accuser says, divine law and human law reasonably establish that the testimony of the witnesses should prevail. And so two witnesses in agreement are required for conviction, or, for greater certitude, three (Q. 70, A. 2).

Testimony has probable, not absolute, certitude, and so any probability to the contrary renders testimony unreliable. Sometimes fault on the part of the witnesses (e.g., unbelievers, the notorious, public criminals) make it probable that their testimony is unreliable. Other times, the testimony of faultless witnesses is unreliable because they lack the use of reason (e.g., children, the insane, and women [!]), because of emotional dispositions (e.g., enemies, closely associated persons, household members), or because of an external condition (e.g., paupers, slaves, and subordinates of the accuser or the accused) (Q. 70, A. 3).

False testimony is always a mortal sin, since it is perjury and contrary to justice (Q. 70, A. 4).

Injustice by Lawyers

Lawyers cannot and need not offer counsel to all the poor, but they should do so when the counsel is relatively necessary and should give the highest consideration to those poor who are most closely connected to them. Were they to give counsel to all the poor, lawyers would need to put aside all other business and attend only to the suits of the poor. And we should say the same thing about doctors regarding care of the poor (Q. 71, A. 1).

Some persons are barred from the legal profession because they lack the requisite capacity. Some lack sufficient use of reason (the insane and children), and others lack sufficient means of communication (e.g., the deaf and the dumb). Some are unsuitable because they are obliged to do greater things (e.g., priests and monks). Others are unsuitable because of a personal defect (e.g., the blind, persons of ill repute, and those convicted of a serious crime). But necessity outweighs unsuitability, and so unsuitable persons can exercise the office of lawyer for themselves or persons closely associated with them. And so also clerics can be lawyers for their churches, and monks for their monasteries (Q. 71, A. 2).

If a lawyer knowingly defends an unjust cause, the lawyer sins grievously and is obliged to make restitution of the loss that the other party unjustly incurs because of the lawyer's help to the plaintiff (Q. 71, A. 3).

Aquinas poses an objection: It is lawful to desist from any sin. But lawyers are punished if they abandon their cases. Therefore, a lawyer does not sin by defending an unjust cause if the lawyer has undertaken its defense. He replies that if a lawyer initially believed a cause just, and it should become evident later in the process that the cause is unjust, the lawyer is not obliged to give it up so as to help the other party, or to reveal secrets of the case to the other party. But the lawyer can and should abandon the case, or induce his client to yield or compromise, without loss to the other party.

Lawyers may justly receive moderate compensation for their services to clients, and the same is true about compensation of doctors (Q. 71, A. 4).

Injustice in Speech

Aquinas in QQ. 72–76 deals with injustice in various forms of speech: insult, detraction, gossip, derision, and cursing.

Fraud in Buying and Selling

Exchanged goods should be of the same value. The price paid for goods measures their value, and money was invented for this purpose. And so selling goods more dearly, or buying them more cheaply, than they are worth is unjust. But the seller may raise the price to compensate for a particular disadvantage that the seller would suffer by the sale, and buyers greatly benefited by the sale may freely pay the seller something extra, although the buyer is not obliged to do so (Q. 77, A. 1).

The seller who knowingly sells goods that are different from the type of goods, the quality of the goods (e.g., a lame horse as a healthy horse), or the quantity the buyer contracts to buy commits fraud and is bound to make restitution. If the seller unknowingly sells goods with such defects, he does not commit fraud but is bound to make restitution when notified of the defects. Likewise, the buyer who knowingly buys goods that are essentially superior to what the seller contracts to sell (e.g., gold bought as copper) commits fraud and is bound to make restitution (Q. 77, A. 2).

It is always unlawful to occasion danger of loss to another, although human beings need not always give help or counsel to another regarding anything to the other's advantage. Rather, they need to do so only in particular cases (e.g., when another is subject to one's care, or when no one else can help). The seller in offering something defective for sale could occasion monetary loss or even danger to the buyer because of the defect. And so, if such defects are hidden, and the seller does not disclose them, the sale will be unlawful and deceitful, and the seller obliged to make restitution. But if the defect is evident (e.g., when a horse has only one eye), and if the seller proportionately reduces the price, the seller is not obliged to point out the defect. Sellers may lawfully look to their own security by keeping quiet about such a defect (Q. 77, A. 3). (Note that this is the familiar legal principle of caveat emptor—let the buyer beware.)

Household managers and statesmen exchange one thing for another, or something for money, in order to provide for the needs of life, and this kind of exchange is praiseworthy. There is another kind of exchange of money for money, or things for money. This kind of exchange is the business of trading for the sake of profit, not to provide for human needs. Nevertheless, although profit does not essentially signify anything worthy or necessary, it does not signify anything sinful or contrary to virtue. And so nothing prevents profit from being directed to a necessary or worthy end. And then the business of trading is lawful. For example, a businessman may direct a moderate profit to maintaining his household or helping the needy. Or one may engage in the business of trading for the benefit of the public, namely, lest one's country lack things necessary for life, and seek profit as payment for one's labor, not as an end (Q. 77, A. 4).

The Sin of Interest-Taking

The ownership of real and personal property such as furniture is separable from its use (e.g., one person may own a house, and another person may rent it). But some things are consumed in their very use (e.g., food, wine), and the ownership and use of such things cannot be separated. Therefore, one cannot seek separate payment for the ownership and use of such things. According to Aristotle and Aquinas, money is such a thing, since its chief use is as means of exchange, and the value of money as a means of exchange is consumed in its use in exchanges. (Coins and metals, of course, have commercial value as commodities.) Therefore, one may not lend money at interest and is obliged to make restitution if one has. Interestingly, Aquinas does not ask whether lending at interest is always a mortal sin, as he frequently does in other cases of injustice. It is perhaps plausible to infer that he thinks that lending at a low rate of interest is only a venial sin, like that of small thefts (Q. 78, A. 1).

Those who by tacit or explicit contract receive anything that money can measure (e.g., use of the borrower's property) incur the like sin and are obliged to make restitution. But a lender does not sin if the lender receives something as a free gift from the borrower, and it is lawful to require in exchange for a loan recompense of things that money does not measure (e.g., benevolence and love of the lender) (Q. 78, A. 2).

Aquinas poses a number of objections that give him the opportunity to make further distinctions. One objection runs as follows: Persons can lawfully take into account compensation against loss. But persons sometimes suffer loss because they lend money. Therefore, it is lawful for them to expect or even require something for their loss over and above the money lent. He replies that lenders can without sin contract with borrowers to compensate them for loss of things that they should have, since this is to avoid loss, not to sell the use of money. And borrowers may avoid greater loss than lenders will incur, and so borrowers out of their gains recompense the loss of lenders. But lenders may not contract with borrowers to be compensated for loss of profit from the money lent, since lenders should not sell what they do not yet have and can in many ways be prevented from having.

A second objection runs as follows: Those who transfer the ownership of money by lending it alienate it more than those who invest money with merchants or craftsmen. But it is lawful to receive profit from money invested with merchants or craftsmen. Therefore, it is also lawful to receive profit from money lent. He replies that lenders transfer ownership of money to borrowers. And so the borrower possesses it at the borrower's risk and is obliged to return all of it, and the lender should not require more. But one who invests money with a merchant or craftsman by forming a partnership does not transfer ownership of the money to the merchant or craftsman. Rather, the money remains the investor's, so that the merchants carry on their business, and craftsmen their craft, with risk to the investor. And so investors may lawfully expect to share in profits from the business or craft, as something that belongs to them.

A third objection runs as follows: A person can take security for money lent (e.g., borrowers give their farms or homes to lenders as security), and lenders could sell use of the security. Therefore, it is lawful to make profit from money lent. He replies that if borrowers should give, as security for money lent to them, things whose use money can measure, lenders should calculate use of the things toward repayment of what they lent. Otherwise, if lenders should want free use, as it were, of the things in addition to repayment, this is the same as if they were to receive money for their loan. This is to take interest, unless the things were perhaps such as friends usually grant the use of without charge, as is evidently the case with borrowed books.

A fourth objection runs as follows: Because of loans, persons sometimes sell things more dearly or buy things more cheaply, or increase the price of their goods in return for giving buyers a longer time to repay the loans, or lower the price of the goods in return for buyers repaying the loans earlier. In all of the above cases, recompense seems to be made for lending money, as it were. But this is not clearly unlawful. Therefore, it seems that it is lawful to seek or even require an advantage for money lent.

Aquinas replies that persons evidently take interest if they should want to sell their goods on credit for more than the just price, since such credit has the nature of a loan. And so everything required in exchange for such credit beyond the just price is like a charge on the loan, which belongs to the nature of taking interest. Likewise, if buyers should want to buy goods more cheaply than the goods' just price by paying for the goods before delivery, this is the same as taking interest, since such prepayment has the nature of a loan, the charge for which is the reduction of the just price of the goods purchased. But if the sellers should want to reduce the price to less than the just price in order to get their money sooner, they do not commit the sin of taking interest.

Things whose use consists of their consumption have no use separate from it. And so, if lenders have extorted such things (e.g., wheat, wine, and money) through the taking of interest, they are obliged to return only what they took, since anything they obtain out of these things is the fruit of their human effort, not that of the things. There would be an exception if the borrower, by losing some goods as interest, were to suffer loss through the lender's retention of the goods, since the lender is bound to indemnify the harm to the borrower. But there is a separate use of things whose use does not consist of their consumption (e.g., houses, farms). And so, if lenders were to have extorted the house or farm of another by taking interest, they would be obliged to return both the house or farm and the fruits derived from them, since the latter are the fruits of property owned by the other and so fruits owned by the other (Q. 78, A. 3).

Although it is never lawful to induce a person to commit the sin of taking interest, it is lawful to borrow at interest from those who are ready to lend at interest and make a practice of doing so, if one borrows for some good purpose, namely, to alleviate one's own need or another's. This is not different from a victim handing over possessions to a robber in order to avoid being killed (Q. 78, A. 4).

The Integral Parts of Justice

Doing the good one owes to God and the community, and avoiding the contrary evil, are the constitutive parts of justice in general. Doing the good one owes to one's neighbor, and avoiding the contrary evil, are the constitutive parts of particular justice (Q. 79, A. 1).

Aquinas poses an objection that allows him again to distinguish justice from the other moral virtues. It belongs to every virtue to do good deeds and avoid evil deeds. But parts do not exceed the whole. Therefore, avoiding evil and doing good should not be parts of justice, which is a special virtue. He replies that we understand good and evil deeds here under a special aspect by which they are applied to justice. And so we posit good and evil as parts of justice by a special aspect of good and evil, not the aspect of any other moral virtue, since other moral virtues regard emotions. In the latter, doing good consists of arriving at the mean, namely, avoiding the extremes as evils. And so, regarding the other virtues, doing good and avoiding evil amount to the same thing. But justice regards external actions and things, in which it is one thing to establish equality and another thing to destroy the established equality.

Transgression is one constitutive part of injustice. It consists of doing something prohibited by a negative precept of the natural or divine law. In a material sense, transgression can be contrary to all kinds of virtue, since human beings transgress divine precepts by any kind of mortal sin. But in a formal sense, transgression is a special sin in two ways. It is a special sin in one way in that, as it belongs to legal justice to consider the obligation of a precept, so it belongs to the proper nature of transgression to consider the contempt of a precept. Transgression is a special sin in a second way insofar it is distinguished from omission, which is contrary to an affirmative precept (Q. 79, A. 2).

Omission signifies the omission of an obligatory good, not any good. But good under the aspect of being obligatory belongs strictly to legal justice if we should understand obligation in relation to divine or human law, and to particular justice insofar as we consider obligation in relation to one's neighbor. And so, in the way in which justice is a special virtue, omission is also a special sin different from sins contrary to other virtues (Q. 79, A. 3).

Aquinas poses an objection: For any special sin, one needs to determine when it begins. But one does not fix a particular time when a sin of omission begins, since one is similarly disposed whenever one does not do something, but one does not always sin in not doing something. Therefore, omission is not a special sin.

He replies that as sins of transgression are contrary to negative precepts, which belong to avoiding evil, so sins of omission are contrary to affirmative precepts, which belong to doing good. Affirmative obligations oblige in relation to a fixed point of time, not at all times, and a sin of omission begins at that time. One may at that time be unable to do what one ought to do, and a person does not commit a sin of omission if the inability to do it is blameless on the part of the person.

But if the inability to do what one ought to do is due to one's prior sin (e.g., if a monk got drunk the night before and was unable to get up for matins, which he was obliged to do), some say that the sin of omission began when the monk committed himself to the unlawful action incompatible with the obligatory action (that is, drinking to excess the night before). But this does not seem to be true since, were someone to rouse the monk forcibly, and were the monk to go to matins, the monk would not omit attending matins. And so it is clear that the prior drunkenness caused the absence from matins and was not the omission itself. And so we should say that an omission begins to be imputed to a person as a sin when it was time for the person to do something, but the omission is imputed to the person because of the prior cause, which renders the subsequent omission voluntary.

Transgression, absolutely speaking, is a more serious sin than omission, since doing evil is absolutely contrary to doing good, but not doing good is not always evil, although a particular omission may be more serious than a particular transgression (Q. 79, A. 4).

The Potential Parts of Justice

Certain virtues are connected or related to justice, but fall short of its perfect character. Religion, filial devotion, and respect for the virtuous are connected to justice, but fall short of its perfect character, since there is no equality between what persons owe to God, their parents, and the virtuous, and what persons can render to them. Truth, gratitude, and retribution are so necessary that one cannot maintain moral rectitude without them, but they fall short of the perfect character of justice, since they lack the characteristic of strict legal obligation (Q. 80, A. 1). Aquinas treats of each of these virtues in QQ. 81–119.

Equity

Established laws cannot anticipate all contingencies, and it is sometimes contrary to the equality of justice and the common good to observe the letter of the law (e.g., to return a gun to an owner who is insane). And so one should sometimes not follow the letter of the law but do what justice and the common good require. This is equity and is a virtue (Q. 120, A. 1).

Aquinas poses an objection: It seems to belong to equity to consider the intention of the lawmaker. But it belongs only to the ruler to interpret the intention of the lawmaker. Therefore, an act of equity is unlawful, and equity is not a virtue. He replies that there is room for interpretation in doubtful matters, in which it is not lawful to depart from the letter of the law without the ruler so determining. But in clear matters, one needs to execute the law, not interpret it.

Equity, as a certain kind of justice, is part of justice in the general sense. And so equity is a subjective part (species) of justice. And predicating *justice* of equity has priority over predicating *justice* of legal justice, since equity governs justice. And so equity is the higher rule of human actions (Q. 120, A. 2).

The Ten Commandments and Justice

The Ten Commandments are the primary precepts of the natural law, and natural reason at once assents to them as most evident. The characteristic of obligation, which is necessary for a precept, is most clearly evident in justice, which governs relations to others. In that regard, it is clearly evident that human beings are obliged to render to others what is due them. And so the Ten Commandments necessarily belong to justice. The first four commandments of the Hebrew Bible (the first three of the Vulgate) concern acts of religion, which is the most important part of justice. The fifth (Vulgate's fourth) concerns acts of filial devotion, which is the second part of justice, and the other five (six in the Vulgate) are laid down about acts of justice in the general sense, namely, about equals (Q. 122, A. 1).

17

FORTITUDE

Fortitude in Itself

Fortitude is the moral virtue by which one resists difficulties that repel the will from acting according to reason. Fortitude of mind is required to take away such difficulties, just as human beings overcome and repel physical impediments to bodily strength (Q. 123, A. 1).

Aquinas poses an objection: Human virtue, since it is good quality of mind, most belongs to the soul. But fortitude seems to belong to the body, or at least to result from one's bodily constitution. Therefore, it seems that fortitude is not a virtue. He replies that we posit fortitude of the soul as a virtue and speak of it by analogy to bodily strength. But it is not contrary to the nature of virtue that one has a natural inclination to a virtue by reason of one's natural constitution.

It is a special virtue insofar as it signifies firmness to endure and resist the greatest difficulties (Q. 123, A. 2). It concerns fear of the difficulties and boldness in attacking them (Q. 123, A. 3). It most concerns mortal dangers, since death takes away all bodily goods (Q. 123, A. 4).

Aquinas poses several objections. One runs as follows: Fortitude is love that readily endures everything for the sake of what is loved, and fears neither death nor any other adversity. Therefore, fortitude concerns mortal dangers and all other adversities. He replies that fortitude well disposes one to bear all adversities. But we consider human beings brave only because they bear the greatest evils well, not because they bear any kind of adversity well. We call persons brave in one respect because they bear adversities other than death well.

Another objection runs as follows: No virtue consists of extremes. But fear of death consists of an extreme, since such fear is the greatest one. Therefore, the virtue of fortitude does not concern fear of death. Aquinas replies that we consider extremes in relation to virtues by what exceeds right reason. And so it is not contrary to virtue if one should undergo the greatest dangers in accord with reason.

It is in order to seek some good that human beings do not flee from the danger of death. The danger of death in combat directly threatens human beings insofar as one is defending the common good in just combat, whether in the case of soldiers waging just war or a person adhering to just judgment against the threat of life-threatening force. But a brave person is also rightly disposed regarding the danger of death from infection in course of attending a sick friend (Q. 123, A. 5).

Endurance in the face of danger, that is, resisting fear, is more important than attacking causes of danger, since it is more difficult to suppress fear than to moderate boldness (Q. 123, A. 6). The brave person acts for the sake of the goodness of the virtue of bravery and expresses the likeness of the virtue in brave acts (Q. 123, A. 7).

A person acting bravely derives spiritual pleasure from the virtuous action, but the person also experiences spiritual sorrow because of the risk of death and the presence of physical pain.

The pleasure in virtue overcomes spiritual sorrow, since a virtuous person prefers the goodness of virtue to physical life and the properties of life (Q. 123, A. 8).

Aquinas poses an objection: Something stronger conquers something weaker. But brave persons love virtuous good more than their own body, which they expose to mortal dangers. Therefore, pleasure regarding the virtuous good overcomes physical pain, and the brave person acts entirely with pleasure. He replies that the pleasure in virtue conquers spiritual sorrow in a brave person. But since physical pain is more sensibly perceptible, and sense perception more apparent to human beings, great physical pain causes spiritual pleasure, which concerns the purpose of virtue, to disappear.

A brave person should think about threatening dangers beforehand, but a person most manifests bravery without forethought in the face of sudden dangers (Q. 123, A. 9).

Aquinas reconciled the views of Aristotle, who held that the virtuous should use anger and other emotions of the soul as moderated by the commands of reason, and the Stoics, who held that anger, like any other emotion of the soul, is intrinsically immoderate and to be shunned. Aquinas held that a brave person uses moderate—but only moderate—anger in acts of bravery (Q. 123, A. 10).

Aquinas poses an objection: As some persons carry out brave acts more forcibly because of anger, so also some do so because of sorrow or desire. But fortitude should not use sorrow or desire to assist brave acts. Therefore, neither should fortitude use anger. He replies that fortitude involves two activities, namely, enduring and attacking. But fortitude uses anger to assist the activity of attacking, not the activity of enduring, since only reason causes endurance. Fortitude uses anger rather than other emotions for attacking because it belongs to anger to attack the cause of sorrow, and so anger directly assists fortitude in attacking. But sorrow by its nature yields to sorrowful things, although sorrow incidentally helps one to attack, either because sorrow causes anger, or because one exposes oneself to danger in order to escape sorrow. Likewise, desire by its nature tends to pleasurable good, and attacking in the face of danger is intrinsically contrary to that good, although desire sometimes incidentally helps attacking, namely, because one prefers to risk danger than to lack something pleasurable.

Since standing fast in the good of reason is a common condition of virtue, and since fortitude stands fast against the greatest difficulties, namely, physical pain and the threat of death, fortitude is a cardinal virtue (Q. 123, A. 11). But prudence and justice are more important cardinal virtues than fortitude, which acts to preserve virtue only by controlling fear and moderating boldness (Q. 123, A. 12).

Fear

When one's will avoids things that reason dictates should be endured in order not to desist from other things that one should do, the fear is inordinate and sinful. But when one's will out of fear avoids what one according to reason should avoid, the will is neither inordinate nor sinful (Q. 125, A. 1).

Every fear derives from love, since one fears only the contrary of what one loves. Inordinate fear is included in any sin. For example, a miser fears the loss of money, which he loves, and an intemperate person the loss of pleasure, which he loves. But inordinate fear of mortal dangers is contrary to fortitude, and we accordingly say by synecdoche that timidity is contrary to fortitude (Q. 125, A. 2). Inordinate fear of mortal dangers is a mortal sin if and only if the will consents to such fear (Q. 125, A. 3).

A person should avoid some evils (e.g., loss of one's life) more than others (e.g., loss of one's property), and so one may yield property to robbers in order to save one's life, but one may not commit sin, which involves death of the soul, in order to avoid bodily harm or death. Fear of imminent mortal dangers lessens but does not excuse sin committed because of such fear, since acts done out of fear, although partially involuntary, are nonetheless partially voluntary (Q. 125, A. 4).

Aquinas poses an objection that allows him to affirm that temporal goods are human goods. Every fear is either of a temporal evil or a spiritual evil. But fear of a spiritual evil cannot excuse one from sin, since such fear does not induce one to sin but draws one away from it. Nor does fear of a temporal evil excuse one from sin, since one need not fear poverty, sickness, or anything other than what comes from one's own wickedness. Therefore, fear never excuses one from sin. He replies that the Stoics held that temporal goods are not human goods, and so temporal evils are not human evils and should never be feared. But Augustine and Aristotle held that such temporal things are goods, although the lowest, and so one should fear contrary things but not so much that one in the face of them retreats from virtuous good.

Lack of Fear

Nature endows one to love one's own life and the things ordered to it, though in the proper way, namely, that one should love such things insofar as one uses them for the sake of one's final end, not as if they constitute one's end. And so not loving them in the way one should is contrary to the inclination of nature and is therefore a sin. One never completely falls away from love of one's life, and so those who kill themselves do this out of love of their flesh, which they wish to free from present distresses. And so it can happen that one fears death and other temporal evils less than one should because one loves their contraries less than one should. This lack of fear arises out of presumptuous spiritual pride in oneself or sheer stupidity (Q. 126, A. 1).

The fear tempered by reason belongs to fortitude, namely, that human beings fear what they should fear, and when they should fear, and so forth. But excess and deficiency can destroy this measure of reason. And so, as timidity is contrary to fortitude by too much fear, so also temerity is contrary to fortitude by too little fear, inasmuch as one does not fear what one should fear (Q. 126, A. 2).

Boldness

Boldness is an emotion. But emotion sometimes lacks the measure of reason, whether by excess or deficiency, and emotion is sinful in this respect. And so boldness, if we understand it to mean excessive boldness, is a sin (Q. 127, A. 1). Boldness in this sense is clearly contrary to the virtue of fortitude, which concerns both boldness and fear (Q. 127, A. 2).

The Parts of Fortitude

There are no subjective parts, that is, species, of fortitude, since fortitude itself has a very specific subject matter, namely, mortal dangers.

There are four integral, or constitutive, parts of fortitude: confidence, magnificence (nobility of character), patience, and perseverance. Acts attacking the causes of mortal dangers require confidence and magnificence. Acts of endurance require patience and perseverance.

The integral parts, if related to other, less difficult subject matter, are potential, that is connected, parts of fortitude. The connected virtue of magnanimity (high-mindedness), which Aquinas regards as equivalent to confidence, concerns great public honors. The connected virtue of magnificence concerns great expenses for public benefactions. Patience and perseverance, if they are related to difficult matters of any sort, will be virtues different from fortitude but connected to it as secondary virtues (Q. 128, A. 1). Aquinas considers these connected virtues and the sins contrary to them in QQ. 129–38.

18

TEMPERANCE

Temperance in Itself

Human virtue inclines human beings to what is in accord with reason. Temperance inclines human beings to this, since it signifies a moderating or tempering, which reason does. And so temperance is a virtue (Q. 141, A. 1).

Aquinas poses several objections. One allows him to make an important distinction, and runs as follows: No virtue is contrary to an inclination of nature. But temperance draws a person away from pleasures of the senses, to which nature inclines the person. Therefore, temperance is not a virtue. He replies that nature inclines things to what befits each thing. And so human beings by nature seek the pleasure befitting them. But since human beings as such are rational, pleasures that are in accord with reason befit them, and temperance draws human beings away from pleasures that are contrary to reason, not those that are in accord with reason. And so temperance is evidently in accord with, not contrary to, the inclination of human nature, although it is contrary to the inclination of an animal nature not subject to reason.

Another objection runs as follows: Virtues are interrelated. But some persons have temperance without having other virtues (e.g., many persons are temperate but greedy or cowardly). Therefore, temperance is not a virtue. Aquinas replies that temperance, insofar as it fully possesses the character of virtue, does not exist apart from prudence, which sinners lack. And so those who lack other virtues, being subject to contrary sins, do not have the temperance that is a virtue. Rather, they perform temperate acts from a natural disposition, as some imperfect virtues are natural to human beings or acquired by habituation, which does not have the perfection of reason apart from prudence.

Temperance is virtue in general insofar as reason moderates all human actions and emotions, but it is a special virtue insofar as reason restrains desires and pleasures of the senses (Q. 141, A. 2). Temperance chiefly concerns emotions tending toward sensibly perceptible goods—namely, the emotions regarding desire and pleasures of the senses—and so concerns the sorrows that result from the absence of such pleasures (Q. 141, A. 3).

Aquinas poses an objection: Temperance is the firm and moderate mastery of reason over sexual lust and other evil impulses of the spirit. But we call all emotions of the soul impulses of the spirit. Therefore, temperance does not concern only sense desires and pleasures. He replies that emotions that belong to avoiding evil presuppose emotions that belong to seeking good, and emotions of the irascible power presuppose emotions of the concupiscible power. And so, while temperance directly moderates emotions of the concupiscible power tending toward good, temperance as a result moderates all other emotions, since moderating prior emotions results in moderation of subsequent emotions. For one who desires moderately then hopes moderately and is moderately saddened about the absence of sensibly desirable things.

Temperance concerns desires of the greatest sense pleasures, and the more natural the actions that result in sense pleasures, the more vehement the pleasures are. But the actions most natural to animals are those that preserve the individual through food and drink and preserve the species by the sexual union of male and female. And so temperance in the strict sense concerns the pleasures of food and drink and the pleasure of sex. But such pleasures result from the sense of touch. And so temperance concerns the pleasures of touch (Q. 141, A. 4). Temperance chiefly regards the pleasure of touch, which intrinsically results from the very use of things necessary for the preservation of the individuals and the species (food, drink, and women), the entire use of which consists of touching them. There is also temperance or its lack in a secondary role regarding the pleasures of taste or smell or sight, since the sensibly perceptible objects of these senses contribute to the pleasurable use of the necessary things (Q. 141, A. 5).

Temperance takes the needs of this life as the rule regarding the pleasurable things that one uses: one should use pleasurable things insofar as the needs of this life require their use (Q. 141, A. 6).

In an answer to an objection, Aquinas gives a further explanation of the needs of this life. We say in one way that that without which something cannot at all exist is necessary for it (e.g., food is necessary for animals). In a second way, we consider the needs of human life as we say that that without which something cannot exist in a suitable way is necessary. Temperance considers the needs of human life in both senses, and so the temperate person seeks pleasurable things for the sake of health or a good constitution. We can consider other things, things unnecessary for human life, in two ways. For some things are impediments to health or a good constitution, and a temperate person in no way uses such things, since this would be a sin against temperance. But other things are not impediments to health of a good constitution, and a temperate person uses these things moderately, according to the right place, the right time, and the thing's compatibility with those with whom the person lives. And so a temperate person also seeks other pleasurable things, namely, those unnecessary for health or a good constitution, if the things are not impediments to one's health or constitution.

Moderation is chiefly praiseworthy in connection with the pleasures of touch, which are more natural, more necessary for the present life, and more difficult to resist, and so temperance is a cardinal virtue (Q. 141, A. 7). The good of the people is more excellent than the good of the individual. And so the more a virtue belongs to the good of the people, the better it is. But justice and fortitude belong to the good of the people more than temperance does. Justice consists of exchanges, which are in relation to others, and fortitude consists of the dangers in wars, which are sustained for the common welfare, while temperance moderates only the sense desires and pleasures of things that belong to the individual person. But prudence and the theological virtues (faith, hope, and charity) are better than justice and fortitude (Q. 141, A. 8). (In answer to an objection, Aquinas admits that temperance is in one respect better than both fortitude and justice, namely, in the frequency one needs to exercise it).

Contrary Sins

The natural order requires that human beings use pleasures necessary for preserving the individual human being and the human species, and one would sin if one should act contrary to the natural order. But it is sometimes praiseworthy to abstain from the pleasures of food, drink, or sex for the sake of a greater good. For example, some abstain from them for the sake of bodily health or executing a function, as athletes and soldiers do, or for the sake of the health of their souls, as penitents do. And human beings wishing to be free for contemplation and divine things need to withdraw themselves from things of the flesh. Such abstinence is in accord with right reason (Q. 142, A. 1).

Aquinas poses an objection that claims that total abstinence from sensual pleasures most advances human beings in the good of reason. He replies that human beings cannot use reason apart from sense powers, which need bodily organs, and so they need to sustain their bodies in order to use their reason. But pleasurable actions, namely, eating and drinking, cause sustenance of the body. And so the good of reason cannot be in human beings if they were to abstain from all pleasurable things. But human beings who have assumed responsibility to be free for contemplation and to transmit spiritual goods to others laudably abstain from many pleasurable things.

An intemperate person is like a child seeking base things, becoming increasingly self-indulgent and needing correction (Q. 142, A. 2). Intemperance is a more serious sin than cowardice in regard to the respective subject matter of each, since the desire for pleasure is not so great as the desire to avoid mortal dangers. Temperance is also a more serious sin than cowardice regarding the sinner, since the desire for pleasure, unlike the fear of mortal danger, does not paralyze the mind, since intemperance is more voluntary, and since intemperance is easier to remedy (Q. 142, A. 3). Intemperance is most worthy of reproach because it is most contrary to human excellence regarding pleasures common to human beings and irrational animals, and because it is the most contrary to the beauty of human beings produced by the light of reason (Q. 142, A. 4).

Parts of Temperance

There are two integral (constitutive) parts of temperance: a sense of shame, which draws one away from base behavior, and an honorable character, which draws one toward the beauty of moderate behavior.

Different subject matters or objects distinguish the subjective parts (species) of a virtue. Temperance concerns pleasures of touch, of which there are two kinds: pleasures related to nourishment and pleasures related to reproduction. Regarding the former pleasures, there are two subjective parts of temperance: abstinence regarding food and sobriety regarding alcoholic drink. Regarding the latter pleasures, there are also two subjective parts: chastity regarding sexual intercourse and sexual modesty regarding incidental pleasures (kisses, touches, embraces).

Virtues that moderate pleasures in other subject matters and restrain other appetites are potential (connected) parts of temperance. Regarding internal movements of the will, continence restrains inordinate desires, humility restrains inordinate hope, and meekness and mercy restrain inordinate anger. Regarding bodily movements and actions, modesty causes good order, proper attire, and gravity in conversation. Regarding external things, parsimony, or self-sufficiency, causes human beings not to demand superfluous things, and moderation, or simplicity, causes human beings not to demand things that are too special (Q. 143, A. 1). Aquinas explains in detail the potential virtues of temperance and their contrary sins in QQ. 155–62, 166–70.

The Integral Parts of Temperance

SHAME Shame is fear of disgrace, which no person of habitual virtue deems possible or difficult to avoid. And so shame, properly speaking, is not a virtue. But broadly speaking, we sometimes call a sense of shame a virtue, since it is sometimes a praiseworthy emotion (Q. 144, A. 1). Shame chiefly concerns reproach, that is, censure, on account of one's sins (Q. 144, A. 2). We feel greater shame from the censure of close associates (Q. 144, A. 3). Even the virtuous have a hypothetical sense of shame, that is, they are so disposed that they would feel shame if there were anything disgraceful in them (Q. 144, A. 4).

HONORABLE CHARACTER Honorable refers to the same thing as virtue (Q. 145, A. 1), and virtue is the same thing as beauty, which is the spiritual radiance of a well-proportioned reason (Q. 145, A. 2). The honorable and the useful and the pleasurable coincide in the same subject, but they differ conceptually. Something is honorable insofar as it has an excellence worthy of honor because of its spiritual beauty, and something is useful insofar as it is related to something else, namely, happiness, and something is pleasurable insofar as it satisfies a befitting desire (Q. 145, A. 3). Honorable character is a spiritual beauty, and so we reckon it an integral part of temperance as a precondition, not as a subjective part or as connected virtue (Q. 145, A. 4).

Subjective Parts of Temperance Concerning Food and Drink

ABSTINENCE Abstinence is restraint in the consumption of food. Insofar as reason governs such restraint, abstinence is a moral virtue (Q. 146, A. 1). Abstinence concerns restraint in the desire for the pleasures of food (Q. 146, A. 2).

GLUTTONY Gluttony is an inordinate desire to eat food and drink (nonalcoholic) liquids, and so it is a sin (Q 148, A. 1). It is a mortal sin if human beings seek gluttonous pleasures as their end, for the sake of which they are willing to act contrary to God's laws. It is a venial sin if one seeks gluttonous pleasures only as a means of happiness, not as something contrary to God's laws (Q. 148, A. 2). The sin of gluttony will not be the most serious by reason of its subject matter, since sins against divine things are the greatest. Nor is gluttony the greatest regarding the sinner, since human beings need to consume food, and it is difficult to discern and regulate what is proper in consuming food. But regarding the effect resulting from it, it is a serious sin, since it occasions other kinds of sin (Q. 148, A. 3).

There can be disordered desire in gluttony in two ways. First, regarding the substance or kind of food, a glutton seeks fine food or delicately prepared food or simply too much food. Second, regarding the way of consuming food, a glutton may seek to eat too fast or too rapaciously (Q. 148, A. 4). Gluttony is a capital sin because it incites human beings to sin in many ways (Q. 148, A. 5). Gluttony incites human beings to other sins: dullness of the senses necessary for the use of reason, unbecoming joy, garrulousness, buffoonery, and inordinate discharge of bodily fluids (Q. 148, A. 6).

SOBRIETY Moderate consumption of intoxicating drink is very beneficial, and immoderate consumption very harmful, since the latter prevents the use of reason even more than excess of food does. And so we call sober one who observes the proper measure in drinking alcoholic beverages (e.g., wine, beer, and brandy), which are of such a nature as to disturb the brain (Q. 149, A. 1). Sobriety is a special virtue preserving reason from the impediments caused by intoxicating drink (Q. 149, A. 2). Drinking alcoholic beverages is morally permissible unless one is in no fit condition to do so or has vowed not to drink alcohol, or the amount drunk is excessive, or the drinking scandalizes others (Q. 149, A. 3). Sobriety is more necessary for youth, women, the elderly, clerics, and rulers (Q. 149, A. 4).

DRUNKENNESS The act whereby one becomes drunk is sinful if one inordinately desires and consumes too mush alcohol, but not if one drinks too much by accident, that is, without knowledge of the drink's strength (Q. 150, A. 1). Drunkenness is a venial sin if one knows that one's drinking is excessive but underestimates its power. Drunkenness is a mortal sin if one knows that one's drinking is excessive and overpowering but chooses to get drunk (Q. 150, A. 2).

Aquinas poses an objection that allows him to make an important point: One should never commit a mortal sin for a medicinal purpose. But some drink excessively on a doctor's advice in order to induce purgative vomiting, and drunkenness results from this excessive drinking. Therefore, drunkenness is not a mortal sin. He replies that we should moderate food and drink as they befit the body's health. And so, as it sometimes happens that the food and drink moderate for a healthy person are excessive for a sick person, so also, conversely, it can happen that the food and drink excessive for a healthy person are moderate for a sick person. Accordingly, we should not consider food or drink excessive if one eats or drinks a great deal on a doctor's advice in order to induce vomiting. (But it is not necessary that drinking should be intoxicating in order to induce vomiting, since even drinking warm water causes vomiting, and so one is not for this need excused from drunkenness.)

Sins contrary to God are more serious than drunkenness (Q. 150, A. 3). If the prior act of the will causing drunkenness is not culpable, then a subsequent sin will be completely blameless, since drunkenness causes acts to be involuntary due to one's ignorance. On the other hand, if the prior act causing drunkenness is culpable, then one is not completely excused from the subsequent sin, since it is rendered voluntary because one willed the prior act. Still, the subsequent sin is lessened, since the voluntary character of the act is lessened due to one's ignorance (Q. 150, A. 4).

The Subjective Parts of Temperance Concerning Sex

CHASTITY Chastity is a virtue, since it consists of reason moderating desire (Q. 151, A. 1). It is a special virtue in that it restrains desires for sexual pleasure (Q. 151, A. 3).

MODESTY Human beings are most ashamed of sexual intercourse, even marital intercourse, and external signs of sexual desire (e.g., lewd looks, kisses, and touches). But signs are more likely to be witnessed, and so modesty concerns them more than sexual intercourse itself. Modesty expresses a condition of chastity, not a virtue distinct from it (Q. 151, A. 4).

VIRGINITY Virginity is a special virtue and signifies that a woman is free of desire for sexual pleasure. The unbroken seal of virginity is incidentally related, the absence of sexual pleasure is materially related, and the intention to forego sexual pleasure is formally and perfectly related, to the moral disposition of a virgin (Q. 152, A. 1). It is in accord with right reason for human beings to abstain from bodily pleasures in order to be freer to contemplate truth, and religious virginity abstains from all sexual pleasure in order to be freer for divine contemplation. And so virginity is praiseworthy, not something contrary to virtue (Q. 152, A. 2).

Aquinas poses a fundamental objection: Everything contrary to a precept of the natural law is unlawful. But as there is a precept of the natural law for the preservation of the individual, so also there is a precept of the natural law for the preservation of the species. Therefore, as one who were to abstain from all food would sin by acting contrary to the good of the individual, so also one who completely abstains from the act of reproduction sins by acting contrary to the good of the species.

He replies that a precept has the nature of something required, but something is required in two ways. In one way, an individual should fulfill, and cannot without sin omit, what is required. In the second way, the community should fulfill what is required. Not every human being is obliged to fulfill such a duty, since one individual does not suffice to fulfill many things necessary for the community, and the community fulfills them when one individual does one thing, and another does another thing. Therefore, individual human beings need to fulfill the precept of the natural law laid down for them about eating, since an individual could not otherwise be preserved. But the precept laid down about reproduction concerns the whole human community, for which it is necessary that it both increase materially and progress spiritually. And so it is sufficiently provided for the human community if some persons should devote themselves to carnal reproduction, and other persons, abstaining from such activity, should be free to contemplate divine things for the adornment and welfare of the whole human race. Just so, some soldiers guard the camp, some bear the army's standards, and some fight, but all of these are required for the army as a corps, and so no one unit of the army can fulfill all of the requirements.

Virginity, preserving oneself free of the experience of sexual pleasure, is more praiseworthy than preserving oneself free of disordered sexual pleasure, and so virginity is a special virtue (Q. 152, A. 3). Virginity is more excellent than marriage because the divine good, which religious virgins contemplate, is more important than the human good, since the good of the soul is preferable to the good of the body, and the good of the contemplative life is preferable to the good of the practical life (Q. 152, A. 4)

Aquinas poses an objection that allows him to make an important distinction. Praise of a virtuous person depends on the person's virtue. Therefore, if virginity were preferable to marital moderation, every virgin would be preferable to any spouse. But this conclusion is false. Therefore, virginity is not preferable to marriage. He replies that although virginity is preferable to marriage, a spouse may nonetheless be better than a virgin. First, a spouse may be better than a virgin regarding chastity itself, namely, if the spouse should have a more ready mind to preserve virginity, if it were needed, than one who is actually a virgin does. Second, the spouse may be better than the virgin because the spouse may have more excellent virtue.

Virginity is the most excellent virtue in the genus of chastity, but the theological virtues (faith, hope, and charity) and acts of religion are preferable to virginity (Q. 152, Q. 5).

LUST We most consider lust regarding wanton sexual pleasure (Q. 153, A. 1). One can use sex without sin if one does so in the proper way and order, as suitable for human reproduction (Q. 153, A. 2). Anything in the use of sex done contrary to the order of reason is sinful, and so lust is a sin (Q. 153, A. 3). Lust is a capital sin because many sins arise from it (Q. 153, A. 4).

There are six species of lust: sins contrary to nature, simple fornication, incest, adultery, seduction of a virgin, and rape. Sins contrary to nature and simple fornication are contrary to the end of the sex act, namely, reproduction and proper upbringing of children, and the other species are contrary to the proper relation to other persons. Aquinas distinguishes the subject matter of the latter species by the woman involved, since he deems a woman the passive and material party in sexual intercourse (Q. 154, A. 1).

FORNICATION Fornication is a mortal sin because it deprives an offspring of its father's care (Q. 154, A. 2). Fornication is a more serious sin than one against property (e.g., theft) but a lesser sin than one against an existing human life (e.g., homicide) (Q. 154, A. 3).

TOUCHES AND KISSES Touches and kisses are mortal sins only if unmarried people touch and kiss for the sake of sexual pleasure and consent to the pleasure (Q. 154, A. 4).

Aquinas poses an objection: We call fornication a mortal sin because it prevents the good of the offspring to be begotten and brought up. But kisses, touches, and embraces do nothing to prevent that good. Therefore, there is no mortal sin in those things. He replies that kisses and touches, although they do not in themselves prevent the good of a human offspring, result from lust, which is the cause that prevents that good. And so they have the character of mortal sin.

NOCTURNAL EMISSION Nocturnal emission, being the emission of superabundant fluid while a man is sleeping, is not in itself sinful, but may be if prior carnal thoughts and desires cause it (Q. 154, A. 5).

SEDUCTION OF A VIRGIN Seduction of a virgin, which is the violation of a virgin who is under the supervision of her parents, is a distinct species of lust both because it causes a woman to lose her reputation, and because it lacks respect for her father (Q. 154, A. 6).

RAPE Rape is a distinct species of lust because it involves the use of force against a virgin or against her father if she is abducted from his house, or against both (Q. 154, A. 7).

ADULTERY To commit adultery is to enter the marriage bed of

another, and adultery is a distinct species of lust regarding both the man and the woman committing adultery. (Curiously, Aquinas considers adultery exclusively regarding a man committing adultery with the wife of another man, but a woman also would evidently commit adultery if she had intercourse with the husband of another woman.) The man prevents the good of an offspring's upbringing and hinders the good of the woman's legitimate children. The woman sins against her husband by creating doubts about who is the father of the offspring and against the good of her legitimate offspring. There is no mention of the adultery's potential harm to the spouse of the adulteress or his rights (e.g., loss of reputation) (Q. 154, A. 8).

INCEST There are several reasons why incest, sex between men and women related by blood or marriage, is a special species of lust. First, human beings naturally owe respect to their parents and so to other blood relatives, who closely trace their origin to the same parents, and sexual intercourse by blood relatives would show disrespect to their common parents. Second, if sexual union of blood relatives were permissible, there would be too much opportunity for it, and lust would sap the participants' minds. Third, such unions would prevent human beings from having the broad range of friends that a wife who was not a blood relative would offer. Fourth, such a union would be too ardent and incite lust (Q. 154, A. 9).

Aquinas posits an objection that allows him to make a fundamental distinction. Whatever does not of itself signify a deformity does not constitute a distinct species of sin. But sex between men and woman related by blood or marriage is not in itself deformed. Otherwise, it would never have been lawful, as it was in the Old Testament. Therefore, incest is not a distinct species of lust. He replies that there is something in itself unbecoming and contrary to natural reason in the sexual union of some blood relatives (e.g., of parents and their own children), Parents and children being directly and immediately related, children naturally owe respect to their parents. But other persons not immediately related but indirectly related to one another through their parents do not of themselves have unsuitability for such sexual union. Rather, becomingness and unbecomingness in this regard vary according to custom and human or divine law. This is because the use of sex is ordered to the common good and so subject to law.

SACRILEGE Sacrilege can be a special species of lust if one's lust violates something belonging to the worship of God (e.g., sexual union with a woman who has a religious vow of virginity) (Q. 154, A. 10).

SINS CONTRARY TO NATURE Sins contrary to nature, which are contrary to the natural order of the sex act, are a distinct species of lust. This happens in four ways: (1) procuring emission of semen without intercourse (masturbation); (2) intercourse with animals (bestiality); (3) intercourse with another of the same sex (sodomy); and (4) use of an improper instrument or way of copulating (principally contraception) (Q. 154, A. 11).

RANK In sins contrary to nature, human beings transgress what nature prescribes about the use of sex, and so such sins are the most serious sexual sins. Incest is the next most serious, since it is contrary to the respect one owes to one's relatives. The next most serious sexual sins involve injury to another (adultery, seduction of a virgin, and rape). Fornication is the least serious species of lust. Adultery is more serious than abduction of virgin, since it is a greater wrong to abuse a woman subject to the power of another in the matter of sexual intercourse than to abuse her only with respect to her custody. The rape of a woman is more serious than her seduction, since rape involves the use of force, and the rape of a married woman is more serious than adultery. The aspect of sacrilege makes all of these more serious (Q. 154, A. 12).

Aquinas poses several objections. One runs as follows: The more contrary to charity a sin is, the more serious the sin is. But adultery, seduction of a virgin, and rape, which tend toward injury of neighbor, seem more contrary to the love of neighbor than sexual sins contrary to nature, which injure no one else. Therefore, sins against nature are not the greatest species of lust. He replies that as the order of right reason is from human beings, so the order of nature is from God himself. And so, in sexual sins contrary to nature, in which one violates the very order of nature, there is a wrong against God himself, who establishes the order of nature.

In response to another objection, Aquinas ranks the different sins contrary to nature. He says that we note the gravity of a sin by the abuse of something rather than by the omission of the thing's proper use. And so the sin of self-abuse, or masturbation, which consists merely of the omission of copulating with another, holds the lowest rank of sexual sins against nature. The sin of bestiality, in which one does not observe the right species, is the most serious sexual sin contrary to nature. The sin of sodomy, in which one does not observe the proper sex, is the second most serious sin contrary to nature. The sin of not observing the proper way of copulating is the third most serious sin contrary to nature, and more serious if one should use an improper means than if the disorder should regard any other things belonging to the way of copulating.

GLOSSARY

ACCIDENT: *an attribute that inheres in something else and cannot subsist in itself*. What subsists in itself and does not inhere in another is a substance. John, for example, is a substance, while his height is an accident and resides in him. *See* Actuality, Property, Substance.

ACTION: *activity*. There are two basic kinds of activity. One kind, transitive activity, produces an effect in something else. The other kind, immanent activity, is a perfection of the very being that acts. Immanent action produces effects in finite living beings. Plants have the immanent activities of nutrition, growth, and reproduction. Animals have, in addition, the immanent activities of sense perception and sense appetites. Human beings have, in addition, the immanent activities of intellection and willing. *See* Cause.

ACTUALITY: *the perfection of a being*. Existing is the primary actuality of every being. A specific substantial form actualizes finite beings and distinguishes one kind of being from another. Particular accidental characteristics further actualize finite beings. Joan, for example, is perfected and actualized by her act of existing, her human form, and her particular attributes (her knowledge, her virtue, her physical attributes). *See* Accident, Form, Matter, Potentiality, Substance.

ANALOGY: *predicating perfections of God and creatures in a sense partially the same (as to the presence of the perfection in both) and completely different (as to the way the perfection is in each)*. This is possible because nothing is in an effect (a creature) that is not in some way in its cause (God). *See* Participation.

APPETITE: *the desire or striving of finite beings for some good.* Nonliving material beings have only natural appetites. Plants have, in addition, the vegetative appetites of nutrition, growth, and reproduction. Animals have, in addition, sense appetites. Human beings have, in addition, an intellectual (rational) appetite, the will. *See* Concupiscible, Irascible, Will.

BEATIFIC VISION: *the intellectual intuition of God's essence.* This is the ultimate end of human beings. *See* Happiness.

BEING (1): *an existing thing.*

BEING (2): *the act of existing. Being* as a participle signifies the actuality of existing and is not a copula.

CAUSE: *something that contributes to the being or coming to be of something else.* The term refers primarily to an efficient cause, that is, a cause that by its activity produces an effect. For example, a builder and his workers are the efficient causes of the house they construct. A final cause is the end for the sake of which an efficient cause acts. For example, a builder builds a house to provide a dwelling suitable for human habitation (objective purpose) and to make money if the house is to be sold (subjective purpose). An exemplary cause is the idea or model of a desired effect in the mind of an intellectual efficient cause preconceiving the effect. Efficient, final, and exemplary causes are extrinsic to the effects they produce. In addition, form, which makes an effect to be what it is, and matter, which receives the form, are correlative intrinsic causes. For example, a house is composed of bricks and mortar (its matter), which are given a structure or shape (its form). *See* End, Form, Matter.

CHARITY: *the infused supernatural virtue that characteristically disposes human beings to love God above all things and to love one's neighbor and all other things for his sake. See* Virtue.

COMING TO BE, PASSING AWAY: *The process of substantial change.* In substantial change, prime matter acquires a new substantial form, and so a new material substance comes to be. The same matter also loses its old substantial form, and so the previous material substance ceases to exist. *See* Form, Matter.

CONCUPISCENCE: *the inclination of human beings' sense appetites toward actions contrary to reason. The inclination is not completely subject to reason.* Concupiscence is not to be identified with the concupiscible appetites as such. See Concupiscible, Will.

CONCUPISCIBLE: *a sense appetite for something pleasant.* Love and hate, desire and aversion, joy and sorrow are emotions of concupiscible appetites. See Appetite, Irascible.

CONSCIENCE: *the dictate of reason that one should or should not do something.* See Synderesis.

EMOTIONS: *movements of sense appetites.* Emotions may be ordinate (in accord with right reason) or inordinate (contrary to right reason). Emotions involve either desire for pleasant things or repugnance regarding difficult things. See Concupiscible, Irascible, Moral Virtues.

END: *the object for the sake of which something acts.* The end may be intrinsic or extrinsic. The end is intrinsic if it belongs to the nature of an active thing. The end is extrinsic if it is the conscious object of a rational being's action. See Cause, Intention.

EQUITY: *fundamental fairness, or natural justice, in human relations.* Human laws cannot anticipate all contingencies, and it is sometimes contrary to justice and the common good to observe the letter of the law (e.g., a law requiring the return of property to its owner in the case of a gun to an owner who is insane). Therefore, one should sometimes follow what justice and the common good require, not the letter of the law. See Law.

ESSENCE: *that which makes things what they substantially are* (e.g., the human essence makes humans beings to be what they are as substances, namely, rational animals). The essence of a being, when considered the ultimate source of the being's activities and development, is called the being's nature (e.g., human nature is the ultimate source of specifically human activities, namely, activities of reason and activities according to reason). See Form, Property (2).

EXISTING: *the primary actuality of every being.* See Actuality.

FAITH: *the infused supernatural virtue that characteristically disposes human beings to believe what God has revealed about himself and his plan for human beings.* See Virtue.

FORM: *that which determines a thing to be the specific kind of thing that it is or to possess additional attributes* (e.g., the human form, namely, the human soul, makes human beings human, and other forms make them so tall and so heavy). Form determines the essence of all finite immaterial substances, but matter is necessary to individuate the form of material things. See Essence, Matter, Species.

FORTITUDE (COURAGE): *the moral virtue consisting of the right characteristic disposition to withstand and resist fear of the greatest difficulties, namely, mortal dangers, which hinder the will from acting in accord with right reason.* Fortitude involves endurance and moderate boldness in attacking the cause of such fear. Secondary virtues related to fortitude concern fear of lesser difficulties (e.g., the virtues of patience and perseverance in physically, psychologically, or morally difficult situations). See Moral Virtues, Virtue.

GENUS: *See* Species.

HABIT: *characteristic human disposition.* Habits concern being or acting in a certain way and belong chiefly to faculties of the soul, namely, the intellect and the will. Habits may be innate or acquired, natural or supernatural, good or bad. For example, the habit of logical argumentation belongs to the intellect; the habit of justice belongs to the will; the habits of the first principles of theoretical and practical reason are innate; the habit of cleanliness is acquired; the acquired habit of courage is natural; the infused habit of faith is supernatural; the habit of generosity is good; the habit of stinginess is bad. Habits belong secondarily to the body, as the latter is disposed or made apt to be readily at the service of the soul's activities. See Virtue.

HAPPINESS: *the perfect attainment of the ultimate good, that is, the ultimate end, for which human beings by nature desire and strive.* Happiness as such is an objective state of perfection, not a subjective state of euphoria, although human beings possessing the state of perfection will experience joy and satisfaction. For Aristotle, human beings become happy, that is, achieve the state of perfection, by engaging in activities of reason and living in accord with right reason. For Aquinas, human beings can only be perfectly happy when they behold God as he is in himself, although activities of reason and activities in accord with right reason bring human beings to a state of imperfect happiness in this life. *See* Beatific Vision, End.

HOPE: *the infused supernatural virtue that characteristically disposes human beings to be confident that they will attain the promised eternal union with God if they behave properly.* See Virtue.

IDEAS (DIVINE): *the forms or natures of actual or possible creatures in God's mind.* Because God knows himself as imitable, he knows the forms or natures of every being that he creates or could create. These ideas are identical with God's knowledge of himself, and his knowledge is in turn identical with his substance.

INTELLECT: *the human faculty of understanding, judging, and reasoning.* Aquinas holds that each human being has two intellectual powers: one active and the other passive. The active intellect causes the passive, that is, the potential, intellect to understand the essence of material things, to form judgments, and to reason deductively. *See* Reason.

INTELLECTUAL VIRTUES: *virtues consisting of the right characteristic disposition of the intellect toward truth.* Theoretical intellectual virtues concern first principles, scientific knowledge, and theoretical wisdom. Practical intellectual virtues concern prudence and skills. *See* Principle, Prudence, Science, Theoretical Wisdom.

INTENTION: *an act of the will tending toward something.* The human will necessarily tends toward the human end (happiness) and freely toward means to this end, which are only imperfectly good and so subject to choice. Human beings are morally responsible for the evil they intend or fail to take reasonable care to avoid. *See* End, Happiness, Will.

IRASCIBLE: *a sense appetite for a useful object that one can obtain only by overcoming opposition.* Fear and anger are emotions of irascible appetites. Unlike the objects of concupiscible appetites, the objects of irascible appetites do not seem pleasant. *See* Appetite, Concupiscible.

JUSTICE: *the moral virtue consisting of the right characteristic disposition of the will to render others what is due to them.* This is the special virtue of justice, and there are two particular kinds. One kind, commutative, concerns the duties of individuals and groups to other individuals and groups (including the community as a corporate entity).

The other kind, distributive, concerns the duties of the community to insure that individuals and groups receive a share of the community's goods proportional to the contributions by the individuals and groups to the community.

But justice in general is moral virtue in general, insofar as all moral virtues can be directed to the common good. Aquinas and Aristotle call such justice legal justice, since the laws of the political community prescribe the moral virtues of citizens. See Moral Virtues, Virtue.

KINGLY PRUDENCE: *the archetype of political prudence, that is, prudence in governance.* See Political Prudence, Prudence.

LAW: *an order of reason for the common good instituted by one with authority, and promulgated.* For Aquinas, the archetypical law is God's plan for the universe and each kind of creature he creates. Aquinas calls this plan the eternal law. Human beings, as rational creatures, can understand God's plan for them as human beings and can judge what behavior it requires of them. Aquinas calls this participation in the eternal law the natural law. The most general precepts of the natural law are that human beings should preserve their lives, mate, educate offspring, seek truth, and live in community with other human beings. Human laws either adopt conclusions from the general precepts (e.g., do not commit murder) or further specify the precepts (e.g., drive on the right side of the road). He calls those human laws that are proximate conclusions from the general precepts of the natural law the common law of peoples. He calls those human laws that are more remote conclusions from, or further specifications of, the general precepts civil laws. There is, in addition, divine law: the Old Law for the Jewish people before the coming of Christ and the New Law after his coming. See Political Community.

MATTER: *the stuff or subject matter out of which material things are constituted.* See Cause, Form.

MORAL VIRTUES: *virtues consisting of the right characteristic disposition of the will toward the ends that reason prescribes for human actions, namely, that they be just, courageous, and moderate.* The ends of moral virtues preexist in practical reason as habitual self-evident principles, and prudence (practical wisdom) chooses the means to achieve those ends. Moral virtues concern the mean between too much and too little. The chief moral virtues are justice, fortitude, and temperance. Justice concerns external things, and fortitude and temperance concern control of emotions. *See* Emotions, Fortitude, Justice, Prudence, Temperance, Virtue.

NATURE: *See* Essence.

PARTICIPATION: *the sharing in being.* Since being is both one and many, philosophers have attempted to explain the fact by invoking participation, namely, that being is one and infinitely perfect in God, and that other beings share finitely in its perfection.

PASSING AWAY: *See* Coming to Be.

POLITICAL COMMUNITY: *the organized society in which human beings seek their proper well-being and excellence.* Like Aristotle, Aquinas holds that human beings are by their nature social and political animals. Human beings need to cooperate with one another for their full intellectual and moral development. Only an organized community of a certain size can be self-sufficient to achieve these goals. Political community thus differs from the state, which is the supreme agency responsible for organizing the community, and from government, which is the machinery and personnel of the state. Unlike Aristotle, however, Aquinas envisions a supernatural end for human beings beyond their temporal well-being and, by reason of that supernatural end, the membership of Christians in another, divinely established community, the Church. The two communities should cooperate with one another to achieve their respective ends. *See* Beatific Vision, End, Happiness, Polity.

POLITICAL PRUDENCE: *the intellectual virtue consisting of the right characteristic disposition to reason about matters of governance.* Kingly wisdom is the archetype of political prudence in rulers, and other kinds of rulers share in this prudence in lesser ways. Citizens or subjects of the rulers have another kind of political prudence, one that consists of the right characteristic disposition to obey the rulers' laws. See Kingly Prudence, Law, Prudence.

POLITY: *the regime or constitution that gives a political community its distinctive form.* For Aquinas, as for Aristotle, polity also has the meaning of a particular regime or constitution that combines features of monarchical rule (rule by the one best person), aristocratic rule (rule by the few best persons), and democratic rule (rule by the people). Such a regime includes only limited popular participation. See Political Community.

POTENTIALITY: *the capacity to be or to become something.* The potentiality of a being limits its actuality. For example, frogs can swim but not fly, and John can go bald. Finite material things can also change from one substance into another. For example, grass, when consumed by a cow, becomes part of the cow. Potentiality in the active sense is the same as power. See Accident, Actuality, Matter, Power.

POWER: *the active capacity to perform a certain kind of activity.* For example, the intellect and the will are powers of human beings to perform specific acts.

PRINCIPLE: *the major premise of an argument.* Principles presupposing no other principles, or at least no other principle than the principle of contradiction, are first principles. There are theoretical first principles (e.g., everything coming to be has a cause) and practical first principles (e.g., do good, avoid evil). See Intellectual Virtues, *Synderesis.*

PROPERTY (1): *any material possession.*

PROPERTY (2): *a quality or characteristic that necessarily belongs to something but is not part of its essence or definition.* For example, the ability of human beings to use speech to convey their thoughts is a characteristic proper to them and so one of their properties, but not part of their essence or definition, namely, rational animal.

PRUDENCE (PRACTICAL WISDOM): *the intellectual virtue consisting of the right disposition to reason about what human beings should or should not do.* Prudence concerns human action and so differs from theoretical wisdom, which concerns the ultimate causes of things without regard to human action. The ends of moral virtues preexist in practical reason as habitual self-evident principles, and prudence chooses the means to achieve those ends. As the most important natural virtue connected with human action, prudence is sometimes listed as a moral virtue. *See* End, Habit, Happiness, Moral Virtues, Political Prudence, Theoretical Wisdom, Virtue.

REASON: (1) *the process of drawing conclusions from principles;* (2) *the power to draw conclusions from principles;* (3) *the power of the intellect in general.* Aquinas often uses the term in the third sense. *See* Intellect, Principle.

REGIME: *See* Polity.

RIGHT: *the objectively right, that is, just, order of human relations.* Natural law, divine law, and human law determine the order of human relations. Aquinas is concerned about the duties that human beings owe one another, not the rights that individual human beings possess, although the rights of some human beings are necessarily correlative to the duties that other human beings owe them. *See* Justice, Law.

SCIENCE (ARISTOTELIAN): *Knowledge of things through knowledge of their causes.* Science studies the efficient, final, material, and formal causes of things. Physical, psychological, and social sciences study the secondary causes of material and human things, and philosophy (metaphysics) studies the first causes of being as such. For Aristotle, philosophy is the highest science. For Aquinas, theology, the study of God in the light of Christian revelation, is the highest science. *See* Cause, Intellect, Intellectual Virtues, Theoretical Wisdom.

SENSES: *faculties of perception through bodily organs.* The external senses (sight, hearing, smell, taste, touch) have proper objects, that is, objects that only one sense perceives, and common objects, that is, objects related to quantity that more than one sense perceives. The internal senses (the common or unifying sense, imagination, memory, and the cognitive sense) derive from data provided by the external senses.

SKILLS: *practical intellectual virtues that consist of right reasoning about how to make things.* *See* Intellectual Virtues.

SLAVERY: *involuntary servitude*. In medieval society, war captives became slaves, and their servitude was terminated by ransom or treaty. The feudal institutions of serfdom and vassalage were similar to slavery in that serfs, vassals, and their children were bound to certain lifelong duties to their lords and masters. But serfs and vassals, unlike the manual slaves of ancient Greece and Rome and those of the antebellum American South, had rights that their lords and masters were in theory bound to observe.

SOUL: *the substantial form of a living material thing*. The soul is the ultimate intrinsic source whereby living material things differ from nonliving ones. There are three kinds of souls: the vegetative soul capable of nutrition, growth, and reproduction; the sensory soul capable of sense perception; the rational soul capable of intellection. According to Aristotle and Aquinas, the only soul in human beings is the rational soul, which also has the powers of the vegetative and sensory souls. The rational soul is intrinsically independent of matter for its existence and activity. *See* Form, Substance.

SPECIES: *the substantial identity of material things insofar as the identity is common to many things*. The species concept (e.g., human being) is composed of a genus concept (e.g., animal), which indicates the essence of a material thing in an incompletely determined way, and a specific difference (e.g., rational), which distinguishes different kinds of things belonging to the same genus. The species concept, or definition, thus expresses the whole substance or essence of a particular kind of material thing. *See* Essence.

SUBJECT (1): *that in which something else inheres*. In the strict sense, subjects are substances underlying accidental characteristics. For example, human beings are the subjects of their powers and acts. In a broader sense, powers are the subjects of the powers' acts. For example, the intellect is the subject of the intellect's acts.

SUBJECT (2): *a human being bound to obey another human being*. British citizens are British subjects, that is, bound to obey British authorities.

SUBSISTENCE: *the ability of something to exist in itself and not in another*. Existing *in* itself is not to be confused with existing *by* itself, that is, as uncaused by another. Both God and finite beings exist in themselves, but only God exists by himself. God has no accidents, but finite beings do (e.g., spiritual beings have spiritual faculties and activities, and material beings have material characteristics and activities). See also Substance, Accident.

SUBSTANCE: *what exists in itself and not in another.* Finite individual substances "stand under" (Latin: *substare*) accidents and persist through accidental changes. For example, human beings are composed of a substance (body-soul) and accidents (size, shape, color, etc.). See Accident, Property, Subject (1).

SYNDERESIS: *habitual understanding of the first principles governing human action.* This habit is innate. The rational nature of human beings disposes them to recognize that they should seek the good proper to their nature and avoid things contrary to it. The human good involves preserving one's life in reasonable ways, mating and raising offspring in reasonable ways, and living cooperatively with others in organized society. Conscience applies these first principles to particular acts. See Conscience, Habit, Law, Principle.

TEMPERANCE (MODERATION): *the moral virtue consisting of the right characteristic disposition to restrain inordinate sense appetites for the greatest sense pleasures, namely, food, alcoholic drink, and sex.* See Moral Virtues, Virtue.

THEORETICAL WISDOM: *the intellectual virtue consisting of the right characteristic disposition to reason about the ultimate causes of things.* See Intellectual Virtues, Virtue.

VIRTUE: *human excellence.* Virtue is an enduring quality and so a characteristic disposition. Aquinas distinguishes three kinds of virtue: intellectual, moral, and theological (supernatural). Concerning theoretical truth, intellectual virtues comprise understanding first principles, scientific knowledge, and theoretical wisdom. Concerning practical truth, intellectual virtues comprise prudence and skills. Moral virtues consist of characteristic readiness to act in practical matters as prudence dictates. Natural prudence and natural moral virtues are acquired. The theological virtues are faith, hope, and charity. These virtues are infused, and supernatural prudence and supernatural moral virtues are infused with charity. *See* Charity, Faith, Habit, Hope, Intellectual Virtues, Moral Virtues, Principle, Prudence, Science, Theoretical Wisdom.

WILL: *the intellectual (rational) appetite of human beings, the intellectual faculty of desire.* In addition to sense appetites, which are common to all animals, human beings have an intellectual (rational) appetite, the will. Human beings can and do will things that reason understands as good for them. The will necessarily desires the ultimate human perfection, happiness, but freely desires particular goods, which are only partially good. *See* Happiness, Intention.

WISDOM: *See* Prudence, Theoretical Wisdom.

GENERAL COMMENTARIES

Aertsen, Jan. *Nature and Creation: Thomas Aquinas' Way of Thought*. Leiden: Brill, 1988.
Clarke, W. Norris. *The One and the Many: A Contemporary Thomistic Metaphysic*. Notre Dame, IN: University of Notre Dame Press, 2001.
Davies, Brian. *The Thought of Thomas Aquinas*. Oxford, UK: Oxford University Press, 1992.
———. *Aquinas*. London: Continuum, 2002. This work includes a comprehensive bibliography up to 2000 A.D.
———, ed. *Thomas Aquinas: Contemporary Philosophical Perspectives*. Oxford, UK: Oxford University Press, 2002.
———. *Thomas Aquinas' Summa Theologiae: A Guide and Commentary*. New York: Oxford University Press, 2014.
Gilson, Etienne. *Thomism: The Philosophy of Thomas Aquinas*. 6th ed. Translated by Laurence K. Shook and Armand Maurer. Toronto: Pontifical Institute of Medieval Studies, 2002.
Kenny, Anthony. *Aquinas on Being*. New York: Oxford University Press, 2003.
Kretzmann, Norman, and Stump, Eleanore. *The Cambridge Companion to Aquinas*. Cambridge, UK: Cambridge University Press, 1993.
McCabe, Herbert. *Aquinas*. London: Continuum, 2005.
Pieper, Joseph. *Guide to Thomas Aquinas*. Translated by Richard Winston and Clara Winston. New York: Pantheon, 1962.
The SCM Press A to Z of Thomas Aquinas. London: SCM Press, 2005.
Stump, Eleanore. *Aquinas*. London: Routledge, 2003.
te Velde, Rudi A. *Aquinas on God*. Aldershot, UK: Ashgate, 2007.
van Nieuwenhove, Rik, and Joseph Peter Wawrykow, eds. *The Theology of Thomas Aquinas*. Notre Dame, IN: University of Notre Dame Press, 2005.
Wippel, John F. *The Metaphysical Thought of Thomas Aquinas*. Washington, DC: The Catholic University of America Press, 2000.

INDEX OF PERSONS

Albert the Great, 3, 7, 21
Alexander of Hales, 3
Aquinas
   on human acts, 30–33
   on the human end, 33–39
   on the human soul and the human being, 21–23
   on God and the world, 13–19, 49–72
   on individuation, 12–13
   life and the *Summa Theologica*, 1–2
   on natural law, 33–38
   on participation, 11–13
   on specific virtues, 38–45
Aristotle, 157
   and Aquinas, 24–25, 32–33, 37
   and Christian faith, 4–5, 18–20
   and the West, 3–7
Augustine of Hippo, 6, 14, 19, 61
Avicenna, 12, 20–21
Averroes, 4–5, 14, 21

Bonaventure, 3, 13–14, 21

David of Dinant, 14
Duns Scotus, 13

Grosseteste, Robert, 4

James of Venice, 4
John of Jandun, 6

Kant, Immanuel, 9

Lombard, Peter, 3

Maimonides, Moses, 15–16
Moerbeke, William of, 4

Nemesius, 19

Paul of Tarsus, 14
Plato, 8–10
Plotinus, 11

Siger of Brabant, 6

TOPICAL INDEX

Abstinence from food, 262–63, 265–67
Apostasy, 161
Appetite
    intellectual (the will), 90–93
    sense, 83–84

Blasphemy, 162
Boldness, 258

Charity
    and contrary sins, 178–85
    in itself, 167–77
    precepts of, 185–86
Chastity, 267
Cognition, human
    intellectual, 84–90
    sense, 81–83
Concupiscence, 101, 130
Conscience, 85, 138
Contention, 181
Creation, 73–76
Custom and law, 139–40

Despair, 165
Discord, 180
Drunkenness, 266–67

Emotions, 33, 113, 123–24, 210, 260
Envy, 180
Evil, 74–76, 110–11

Faith
    and contrary sins, 40–41, 157–62
    in itself, 38–40, 147–57
Fear, 253–56
Food and drink, 265–67
Fortitude, 44–45, 124, 253–58
Free choice, 91–93
Fraud, 220

Gluttony, 265–66
God
    eternity of, 55
    existence of, 49–53
    goodness of, 54
    and governance of the world, 76–77
    and ideal forms of things, 61
    immutability of, 55
    infinity of, 54
    and justice and mercy, 67
    and his knowledge, 59
    and his life, 61–62
    and his love, 66–67
    our knowledge of, 55
    our predication about, 55–59
    perfection of, 54
    power of, 71–72
    and predestination of the elect, 55–59, 69–71
    providence of, 68–69
    simplicity of, 54

God (*cont.*)
   uniqueness of, 55
   and his will, 62–66
   and the world, 73

Habits, 92, 117–20
Happiness, 98–99
Hate, 178–79
Homicide, 229–32
Hope
   and contrary sins, 165–66
   in itself, 163–65
Human acts
   and choice, 91–93
   and consent, 107
   and deliberation, 106–7
   and emotions, 113, 123–24, 260
   external as commanded by the will, 107–9
   external as morally good or evil, 30–32
   in general, 100–109
   and intention, 104
   internal, 30
   and voluntariness, 100–103
   and the will, 102–4
Human end, 97–99

Ideas, divine, 61
Individuation, 9–13
Injustice
   in general, 212–15
   in judicial proceedings, 215–18
   against the person, 229–34
   regarding property, 234–38
Intellect, human
   in general, 84–85
   and knowledge of itself, 89–90
   and knowledge of material things, 85–87, 89
   and knowledge of superior things, 90
Interest-taking, 246–49

Justice
   definition of, 206–15
   and emotion, 210, 260
   and equity, 251–53
   integral parts of, 249–51
   and judicial judgment, 215–18
   as a moral virtue, 38, 43, 206, 210
   as a particular virtue, 209–10
   potential parts of, 251
   and preferential treatment of persons, 228
   as a real mean, 124, 211
   and restitution, 223–28
   and retaliation, 221–22
   subjective parts of, 218–22
   and the Ten Commandments, 252
   as virtue in general, 209

Law
   definition of, 127–38
   divine, 129–30, 141–44
   effects of, 130–31
   eternal, 128, 131–33
   human, 129, 137–43
   kinds of, 128–30
   natural, 128–29, 133–37
Love
   God's, 66–67
   human, 114–15
Lust, 269–70
   adultery, 270–71
   fornication, 270
   incest, 271–72
   nocturnal emission, 270
   rape, 270
   and sacrilege, 272
   seduction, 270
   sins contrary to nature, 272–73
   touches and kisses, 270

Neo-Platonists, 6–7, 11
Nominalists, 7–9

Participation
    and Aquinas, 11–13
    and Augustine, 6–7
    and classical Greek philosophy, 9–11
    and Franciscan school, 13
    and Hellenic Greek philosophy, 11
Predestination, 69–71
Preferential treatment of persons, 228
Providence, 68–69
Prudence
    as command, 189
    and deliberation, 189, 199–200
    domestic, 190
    and grace, 190
    and imprudence, 201–3
    individual, 189–90
    innate, 188–89
    integral parts of, 192, 193–96
    in itself, 187–97
    and judgment according to the general law, 189
    and judgment according to higher principles, 201
    kingly, 190, 196–98
    loss of, 192
    military, 192
    and moral virtue, 188–89
    negligence as sin against, 203
    political, 190–98
    potential parts of, 193, 199–203
    and reason, 189, 195
    sins contrary to but resembling, 204–5
    subjective parts of, 192, 196–203
    true and perfect, 191

Restitution, 223–28
Retaliation, 221–22
Right, 206–7

Scandal, 183–85
Schism, 181
Sedition, 182–83

Senses, 81–84
Shame and honor, 264–65
Skills, 122
Sobriety, 266
Solicitude, 189, 204–5
Soul
    appetitive intellectual power of, 90–93
    cognitive intellectual powers of, 84–85
    cognitive sense powers of, 81–84
    essence of, 78
    and how it knows itself, 89–90
    and how it knows superior things, 90
    and how it understands material things, 85–87
    and manner and process of understanding, 87–90
    production of, 93
    union of with the body, 78–80
    vegetative powers of, 80
    and what it knows about material things, 89
Spiritual apathy, 179–80
Stoics, 125, 257
Strife, 182
Synderesis, 85

Temperance
    in itself, 259–62
    integral parts of, 263–65
    as a moral virtue, 259–60
    potential parts of, 264
    sins contrary to, 262–63, 265–67, 269–73
    subjective parts regarding food and drink, 265–67
    subjective parts regarding sex, 267–73
Ten Commandments, 252
Theft and robbery, 234–38
Theoretical wisdom, 24, 122

Universals, 7–9
Universities, medieval, 3–6
Virginity, 267–69
Virtue
    essence of, 121
    intellectual, 121–25
    moral, 123, 125
    relation of moral to intellectual, 125–26
Virtues
    abstinence from food, 265
    charity, 167–86
    chastity, 267
    faith, 147–62
    fortitude, 253–58
    hope, 163–66
    justice, 206–52
    prudence, 187–205
    sobriety, 266–67
    temperance, 259–75
    virginity, 267–60

War, 182